Crossover Readers' Advisory

Crossover Readers' Advisory

Maximize Your Collection to Meet Reader Satisfaction

JESSICA E. MOYER, EDITOR

LIBRARIES
UNLIMITED™
An Imprint of ABC-CLIO, LLC
Santa Barbara, California • Denver, Colorado

Crossover Readers' Advisory
Library of Congress Control Number: 2016954759

ISBN: 978–1–4408–3846–0
EISBN: 978–1–4408–3847–7

21 20 19 18 17   1 2 3 4 5

This book is also available as an eBook.

Libraries Unlimited
An Imprint of ABC-CLIO, LLC

ABC-CLIO, LLC
130 Cremona Drive, P.O. Box 1911
Santa Barbara, California 93116-1911
www.abc-clio.com

This book is printed on acid-free paper ∞

Manufactured in the United States of America

Contents

Introduction

Jessica E. Moyer

If someone told you that you could better meet reader needs without adding new titles to your collection, what would you say? This book asserts just that and shows you how to do it.

It is fairly well known among librarians that many adults enjoy what publishers have designated as "Young Adult Fiction"; and likewise, that many teens enjoy reading "adult fiction and nonfiction." Many teens, especially those who read genre fiction, begin reading adult-designated titles and authors, and too often librarians do not know how to help. For example, in a recent roundtable discussion, science fiction and fantasy authors listed the books that started their love of the genre and adult authors like Anne McCaffrey, Robert Heinlein, Mercedes Lackey, and Ursula Le Guin were mentioned multiple times as favorite teen reads.[1] Youth services librarians, who are not that familiar with adult titles, may not know which of these to suggest to their teen readers. Likewise, adult services librarians may be wary of working with teens and may not know which adult titles are most likely to appeal to teen readers.[2]

At the same time, the number of adults who are reading and enjoying YA titles is growing every year and constitutes an important part of the YA book market.[3] These readers can be even more lost in the library: Many adult readers are reluctant to venture into the youth services area to find a teen specialist, and adult services librarians are often unfamiliar with YA fiction, and do not know which titles to suggest.[4] Moreover, it does not help when society condemns adults for reading teen materials, like in the controversial *Slate Book Review* article, "Against YA."[5]

At the 2010 PLA Conference, I led a popular session on "crossover advisory," available to both physical and virtual conference attendees. By the level of interest from librarians who attended the conference, as well as from those who contacted me after the conference, I realized there was a gap in the professional literature and a need for a guide to this body of literature. Conversations with librarian colleagues over the next few years reinforced the need for a resource, and I also experienced a groundswell of interest in contributing to such a volume.

Which titles can the readers' advisor confidently recommend to these two audiences without risking a turn-off? This book takes the guesswork out of "crossover readers' advisory," employing the knowledge of expert readers' advisors from both adult and teen services. Designed to fill a gap in the existing professional development literature on readers' advisory services and genre titles, it offers a valuable approach. Many readers' advisory guides include YA notes, but these are not always searchable or easy to find. Although *Booklist Online* includes YA notes for many of its adult book reviews that requires a subscription and the ability to search and select from hundreds of reviews. This guide offers a more concise and focused approach and is designed to be used by the busy librarians. Focusing exclusively on titles and authors that have strong appeal outside of their publisher-ordained readership, this book is meant to help the many teen readers who read adult books, and the many adult readers who enjoy YA titles.

Scope and Organization

Each chapter in this volume is dedicated to a single genre. Part I focuses on adult books for teen readers, while Part II covers teen books for adult readers. Many genres are covered in both parts (i.e., science fiction, fantasy, and romance), while others appear in just one section (i.e., thrillers, graphic novels, and new adult) as a result of their appeal and popularity to the targeted age group. Each chapter is also divided into two parts. In the first narrative section, you will find genre definitions, tips on working with readers, lists of tools and resources, and collection development advice. The second part of each chapter provides an annotated list of suggested titles in three major subareas of each genre, with descriptive annotations focusing on appeals and crossover concerns. Classic titles and authors are mentioned, but the focus is on recent and in-print titles that reflect the most recent developments and trends.

Conclusion

By covering a variety of genres that have specific appeal to this crossover readership, including general guidance and suggestions of specific titles and authors, this book is designed to meet the needs of public services staff who work with teen or adult populations. It will be useful for public librarians who work with both adult and teen services populations, as well as school librarians who may need to suggest adult titles to their leisure readers (see the popularity of *School Library Journal*'s Adult Books for Teens blog) as well as suggest YA titles to their teacher colleagues. Above all, this is a guide for readers and those who want to help readers of all ages find their next great read.

Notes

1. "Mind Meld: The Books That Made Us Love Science Fiction and Fantasy," SF Signal, October 7, 2015, http://www.sfsignal.com/archives/2015/10/mind-meld-books-made-love-sff/.

2. The Alex Awards from the Young Adult Library Services Association recognizes this need with their annual list of best adult books for teen readers. YALSA's Alex Awards, http://www.ala.org/yalsa/booklists/alex.

3. Howlett, Georgina, "Why Are So Many Adults Reading YA and Teen Fiction?" *The Guardian*, February 24, 2015, http://www.theguardian.com/childrens-books-site/2015/feb/24/why-are-so-many-adults-reading-ya-teen-fiction.

4. Cait@PaperFury, "10 Problems of Being an Adult Reading YA." Paper Fury, May 15, 2015, http://paperfury.com/10-problems-of-being-an-adult-reading-ya/.

5. Graham, Ruth, "Against YA," *Slate Book Review*, June 5, 2014, http://www.slate.com/articles/arts/books/2014/06/against_ya_adults_should_be_embarrassed_to_read_children_s_books.html.

PART I
Adult Books for Teens

.

1

Mystery and Detection

Ann Chambers Theis

Introduction to the Genre

Definition

Mystery and detection is a form of narrative fiction using a structured plot focused on investigation and crime solving. The emphasis is on who, how, and why "dunit," the detection process, and the resolution. These imaginative stories often involve suspense and intrigue as well as solving crimes. Series are popular in this genre, and detectives, secondary characters, and sidekicks are absorbing creations that engage readers.

Mystery and detection is a part of a large and diverse category of crime fiction that also includes thrillers as well as the subgenres of legal, technological, and espionage. Many espionage, legal, and thriller stories are included in the adrenalin chapter by Jennifer Haas Thiele. Within mystery and detection are numerous subgenres including traditional, female sleuths, hard-boiled, international crime, historical, police procedurals, and private eyes.

Appeals

The clear focus of this genre is the cerebral puzzle component. The pleasure of unraveling the mystery provides a satisfying conclusion for readers. Mystery and detection books may also appeal to our desire for order and justice, which may be of particular interest to teen readers. These books provide intellectual enjoyment and opportunities to learn about other cultures, locations, and the past as well as explore social and political issues and cultural concerns. While the overall emphasis is on the intellectual aspects of solving crime, key characters are often an important draw in engaging readers, resulting in numerous successful series. Tone and pacing are important since the mystery and detection genre is an amalgamation of many diverse subgenres. Like all good reads, the power of a good story, well paced and well told, is a crucial factor in the enjoyment of this genre.

Mystery and detection remains one of the most popular genres for readers of all ages. Edgar Allen Poe, Arthur Conan Doyle, Agatha Christie, and Dashiell Hammett are just a few seminal writers who retain current popularity.

Younger readers enjoy reading widely in this genre and continue to do so as they age. Many well-known authors are now writing for juvenile, teen, and adult readers. A few such authors are John Grisham, James Patterson, and David Baldacci.

Working with Readers

The wide range of subgenres means that there is something to please most readers and also perhaps something to disturb some readers. It is important to understand the interests and personal requirements of readers. There are a slew of useful Readers Advisory resources for tracking this genre. NoveList/NoveList Plus is an EBSCO subscription service providing Readers' Advisory tools for both readers and librarians. Other subscription services include Bowker's Fiction Connection and Gale's What Do I Read Next? Two key reference book series are the Readers' Advisory Reference Guides (American Library Association) and the Genreflecting series of books (Libraries Unlimited). As many mystery and detection books feature series, make sure to use What's Next and Goodreads for tracking series titles.[1] Many library websites are packed with reading lists, book club information, and other useful material for readers and librarians.

Numerous movies and TV shows are excellent tie-ins or are based on mystery and detection books. These include Veronica Mars, Longmire, Miss Fisher's Murder Mysteries, Bones, and Sherlock Holmes and can be a great starting place for teens new to crime fiction books.

Tools and Resources

Edelweiss[2] is an online service providing access to numerous publisher catalogs, advance reading copies, marketing, and information about book buzz from librarians, booksellers, and professional resources. Vendor sites such as iPage and TS360 provide information about demand, BISAC genre categories, and reviews.[3] EarlyWord is an online resource for collection development and readers advisory with an assortment of valuable information for librarians. EarlyWord's Twitter-based galley chats (adult and young adult) are great for networking with peers and discovering what new books librarians and publishers are promoting.[4] Professional review journals like *Booklist*, *Kirkus*, *Library Journal*, and *Publishers Weekly* all devote attention to genre fiction.

Stop, You're Killing Me! is an Anthony Award-winning website listing over 4,700 authors, with chronological lists of their books (over 55,000 titles), both series (5,600+) and non-series.[5]

Collection Development

There are several key areas essential for keeping current with professional developments.

- ## Review Journals

  Booklist, *School Library Journal*, and *VOYA* all note information about adult books that have teen appeal. *School Library Journal*'s Adult Books for Teens is a worthy resource for collection development and readers advisory and Overbooked also tracks notable adult books suggested for teens from key review journals.[6]

- **ALA and Other Library Organizations**

  Young Adult Library Services Association (YALSA) is the American Library Association (ALA) division that focuses on services for teens. Abundant opportunities for networking and professional development are available for members and nonmembers. Annual booklists and awards include the Alex Awards (Adult Books for Young Adults). The Teen Book Finder app (Android and iOS) includes the ability to search for books by author, title, award/list year, genre, award, and book list. The Hub provides connections to Teen collections.[7]

- **Library Metrics and Demographic Studies**

  Integrated library system (ILS) circulation statistics, turnover, and holds data are just a few useful ways to track the impact of library collections. Reports from other vendors, such as OverDrive and Hoopla, also have useful reporting functions. Locally produced demographic reports and Census data are helpful in monitoring trends in population. CollectionHQ and Edelweiss Analytics are products that provide data-driven insights into library collection use to help manage and promote materials.[8] Genre-related organizations and conferences include Mystery Writers of America, Sisters in Crime, International Thriller Writers, Malice Domestic, and Bouchercon.[9] Librarians looking for teen-related popular culture should check out Teen Ink, Connect with Your Teens, and VOYA Pop Culture Quizzes.[10]

The Literature

Cozys and Critters: The Humorous Side of Mystery and Detection

Cozys

Cozys are a subgenre of crime fiction without graphic violence or explicit sex and can cover a wide range of subject matter. Protagonists are typically likeable amateur sleuths solving crimes with a focus on detection in conjunction with compelling action. Cozys are often infused with a comedic sensibility. This genre is closely associated with the traditional mystery subgenre, which is tied to such classic British authors as Agatha Christie. Other classic cozy/traditional authors include Nicholas Blake, Edmund Crispin, Dorothy L. Sayers, and Josephine Tey. More recent authors include Susan Wittig Albert, Simon Brett, Ann Cleeves, Diane Mott Davidson, Carolyn Hart, Alexander McCall Smith, and Julia Spencer-Fleming.

Lourey, Jess. *February Fever*. Murder-by-Month Mysteries #10. 2015.
Librarian, reporter, and budding PI, Mira James is booked on the single's oriented Valentine train on her way to a Private Investigators conference when her trip is derailed by murder. This acclaimed and enjoyable series is fast paced, is filled with great characters, and has a winning combination of humor and suspense. (paperback, ebook)

Lutz, Lisa. *The Spellman Files*. Izzy Spellman Mysteries #1. 2007.
"Get Smart" loving Izzy Spellman wants some distance from her maddeningly dysfunctional family of detectives and their constant snooping, but her sister Rae's sudden disappearance requires the talents of all the

Spellman's to track her down. The outrageous humor and Izzy's fresh voice are the main attractions of this series. Give this Alex Award-winner to fans of Janet Evanovich, Meg Cabot (Heather Wells series), *Harriet the Spy*, and Veronica Mars. (print, ebook, audio)

Racculia, Kate. *Bellweather Rhapsody*. 2014.
Fifteen years after a grisly murder-suicide in room 712, the Bellweather Hotel is hosting the best high school students at the Statewide Music Festival. Alice Hatmaker and her roommate are assigned to room 712. Alice is stunned to find the body of her roommate hanging and more stunned when the body disappears. Racculia's book is an adroit mix of mystery, adult and teen romance, high school drama, and coming-of-age story wrapped up in a celebration of music. The somewhat dark and multilayered plot is lightened by droll wit and an emotionally satisfying story that nods to Agatha Christie. (print, ebook, audio)

Yancey, Rick. *The Highly Effective Detective*. Highly Effective Detective #1. 2006.
After his mother dies, lovable but bumbling Teddy Ruzak quits his job as a night watchman to live his dream of being a private investigator. His first case, which involves a hit-and-run killing of a gaggle of goslings, soon escalates into a murder investigation. Teddy is out of his league as he attempts to be a highly effective detective in this funny and touching series. Rick Yancey is known for his award-winning young adult books. (print, ebook, audio)

Critter Cozies
Critter Cozies feature animals (usually cats or dogs) as either the principal investigator or sidekick to a human partner. Many books in this subgenre overlap with cozies in their tone. Classic authors include Lilian Jackson Braun (Cat Who series), Shirley Rousseau Murphy (Joe Grey series), Rita Mae Brown (Sneaky Pie series), and Susan Conant (Holly Winters series). Many books in this subgenre include paranormal aspects, notably when the animals speak English to humans.

Clement, Blaize. *Curiosity Killed the Cat Sitter*. Dixie Hemingway #1. 2005.
Leaving behind a stressful career in law enforcement and hoping to recover from a family tragedy, Dixie Hemingway is working as a pet sitter when she discovers a body face down in the cat bowl. When her human client turns up dead, Dixie becomes a person of interest and works to clear her name. Interesting subplots (including one involving a gay teen) and the inherent humor of the pet sitting business mixed with a more traditional and slightly darker mystery provide an engaging start to a strong series. (print, ebook, audio)

Lyle, Dixie. *Deadly Tail*. Whiskey Tango Foxtrot Mystery #4. 2016.
Deirdre "Foxtrot" Lancaster is administrative assistant, aka chaos-handler, for wealthy eccentric Zelda Zoransky (ZZ). Foxtrot is assisted by a shape-shifting dog and communicates telepathically with her dead cat, Tango. ZZ's mansion is taken over to film a zombie movie and a real body is produced. The restless spirits emerge from ZZ's pet cemetery to add to the mayhem. A dash of mystery, sprinkle of romance, and a splash of the

supernatural add to the zany charm of this witty series jam-packed with delightful animals. (print, ebook)

Murphy, Shirley Rousseau. *Cat on the Edge: A Joe Grey Mystery*. <u>Joe Grey #1</u>. **1996.**

Joe Grey is contented with life as a gray-and-white tomcat until observing a murder shocks him into the ability to understand and speak like a human. Soon joined by the orange and green-eyed tabby, Dulcie, these two clever cats use cell phones to leak information to the police, and in Joe's case to demand better food at home. These clever kitty crime busters sparkle in this long-running series. (print, ebook, audio)

Quinn, Spencer. *A Fist Full of Collars*. <u>Chet & Bernie #5</u>. **2012.**

Bernie is the owner of the Little Detective Agency and Chet is his canine companion and narrator of their adventures. In their fifth outing, Chet and Bernie "go Hollywood" when they are hired to protect the badly behaved star of a big budget Western and his cat Brando. This ongoing series combines engaging mysteries with humor often related to the relationships between dogs and humans. Point social media loving teens to Chet's blog at http://www.chetthedog.com/. Spencer Quinn is a pseudonym of Peter Abrahams, well known for his works for children and adults and has recently launched the <u>Birdie and Bowser</u> series for middle-grade readers. (print, ebook, audio)

Simon, Clea. *Dogs Don't Lie: A Pru Marlowe Pet Noir*. <u>Pru Marlowe Pet Mysteries #1</u>. **2011.**

Pru Marlowe is an animal behaviorist and animal psychic aided by her snarky tabby Wallis. Pru is compelled to save a client's pit bull after the dog is found covered in blood standing over her owner's body. Pru's struggles with her psychic gift, a well-plotted story, and interesting animal voices get this series off to a good start. Simon's books shine by creating distinctive and plausible animal characters as well as remarkable humans. Simon also writes the <u>Dulcie Schwartz</u> series about a graduate student studying Gothic literature and her deceased cat Mr. Grey. The Schwartz series is slightly darker than other more fluffy cat cozys. (print, ebook, audio)

Historicals and Holmes

Historical mysteries transport readers to another time and place. An exact definition of what time period is considered historical is open to debate; readers often consider anything that happened before their birth historical, which is pretty recent for teen readers. In these texts, accuracy in detail is evident and characters come to life via historical research. The time period's realities (political and social) may impact the course of the story. Common settings are Europe and the United States, but there are series set in many eras and many locations including Egypt, Australia, and Japan. Historical crime fiction can range widely in tone, pacing, and mood, all of which are key factors in attracting readers.

One popular facet of historical mysteries is the use of major historical events, historical figures, and fictional figures. One of those fictional figures is Sherlock Holmes. The popularity of Sherlock Holmes (and his associates) endures and carries on in a wide range of historical mysteries, so much so that we are dedicating an entire section to this iconic detective.

While historical mysteries have been published since the twentieth century, Ellis Peter's *Cadfael Chronicles* (1977–1994) helped popularize the genre. Historical mysteries have become increasingly popular in the twenty-first century, generating numerous *New York Times* bestsellers and award winners. The British Crime Writers' Association and the Malice Domestic Conference honor historical crime fiction with awards as do other mystery conventions. Some classic and key authors are Lindsey Davis, Kerry Greenwood, Laurie R. King, Peter Lovesey, Eliot Pattison, Anne Perry, Ellis Peters, Elizabeth Peters, and Charles Todd.

Historicals

Bebris, Carrie. *Pride and Prescience: Or, a Truth Universally Acknowledged.* Mr. & Mrs. Darcy Mysteries #1. 2004.
      The beloved courting couple from Jane Austen's *Pride and Prejudice* have not even left on their honeymoon when they become entangled in a mystery involving one of their wedding guests. The Darcys are delightful characters comparable to more recent married crime solvers Nick and Nora Charles. Bebris employs genteel prose, country houses, and a Regency backdrop to fine effect. It is lighter in approach than Stephanie Barron's excellent series that features Jane Austen as a sleuth. (paperback, ebook)

Bowen, Rhys. *Malice at the Palace.* A Royal Spyness Mystery #9. 2015.
      Lady Georgiana Rannoch has the advantage of being 35th in line to the English throne, but the disadvantage of limited funds. In this lighthearted series set in the 1930s, the spirited Georgie is called upon to investigate a royal fiancée in a palace rumored to be haunted. A sparkling period piece, a solid mystery, and delightfully amusing characters combine to make this a royal treat for readers. (hardcover, paperback, audiobook narrated by Katherine Kellgren)

Bradley, Alan. *The Sweetness at the Bottom of the Pie.* Flavia de Luce Mysteries #1. 2009.
      Young Flavia is enjoying the summer of 1950 by precociously engaging in her passions for chemistry and poison. Flavia is equally appalled and delighted when she discovers a dying man on the backstep. When Flavia's father is accused of the murder she embarks on a scientific investigation. Flavia's first case is a wickedly entertaining tale of deception, class and society, and a beguiling mystery. Listed as one of ALA's Best Books for Young Adults. (hardcover, paperback, ebook, audiobook narrated by Jayne Entwistle)

Christie, Agatha. *Death Comes as the End.* 1944.
      It is Egypt in 2000 BC. Renisenb believes the death of a concubine by snakebite was not an accident and she seeks to discover the evil lurking in the midst of her family. This standalone by Christie draws upon her knowledge of the archeology of the Middle East and her interest in psychology, and the premise of the story is based on actual ancient Egyptian letters. Christie skillfully brings the past to life as she explores including the story of an ancient serial killer. (print, ebook, audiobook)

Greenwood, Kerry. *Cocaine Blues: A Phryne Fisher Mystery.* Phryne Fisher Mystery #1. 2006.
      Fleeing her boredom with high society, unflappable flapper Phryne Fisher relocates to Melbourne, Australia, early in 1928. Soon she has her hands full as she contends with back alley abortionists, cocaine dealers, and a handsome Russian dancer. Sassy, smart, and sophisticated, Phryne is a fetching character surrounded by an engaging entourage. An excellent period

mystery series that has produced a sparkling and successful television series. (print, audiobook)

Morrell, David. *Murder as a Fine Art*. Thomas and Emily De Quincey #1. 2013.
    Memoirist Thomas De Quincey is the prime suspect in a series of horrific murders that paralyze London. Desperate to prevent more atrocities but crippled by opium addiction, De Quincey is aided by his brilliant daughter, Emily, as well as two determined Scotland Yard detectives. The fast-paced action, interesting characters, gritty period details, and true crime facts will attract more mature teen readers. (hardcover, paperback, ebook)

Thomas, Wil. *The Limehouse Text*. Barker & Llewelyn #3. 2006. *Some Danger Involved*. Barker & Llewlyn #1.
    Victorian enquiry agent Cyrus Barker and his inexperienced assistant, Thomas Llewelyn, are drawn into Limehouse, London's forbidding Chinese district, to track down a rare book on lethal martial arts. Barker draws on his extensive familiarity of the London underworld and his network of allies to navigate opium dens, blood sports, and sailors' hangouts. A visceral outing down the dark streets of London, this fast-paced series owes a debt to the original Victorian-era Sherlock Holmes. (hardcover, paperback, ebook)

Upson, Nicola. *London Rain*. Josephine Tey Mysteries #6. 2015. *An Expert in Murder*. Josephine Tey Mysteries #1.
    The coronation of George VI (1937) provides the background for the fictional adventures of a real-life mystery writer. Josephine Tey is attending rehearsals of her play being adapted for radio. When a BBC announcer involved in a love triangle is murdered, Tey works with her Scotland Yard friend to untangle the secrets of a complicated case. Tey must also untangle her own love triangle when her relationship with her lover Marta goes awry. This series is both fascinating and provocative, filled with vivid characters and incorporating plots that capture the atmosphere of prewar England. (paperback, ebook, audiobook)

Winspear, Jacqueline. *Maisie Dobbs*. Maisie Dobbs Mysteries #1. 2003.
    Maisie is a smart and resourceful sleuth who sets up shop as M. Dobbs, Trade and Personal Investigations in postwar London. Soon after she investigates a community of wounded World War I veterans, she uncovers a disturbing mystery and confronts a ghost that has haunted her. An evolving mystery about love and loss featuring an intriguing heroine who worked as nurse in World War I. Winspear has won many awards, including an Alex Award for *Maisie Dobbs*. (paperback, ebook, audio read by Rita Barrington)

Elementary: The Holmes Canon Continues

Abdul-Jabbar, Kareem and Anna Waterhouse. *Mycroft Holmes*. 2015.
    A rousing mystery featuring Sherlock's older (and smarter) brother. Mycroft is a rising young star in government when he is drawn to Trinidad, home of both his best friend of African descent, Cyrus Douglas, and his own fiancée Georgiana. Tales of spirits luring children to death and other

mysterious events in Trinidad draw Mycroft and Cyrus into a web of treachery. The action moves quickly and incorporates absorbing historical details. The relationship between Mycroft and Cyrus is one of the many strong points of the story and is presented realistically given the time period. (print, ebook, audiobook narrated by Damian Lynch)

Horowitz, Anthony. *Moriarty.* **2014.**
    The game is once again afoot in this riveting mystery from the best-selling author of *The House of Silk.* Sanctioned by the Conan Doyle estate, this story explores what really happened at the Reichenbach Falls. Moriarty's death has left a vacuum in the criminal world and a new mastermind is emerging to assume Moriarty's mantel of evil. (hardcover, paperback, ebook, audiobook narrated by Derek Jacobi)

King, Laurie R. *The Beekeeper's Apprentice.* <u>Mary Russell and Sherlock Holmes #1</u>. **1994.**
    This successful and long-running series begins in the 1910s when recently orphaned teen Mary Russell bumps into a retired Sherlock Holmes as he tends bees on the Sussex Downs. First an apprentice and protégé, Mary and Holmes eventually solidify their partnership and marry between books 2 and 3 (the actual wedding is detailed in the charming short story, "The Marriage of Mary Russell") (2016). World War I forces Holmes out of retirement just as discovering a woman could be his intellectual equal forces Holmes out his Victorian mindset, which leads to globe-trotting series of investigations by Holmes and Russell. (hardcover, ebook)

Meyer, Nicholas. *The Seven-Percent Solution.* <u>Nicholas Meyer Holmes Pastiches #1</u>. **1974.**
    Relates the previously unknown collaboration of Sigmund Freud and Sherlock Holmes as they work to thwart a diabolical conspiracy. Dr. Watson set up a drug intervention for Holmes to obtain treatment from Freud. Meyer discovered, edited, and annotated Dr. Watson's account of the intervention and adventure. Also revealed are the identity of Moriarty, dark secrets of the Holmes brothers, and Sherlock's true whereabouts during the Great Hiatus. *The Seven-Percent Solution* was also a 1976 movie starring Robert Duvall, Alan Arkin, and Vanessa Redgrave. (print)

Robertson, Michael. *The Brothers of Baker Street: A Mystery.* <u>Baker Street Letters #2</u>. **2011.** *The Baker Street Letters.* <u>The Baker Street Letters #1</u>. **2009.**
    The brothers are Reggie and Nigel Heath, whose chambers are located at Sherlock Holmes's Baker Street address and are required by lease to answer all mail addressed to Sherlock Holmes. This sometimes requires a bit of detecting. In this case a modern-day Moriarty schemes to sully London taxis. A romp of a story, fast paced and funny. (hardcover, paperback, ebook, audiobook)

Siciliano, Sam. *The Further Adventures of Sherlock Holmes—The White Worm.* <u>The Further Adventures of Sherlock Holmes #4</u>. **2016.**
    Siciliano deftly employs plot elements from an obscure Bram Stoker novel in his stellar fourth Sherlock Holmes pastiche. Adam Selton is warned away from his fiancée because of a legendary curse about a woman who can shape-shift into a giant serpent and strange events occurring on her family land. Holmes investigates and presents a clever solution. (paperback, ebook)

Off the Beaten Path: Procedurals, PIs, and International Crime

Not your round up of the usual suspects: the good, the bad and the quirky . . .

Private Eyes and Private Investigators

Trouble is the private eye's business. The private eye, or PI, is not a member of official law enforcement. The PI ambience or "code" is part of what draws the reader into the genre and may harken back to the Western cowboy genre, and is a major appeal for teen readers. The solitary and often dangerous character of the detective is crucial. The PI may by a rogue or operate under a strict personal moral code, favor underdogs, or try to right society's wrongs. He or she may work for money while also being motivated by altruism. Even loners may have sidekicks to add depth and help carry the storyline or add a touch of humor. Settings may be urban or rural but tend to be darker and harder edged. Realism is a key element impacting the story, characters, and crime itself. The amount of violence may vary but often leans more toward the hard-boiled tradition. Language is usually grittier and can be explicit. These tales are frequently narrated in the first person and may follow an investigation step by step. This genre is sometimes referred to as the only homegrown American literary genre. Classic and key authors and their PIs: Lawrence Block (Matthew Scudder), James Lee Burke (Dave Robicheaux), Raymond Chandler (Philip Marlowe), Sue Grafton (Kinsey Millhone), Dashiell Hammett (Sam Spade), Laura Lippman (Tess Monaghan), John D. MacDonald (Travis McGee), Walter Mosley (EZ Rawlins), Marcia Muller (Sharon McCone), Robert B. Parker (Spenser), Sara Paretsky (V. I. Warshawski), Mickey Spillane (Mike Hammer), and Rex Stout (Nero Wolfe).

Brackston, P. J. *Gretel and the Case of the Missing Frog Prints: A Brothers Grimm Mystery.* **A Brothers Grimm Mystery #1. 2015.**
Gretel—yes, that Gretel—is all grown up, living in Bavaria with her brother Hansel and working as a PI. Albrecht Durer the Much Much Younger has had his Frog Prints stolen and Gretel takes the case. This series combines mystery and fantasy and blends folk tale whimsicality with a mordant sensibility, larger-than-life characters, and solid plotting. This series should appeal to cozy or traditional fans as well as readers who enjoyed Jasper Fforde's Nursery Crime and Thursday Next series. (print, ebook)

Cha, Steph. *Dead Soon Enough.* **Juniper Song Series #3. 2015.**
Los Angeles–based PI Juniper Song is back in an exciting story about heritage and responsibility, motherhood and genocide. Song is hired to find a surrogate mother who is an activist embroiled in a dispute over an Armenian genocide memorial. Cha takes full advantage of the LA melting pot to produce a complex, tightly plotted, and emotionally involving story. A good bet for Sue Grafton fans. (print, ebook, audio)

Connolly, John. *The Burning Soul.* **Charlie Parker Series #10. 2011.**
Private detective Charlie Parker is hired by convicted murderer Randal Haight to find out who is threatening him. During the course of his investigations, Parker stumbles into a web of deceit involving the FBI and a missing teenage girl. A potent storyline, a likeable and engaging narrator, and a touch of the supernatural are strong draws for teens.

Huston, Charlie. *Already Dead.* Joe Pitt Series #1. 2005.

The high society daughter of a well-known New York family is missing, and her enthrallment with vampyres makes Joe Pitt (private detective and vampyre) a natural for this job. Trouble abounds for Pitt as he runs afoul of the Clans that run the undead to find the missing girl. An original take on the vampire myth combined with a fast-paced, hard-boiled detective story make this a good bet for teens.

Police Procedurals

Noted mystery critic Anthony Boucher is credited with coining the phrase *police procedural* as a new subgenre in 1956. Boucher noted the popularity of the radio program *Dragnet* and books by J. J. Marric and Ed McBain as he molded a subgenre that is constructed around the authentic depiction of law enforcement. Police procedurals track how law enforcement works on the job and are often less concerned with the puzzle element of most mysteries and more concerned with the accurate portrayal of the job and proper crime solving procedures.

Either the entire department or unit is the center of the story or else an individual member is featured as the focus of the story telling. Series are common in this subgenre, and secondary characters with distinctive personalities add depth, interest, and sometimes humor. Books in this subgenre often contain multiple strands of investigations. The details of the investigation process are crucial and authors often incorporate their own expertise or research (forensic, legal) to add realistic details and techniques. Settings vary widely from city homicide departments to rural law enforcement officers from a range of agencies. Realism is a major component across story elements including a "warts and all" approach to the very human officers and the crime itself. Violence is specific and may be gruesomely detailed. Language or dialogue is often explicit and streetwise. Lone wolf detectives like Harry Bosch often have to work within the uncomfortable confines of their agency and also act outside of the normal law enforcement parameters. The popularity of this subgenre continues in print, TV, and movies. Most teens have grown up knowing the clang tone from *Law and Order*. Classic and key authors: Nevada Barr, C. J. Box, Michael Connelly, Elizabeth George, Tony Hillerman, P. D. James, Henning Mankell, Ed McBain, Louise Penny, Ian Rankin, Ruth Rendell, and Karin Slaughter.

Beukes, Lauren. *Broken Monsters.* 2014.

Detective Gabriella Versado investigates the work of a criminal mastermind who creates disturbingly violent tableaus by fusing the remains of murder victims with animals. Versado's geeky daughter, Joono a narcissistic freelance journalist, and TK who is trying to keep a homeless family together are all players in this genre-bending story about a city and people trying to put life back together. Grotesque crime scenes, the blending of detective procedure with atmospheric horror, and compelling characters make this a good choice for older teens. (print, ebook, audio)

Grabenstein, Chris. *Tilt-a-Whirl.* John Ceepak Mysteries #1. 2005.

A billionaire tycoon is found murdered on the Tilt-a-Whirl at a seedy seaside amusement park in the summer tourist town of Sea Haven. Ceepak, a former MP with a strong personal code, heads up the murder investigation along with Danny Boyle, a part-timer more interested in beach activities than policing. Unexpected plot twists, the relationship between Boyle and Ceepak, and punchy, humorous dialogue are good draws for teens. (print, ebook, audio)

Lin, Ed. *This Is a Bust*. <u>Robert Chow Series #1</u>. **2007.**

Robert Chow is on the beat in New York's Chinatown, circa 1976. Still recovering from his time in Vietnam, he is seldom challenged to do more than PR appearances at community events but wants a promotion to detective. The death of an old woman and community unrest force him to take action. Strikingly nuanced portrayal of a community, a time, and a place. Memorable characters, a gritty urban noir tone, and lively, literary writing are key appeal factors. For a different take on Chinatown, teens may want to check out S. J. Rozan's acclaimed series about two NYC private detectives. (print, ebook)

Mizushima, Margaret. *Killing Trail*. <u>Timber Creek K-9 Mystery #1</u>. **2015.**

When a young girl is found murdered in the Colorado Mountains, Officer Mattie Cobb and her police dog Robo are on the case. Hometown secrets and hidden agendas make tracking down the truth tough and dangerous for both Mattie and Robo. A strong start to a new series that will appeal to teens who enjoy books by Nevada Barr and C. J. Box and liked *Suspect* by Robert Crais. (print, ebook)

Nesbø, Jo. *The Snowman*. <u>Harry Hole Series #7</u>. **2011.**

Jonas wakes in the night to find his mother missing and a sinister snowman has appeared in the yard wearing his mother's scarf. Obstreperous maverick Oslo detective Harry Hole realizes a serial killer is at work and may be targeting him. This exceptional crime novel hits all the right notes thanks to stylish writing, a suspenseful and chilling plot, and intriguing characters. (print, ebook, audio)

Conclusion: Trends in Mystery and Detective Fiction

Crime fiction is one of the most popular genres and the range of subgenres continues to grow. The appeal of crime fiction crosses all demographics and the genre offers something for every reader. Teens growing up in the Harry Potter age are used to reading longer and more complicated books. Books with complicated psychological themes are trending for both teens and adults. Many mysteries in all subgenres are engaging in faster pacing to draw in readers. Current trends in mystery and detection include genre crossing and mash ups, supernatural elements, diversity, international crime, and historical fiction.

Reading for pleasure may be a key element in increasing empathy and connectedness. It may improve overall well-being and increase the readers' self-awareness and insight into the world around them. It should be an everyday and lifelong activity. With such a diverse and vibrant genre there are many opportunities for readers of all ages to find pleasure in reading crime fiction.

Notes

1. Kent District Library, "What's Next," http://ww2.kdl.org/libcat/whatsnext.asp, March 31, 2016.

2. Edelweiss, http://edelweiss.abovethetreeline.com/, March 31, 2016.

3. iPage, https://ipage.ingramcontent.com/; Baker & Taylor, https://ts360.baker-taylor.com/.

4. Early Word, http://www.earlyword.com/, March 31, 2016.

5. Stop, You're Killing Me!, http://www.stopyourekillingme.com/.

6. Adult Books for Teens, http://www.slj.com/category/collection-development/adult-books-for-teens/; Overbooked, http://overbooked.com/next-chapter/featured/adult-books-for-teens/.

7. The Hub, http://www.yalsa.ala.org/thehub/.

8. CollectionHQ, http://www.collectionhq.com/); Edelweiss Analytics, http://www.ingramcontent.com/.

9. Mystery Writers of America, https://mysterywriters.org/; Sisters in Crime, http://www.sistersincrime.org/; International Thriller Writers, http://thrillerwriters.org/; Malice Domestic, http://www.malicedomestic.org/; Bouchercon, http://www.bouchercon.info/.

10. Teen Ink, http://www.teenink.com/opinion/pop_culture_trends/; Connect with Your Teens, http://connectwithyourteens.net/; VOYA Pop Culture Quizzes, http://www.voyamagazine.com/tags/teen-pop-culture-quiz/.

2

Science Fiction

Jessica E. Moyer

Introduction to the Genre

Definition

According to librarians Moyer and Donaldson in the readers' advisory text, *Integrated Advisory*, "Science fiction is the literature of the future, ranging from stories set so far in the future Earth is lost to near future stories set only a few possible years from now. Science fiction is stories about space, stories about technology, and stories of bleak, post apocalyptic futures. In the broadest sense, Science fiction stories are speculations on the future of humanity ... [and] science fiction stories all ask 'what if?' "[1] A more popular definition can be found in the *Merriam-Webster* dictionary, which calls it "fiction dealing principally with the impact of actual or imagined science on society or individuals or having a scientific factor as an essential orienting component."[2] This second definition is more inclusive of the recent rise of steampunk that explores alternate histories dominated by steam technology, while the first may prove more useful to librarians providing readers' advisory and collection development. For experts, science-fiction scholar James Gunn provides a technical definition, "The first premise of SF is that humanity is adaptable. To that premise, however, science fiction added another that naturalism never had: Although humanity is as much a product of its environment as the other animals, it possesses a quality that the other animals lack—the intellectual ability to recognize its origins and the processes at work upon it, and even, sometimes, to choose a course other than that instilled by its environment."[3] While denser than popular definitions, Gunn is an acknowledged leader of science fiction scholarship and his many essays on the genre are worth pursuing for librarians and readers interested in learning more about the history of this complex genre.

Appeals

As evinced earlier, science fiction is a complex genre and cannot be easily defined, and that very complexity is what draws in many readers and keeps them engaged with the genre throughout their lives. Nearly all avid science fiction readers will have become hooked as a teen, whether from reading classic authors such as Andre Norton or Robert Heinlein, or jumping straight into adult fiction by the likes of teen favorites Anne McCaffrey or Mercedes Lackey. Today's teens may be more likely to have first encountered science fiction in teen-oriented titles like *Hunger Games* or *Divergent*, but that does not mean they are not ready to embrace adult titles and authors. In fact, many may be eager to move on to the longer and more complex stories of adult science fiction.

Plots and themes unique to science fiction, like post-apocalyptic societies or human exploration of space, often draw in teen readers. These days steampunk elements are equally popular, especially with teens interested in the costuming and creation aspects of steampunk. Characters and characterization is generally not as important and traditionally has not been a strong suit for classic science fiction. Readers are much more likely to be interested in how a character reacts to new technologies or deals with adverse conditions than learning their full backstory and deep inner thoughts. In fact, one of the unique appeals of science fiction is the technology, which at times, can become a character of its own, such as stories that feature robots and artificial intelligences like the classic *2001: A Space Odyssey* by Arthur C. Clarke. Teens with an interest in science and technology may be drawn to these stories as they are generally based on current scientific knowledge and often written by scientists like astrophysicist and Nebula award-winning author Catherine Asaro.

Working with Readers

When working with science fiction readers of any age it is essential not to overlook the multimedia nature of the genre. Science fiction readers enjoy their stories in book, podcast, movie, and TV shows, and successful readers' advisory will incorporate suggestions based on media interests. Science fiction is becoming increasingly mainstream; the success of movies like the *Hunger Games* series or the recent Academy Award-winner *The Martian* has proven that science fiction draws a much larger crowd than it did 10 or 15 years ago. With a plethora of science fiction TV shows, from the superhero-based science fiction shows on CW (*The Flash*) to the recent debut of *The Expanse* on SyFy, smart readers' advisors will capitalize on these shows to create displays and readalikes.

Tools and Resources

- "Adult Books 4 Teens," originally a column in *School Library Journal*, has become an active and popular blog with a dedicated science fiction section, http://blogs.slj.com/adult4teen/category/science-fiction/.
- *Booklist*: With a long history of noting adult titles with teen appeal, the librarians' favorite *Booklist* and its online companion are one of the best resources for finding adult science fiction with strong young adult (YA) appeal. Look for YA notes at the end of adult book reviews.
- Brannen, Jennifer. "All about Science Fiction for Teens" Novelist. https://www.ebscohost.com/novelist/novelist-special/all-about -science-fiction-for-teens. Go here for a quick overview of the genre

and bullet lists of teen appeal. Few specific titles are listed but the basic information is spot on.

* "Locus Online," http://locusmag.com/, is written by fans and genre experts instead of librarians; the online companion to the long-running magazine has plenty of useful content. Lots of reviews are complimented by virtual round tables and round ups of genre news.

Collection Development

In addition to the aforementioned sources, librarians looking to develop their science fiction collection will find plenty of online sources. The science fiction community has a long and active history with the Internet and still remains one of the best places to keep up on the latest news and under the radar titles. Self-publishing has been a large part of science fiction for many years and the success of recent titles like *Wool* by Hugh Howey and *The Martian* by Andy Weir are evidence that this trend is likely to continue. Computer-fluent teens will already be online reading these works, so it is up to librarians to keep abreast of the latest developments to be able to offer readalikes for the next *Martian* long before the print rights are bought by a major publisher. Here are five places to get started:

Lightspeed magazine, http://www.lightspeedmagazine.com/, hosts much of its published works online. With an active short fiction market, new and emerging authors often make their professional debuts with shorter works and this is one of the good venues to find a range of authors. *Lightspeed* is also well known for its special issues starting with "Women Destroy Science Fiction," which came from a crowd-funded campaign as a reaction to ongoing gender controversy.

RT Book Reviews: Science Fiction, http://www.rtbookreviews.com/genre/science-fiction, reviews more than just science fiction romance, and its reader-centric reviews cover a wide range of science fiction stories.

Science Fiction Signal, http://www.sfsignal.com/. This award-winning blog provides regular roundups of free fiction in addition to news and reviews.

Tor.com may be hosted by a major publisher, but it does not seem biased to its own books. In fact, this has become one of the go-to sites for new short fiction as they pay more than the going rate for professional work. The rereads of popular series books like *Harry Potter* or the works of H. P. Lovecraft will enthrall eager fan boys and girls.

Whatever, whatever.com. John Scalzi's long-running blog (it is one of the earliest, still active) first hosted his book, *Old Man's War*, where it was discovered and contracted by science fiction publishing powerhouse Tor. With regular author interviews plus popular culture content, this is a great place to keep on any librarians' list. If a book is going to be popular, or an issue becomes "the topic" of online conversation, it is a guarantee it will appear here.

The Literature

Space Opera

Space opera has been a thriving and beloved subgenre of science fiction since the earliest years of the genre, and it has been of interest to young readers for just as long. Space opera offers teen readers the opportunity to explore outside the confines of their daily lives, whether the exploration of our solar system, the wider galaxy, or different facets of human culture. Adolescence is an important time for identity formation and many teens will want to look outside for new ways of looking at old ideas, or just different takes on controversial issues like gender, identity, or personal freedoms. Space opera allows readers of all ages to explore these big ideas within the safe confines of a story that is both accessible and enjoyable. Space opera with teen characters and/or characters struggling with their identity and place in the world are a classic staple of this area and a sure place to start teen readers looking to explore adult science fiction. Space opera can also satisfy readers who are interested in math, science, or military careers or just feed an amateur interest in cosmology or astronomy.

Asaro, Catherine. *Schism: Book 1 of the Triad*, **2004, and** *The Final Key: Book 2 of the Triad*, **2005.**

Asaro's long-running Skolian Saga has become known for its use of high-level math and physics mixed with military and romantic elements that is written in a style accessible to teen readers. In *Schism* and *Final Key*, Asaro explores the young adult years of heroine Soz, set more than 30 years before series debut *Primary Inversion*. Soz wants to emulate her older brother and become an elite military pilot, but her peace-loving father would much rather she stay home on the pastoral planet that has become a haven for their uniquely valuable family. (print, ebook, digital audio from Audible read by Suzette Weintraub)

Bach, Rachel. *Fortune's Pawn*, **Paradox. 2013.**

Bach turns all the clichés of military space opera and mercenaries upside down when she introduces macho and swaggering Deviana Morris, who will do anything to make her reputation as a powered armor fighter and earn a place in her God-King's elite bodyguard. Which is how she ends up on high-risk ship and voyage that takes her far outside her comfort zone. Devi is a great model for teen girls and the plethora of military details and action scenes helps widen the appeal to male readers. (print, ebook, audio read by Emily Durante)

Corey, James S. A. *Leviathan Wakes*, **The Expanse. 2011.**

Corey's ongoing series is set a few hundred years in the future, when humanity has spread across the solar system, but has yet to escape to the stars. A mix of mystery, romance, and adventure, this is a great introduction to space opera for teens who prefer their science fiction set closer to home. With conflict brewing between the Earth government, the Outer Planets, and dissent from the independent inhabitants of the belt, it is up to rebel sympathizer Jim Holden and Belt cop Miller to figure out why one missing girl is the cause of so many problems. (print, ebook, audiobook from Recorded Books read by Jefferson Mays)

Dozois, Gardner and Jonathan Strahan, eds. *The New Space Opera*, **2007, and** *The New Space Opera 2*, **2009.**

Noted editors and anthologists Dozois and Strahan combine forces to provide an introduction to twenty-first-century space opera stories. With plenty of stories from newer names like Kristine Kathryn Rusch and Nancy Kress, as well as contributions from science fiction stalwarts Peter Watts and Bruce Sterling, this collection is the perfect choice for teens interested in solidly plotted stories and a great introduction to many of today's best science fiction authors. Short stories can be perfect for time-pressed teens with a packed schedule or intermittent time to read. (print, ebook, audio-book—multiple narrators)

Johnson, Jean. *A Soldier's Duty*, <u>Theirs Not to Reason Why</u>. 2011.

One of the few citizens to ever leave her theocratic heavy gravity home-world, Ia is driven by visions of the utter destruction of humanity and the galaxy. She enlists in the Terran Army at the age of 18, leaving behind friends, family, and the only world she knows. Ia's path is long, lonely, and fraught with peril for she can see only one slight possibility of a future for humanity, and she has only so much time to set into action the many events that must occur. Strong female characters, a complex plot in both individual entries and the overall series, and a unique premise add to the teen appeal. (print, ebook)

Lee, Sharon and Steve Miller. *Fledgling*, <u>Liaden</u>. 2009.

Lee and Miller's long-running <u>Liaden</u> series has plenty of appeal for teen space opera fans looking for something on the lighter side. Readers new to the series should start with *Fledgling*, which introduces previous unknown characters; teenage Theo and her parents, both professors, live together on the safe, staid, and human university planet of Delgado. Theo struggles to fit in, especially after her parents separate, when an off-world trip forces Theo (and her mother) to learn about her unique heritage and ties to some of the most famous people in the galaxy. (print, ebook, audible digital audio read by Eileen Stevens)

Scalzi, John. *Old Man's War*. 2005.

How exactly does the Colonial Union Defense Force use its senior citizen volunteers? By transplanting their brains into brand new bodies designed for interstellar warfare. John Perry may be in his 70s but between his new body and new life, he is experiencing all the agony and ecstasy of being a young man trying to find his place in the world. He just happens to be doing it while fighting aliens. Now considered a modern classic, experienced teen science fiction readers will appreciate Scalzi's homages to classic Heinlein science fiction and all will enjoy his humorous tone and well-developed characters. (ebook, print, audio read by William Dufris)

Scalzi continues to write in this series with books for adults as well as teens, marketed as *Zoe's Tale,* about his adopted daughter and her alien protectors.

Shepherd, Mike. *Mutineer*, <u>Kris Longknife</u>. 2004.

From the first pages of *Mutineer* it is easy to see that Kris is not an average officer or daughter of privilege. It is not easy being a descendant of (in)famous politicians, fighters, and businessmen when everyone sees her as "just another Longknife." Over the course of the series Kris grows from a nervous lieutenant to a confident leader, all while repeatedly saving her friends and compatriots from attack and assassination attempts. Fast and light, this series is best for readers concerned about their ability to handle math and science or girls looking for strong female characters. (print, ebook, audio read by Dina Pearlman)

Weber, David and John Ringo, *March Upcountry*. 2001.

Prince Roger knows he is spoiled and not very popular, but it is still a shock when his ship is destroyed over an alien world. During the trek across

Marduk, Roger's big-game hunting skills finally become useful, earning him grudging respect from the Marines trying to protect him from a plethora of violent plants and creatures. Fast paced and full of action, this series is just right for teens who like a plot-driven story, and Roger's personal growth will appeal to teens still struggling to find their place in the world. (print, ebook)

Volumes 1 and 2 (*March to the Sea*) have been reissued as *Empire of Man* (2014).

Steampunk

Technology has always been an important part of science fiction, and the subgenre of cyberpunk and its more recent iteration, steampunk, feature stories with a focus on technologies, new and old. While the technology can sometimes overshadow characters and plots, done right it adds depth to the world building and backstory. Generally using a nineteenth-century setting, steampunk stories are often predicated on great advances in steam-based technologies that never occurred in history. Alternately, other steampunk stories are inspired by Charles Babbage and his analytical engine and include the successful construction and application of a prototype computer. Predicated upon this idea, William Gibson's classic *The Difference Engine* is a must read for completists and historians, but may lack in appeal for readers who have been born since its publication in the 1980s. Steampunk can be fantasy, science fiction, or even a mix of both. The science fiction stories included in this chapter have all the elements of steampunk, yet are just as likely to take place on a remote planet in the far future, than an alternate Victorian England. Most important, the explanations for unusual creatures (zombies or kraken) are always science based and nothing can be solely attributed to the supernatural. Steampunk stories with vampires, werewolves, and magic can be found in the fantasy chapter.

Steampunk appeals to teens as the technology in these stories is both understandable and accessible to readers with a limited sci-tech background, making it more approachable and less intimidating than some of the tech-heavy stories that dominate traditional hard science fiction. Airships of all types, from gargantuan hydrogen-filled ships suited for crossing oceans to portable balloons for daily commutes, are a staple of this imaginative genre, along with plenty of gadgets, goggles, and mad scientists. Steampunk also draws in teen readers who enjoy the cosplaying and pop culture aspects. Creative teens may want to create their own costumes or gadgets, while others will be content to merely immerse themselves in the alternate histories that arise when technology follows another path.

Buckell, Tobias. *Crystal Rain*. 2006.

Nearly 30 years ago, John washed up on the shores of Nanaganda, a colony settled by global warming refugees from the vanishing islands of the Caribbean. Cut off from Earth, technology is limited to steamships and hydrogen-propelled airships, but war is still waged against the human sacrificing Azteca. Heavily influenced by his own Caribbean heritage as well as Aztec history and culture, Buckell has written one of the few truly multicultural steampunk stories, making it an excellent choice for teens from all backgrounds. John's teenage son Jerome will draw in male readers. As the series progresses it veers closer to space opera, making this an easy crossover recommendation. (print, ebook)

Ballantine, Pip and Tee Morris. *Phoenix Rising*, <u>Ministry of Peculiar Occurrences.</u> **2011.**

Set in the late Victorian Age, the <u>Ministry of Peculiar Occurrences</u> series stories are classic steampunk. Agent Wellington Books is an excellent archivist but a terrible field agent, but he is forced outside his basement lair when he is paired with Kiwi agent Eliza Braun. A very modern woman who wears pants and a bulletproof corset, Agent Braun also has a love of explosives, and the willingness to do whatever it takes for the king and the empire. Their action and tech-packed adventures, plus Eliza's modern attitudes and slightly supernatural events, make this appealing to teen readers. (print, ebook, audio)

Brooks, Meljean. *Kraken King*, <u>Iron Seas.</u> **2014.**

Originally published as a serial (like many Victorian era books), *The Kraken King* is an excellent intro point to Brooks's acclaimed <u>Iron Seas</u> series, which mixes steampunk, romance, and science fiction with diverse characters and far-flung settings. Zenobia Fox, spinster, author, and regular kidnapee (thanks to her brother's infamy), travels to Australia and falls into the hands of the legendary Kraken King when her airship is attacked by rogue flyers. Their developing relationship is well balanced by mystery and adventure as they traverse the Antipodean Continent. (print, ebook)

Carr, Viola. *Diabolical Miss Hyde*, <u>Electric Empire.</u> **2015.**

Inspired by the classic science fiction tale of *Dr. Jekyll and Mr. Hyde*, Carr's series features Hyde's daughter, Miss Eliza, who has her own hidden alter ego, the lusty and wild Lizzie. Even in a Victorian London, where having a robotic assistant is normal, women still are not seen as capable of running their own lives and careers. Trained as a doctor but unable to make ends meet, Eliza works as a crime scene specialist, which brings her into contact with Captain Lafayette, dashing young officer with secrets of his own. Eliza's efforts to manage her own affairs, fight to contain Lizzie, and budding romance, all make this series an excellent choice for teens. (print, ebook)

Hodder, Mark. *Strange Affair of Spring Heeled Jack*. **2010.**

A Victorian-era urban myth, Spring Heeled Jack is brought to life in this alt world steampunk story that features a unique spin on historical personages Charles Darwin, Florence Nightingale, and Isambard Kingdom Brunel. After Queen Victoria is assassinated, rival factions of libertines and technologists disrupt society, culture, and politics, ushering in an era of rapid changes and social unrest. Famed explorer Richard Burton, now king's agent, investigates sightings of Jack and werewolves in Whitechapel with the help of friend and aspiring poet Algernon Swinburne. (print, ebook, digital audio)

Mann, George. *The Affinity Bridge*, <u>Newbury and Hobbes.</u> **2008.**

Sir Maurice Newberry, a gentleman investigator for the crown, is a steampunk Indiana Jones, working as an anthropologist at the British Museum when he is not chasing murderers across town. Teamed up with a modern (female!) assistant, Miss Veronica Hobbes, their first case involves a crashed airship, automatons, and a zombie plague. The lively chase and action scenes will draw in male and female readers, as will the description of the many gadgets and steam-driven devices, which continue in this ongoing series of novels and short stories. (print, ebook, audio)

Priest, Cherie. *Boneshaker*, Clockwork Century. 2012.
Zeke has grown up knowing that his father was blamed for the blight gas that covers Seattle and turns all living humans into ravenous zombies. Briar attempts to protect her son by keeping him outside the walled remnants of the ruined city, but Zeke's burning desire to save his father's name takes him into the home of airship pirates, gas mask–wearing refugees, and ruthless criminals. One of the few American set stories, this is the first in an ongoing series starting in the 1880s. (print, ebook, audio)

VanderMeer, Ann. *Steampunk*. 2008.
Readers needing a more moderate dip into the steampunk world should try this excellent collection of stories that introduces readers to many of the classic elements of steampunk, from space faring dirigibles to mad scientists, to corsets and waistcoats. Several stories introduce the classic big questions about the role of technology in a changing society and the dangers of creating artificial intelligence. Contributions from classic authors like Michael Moorcock and James Blaylock make this an excellent starting point for new and experienced steampunk readers. (print, later volumes, *Steampunk II* and *Steampunk III* are also available as ebooks)

Dystopias and the Apocalypse

Anyone familiar with teens will know their predilection for drama, so it should come as no surprise that teens are drawn to the dramatic and exciting stories set in a bleak future. Long a staple of science fiction (*1984* or *Fahrenheit 451*) stories of a future Earth destroyed by human negligence, greed, or violence are another good place to start teen readers, especially those who have enjoyed the popular YA books like *Hunger Games* or *Divergence*. Teens can also bring a unique view to these stories; unlike adults who may be too entrenched in daily life, teens can see that there are ways out of the worst crises if only they are willing to take the chance.

Brooks, Max. *World War Z*. 2006.
Teens may recognize the title from the moderately successful movie of the same name (2013), but the book version's unique storytelling style of relating the end of the world via interviews and documents will definitely appeal to teens. Humanity barely survived the zombie uprising; now the full and true story is being compiled from the stories of survivors across the world. (print, audio, ebook)

Brown, Pierce. *Red Rising*, Red Rising. 2014.
Humanity has colonized Mars, but for the Reds, life is short and hard. Working as miners deep under Mars, they toil away with the promise that future generations will be able to live on a fully terraformed Mars. After a mining tragedy, Darrow joins the shadowy rebel organization, Sons of Ares in an attempt to infiltrate the Golds, the highest level of Martian society. But even at the top, life is not easy on Mars and Darrow finds himself trapped in a testing program that makes the *Hunger Games* seems easy. Violent, and action packed, this cross between the *Hunger Games* and *Ender's Game* will appeal to many teen readers. (print, ebook, audio)

Carey, Jacqueline. *Santa Olivia*. 2009.
Trapped in the militarized border zone between Texas and Mexico, orphan Loup Garron has grown up knowing the only hope of escape is to

defeat the general's champion in a public boxing match. And she just might have a chance since she inherited speed, strength, and stamina from her father, a genetic engineering experiment. In this variation of Robin Hood, Loup lives with the Santitos, fellow orphans and outcasts who spend their nights avenging the many wrongs done to the people of the town even as Loup trains for the fight of her life. (print, ebook, audio)

Cline, Ernest. *Ready Player One.* **2011.**

Teen on the run from an all-knowing evil corporation encounters the biggest Easter Egg of his life in a virtual world, but he will not find it and stop the baddies without his best (virtual) friends in the real world, at last. Full of references to 1980s culture and video games, teen readers will enjoy the historical appeal and the gamer lifestyle portrayed in this somewhat upbeat view of the future.

Howey, Hugh. *Wool.* **2013.**

No one remembers a time when humanity did not live inside 100-story silos sunk deep underground, or when democracy and education were stalwarts of society. Howey's self-publishing success, nine linked stories about the secrets of the silos, explores why humanity must hide deep beneath the earth, constrained by strict rules and a highly classified society. Coming-of-age themes, young adult characters, and a fast-paced plot all make this perfect for teens. (print, ebook, audio)

Stirling, S. M. *Dies the Fire,* The Change. **2005.**

One day anything electrical, using a combustion engine or gunpowder, suddenly and catastrophically fails. Thrown into chaos, groups of survivors attempt to start new communities and live. Some, like the group led by Juniper, become peaceful farmers. Others have become ruthless killers, using their skills from the Society of Creative Anachronism to fight and kill in a world without guns. Teens will be drawn by the "what if?" only to become engaged with the action-packed plot lines. (print, ebook, audio)

Winters, Ben. *The Last Policeman.* **2012.**

In six months, the world as we know will be destroyed when a huge asteroid hits Earth. Policeman Hank Palace still tries to solve crimes, even though no one else seems to care, leaving Hank on his own to investigate a suspicious suicide. The dissolution of society as the asteroid approaches adds tension and world building that makes this more than just another disaster story. (print, ebook, audio)

Conclusion: Trends in Science Fiction

As long as there has been adult science fiction, teens have been reading it and will continue to be a key part of the genre's readership. Without being exposed to science fiction as a teen, few of today's adult science fiction readers would have become the fans they are; therefore, keeping teens interested and connected with adult science fiction is an important part of keeping the science fiction world lively and diverse. Without new voices science fiction could stagnate and become obsolete, so it is up to librarians to make sure that teens of all types are welcomed and provided with the stories they seek.

Notes

1. Moyer, Jessica E. and Christy Donaldson, "Science Fiction" in *Integrated Advisory*, Jessica E. Moyer, ed., Libraries Unlimited, 2011.

2. "Science Fiction," http://www.merriam-webster.com/dictionary/science%20fiction, accessed March 24, 2016.

3. Gunn, James, "The Worldview of Science Fiction" from the *Science of Science-Fiction Writing*, http://www.sfcenter.ku.edu/sfview.htm.

3

Fantasy

Jessica E. Moyer

Introduction to the Genre

Definition

In her chapter on fantasy in *Integrated Advisory Service*, librarian Jessica Zellers writes, "The universal story types—myths, legends, and fables—all pay homage to the fantastic, and even in today's technologically advanced society, fantasy enjoys broad appeal. The first stories that we hear as children, fairy tales, are a subgenre of today's fantasy; the classics of children's literature are predominantly fantastic." It should come as no surprise then that fantasy is one of the most popular adult genres read by teens. Zellers goes on to define fantasy as fiction that "necessarily includes something—a setting, a character, an action—that could not occur in the past, present, or future of the world as we know it." This is an especially useful definition for librarians working with wide range of fantasy as it is inclusive of emerging subgenres of steampunk and urban fantasy, both of which are popular with teen readers.

Appeals

Adult readers of fantasy will often have started reading adult fantasy in their early teens, which was partially a response to the lack of young adult (YA) fantasy. Children raised on fairy tales and children's fantasy, from the picture books of Bill Peet to the chapter books of Roald Dahl, continue to seek out fantasy stories. Before the boom in teen fantasy, led by authors like Tamora Pierce or Robin McKinley, teens would often jump straight to adult fiction and even today, many teens still want to explore adult fantasy books. Of course, one reason is that traditional fantasy books often have young lead characters in their late teens or early 20s, who set off on a quest to discover themselves and save the world. How many teens dreamed of being Rand al'Thor, the secretly world-saving hero of Robert Jordan's *Wheel of Time* saga? While today's fantasy has expanded beyond the traditional quest and sword and sorcery titles of the 1980s and 1990s, younger characters still abound, making it easy for teens to relate to their struggles and adventures.

Of course, the fantastical setting is at least as big a draw for teens as it is for adults. Adolescence can be a challenging and turbulent time in the life of any teen, so being able to escape away to a world that is clearly not their own can be a great draw for many readers. Fantasy provides a full range of alternate realities, from vampires hidden among the world as we know it to the fully fantastical second worlds of authors, such as Robin McKinley or Tamora Pierce. Suggest urban fantasy for teens more interested in real stories and steampunk for those with a strong interest in history, costumes, and gadgets.

Working with Readers

Advisors working with teen readers should consider using their interests in fantasy TV series, movies, and games to connect to adult fantasy books, as well as make readalike recommendations based on known YA authors, such as Naomi Novik's *Uprooted* for fans of Robin McKinley's fairy-based tales like *Spindles End*. Older teens may also be interested in moving to adult books because they are looking for longer and more complex stories. Few YA series extend beyond three or four books, whereas adult fantasy series can be nearly unending. Individual volumes also tend to be longer, many in the 600–800 page ranges, which may appeal to readers who have breezed their way through the YA section. Finally, advisors working with teens need to understand that teens, as a general rule, are excellent self-censors. Rather than give warnings about books being inappropriate for a reader (a guaranteed way to entice rebellious teens), matter-of-fact mentions of violence, sex, or language is all that is needed. Give teens plenty of choices and they will choose the best books for themselves.

Tools and Resources

Most websites and book awards geared to science fiction also cover fantasy, listed next are resources that focus on just fantasy.

- "Adult Books 4 Teens," originally a column in *School Library Journal*, has become an active and popular blog with a dedicated fantasy section, http://blogs.slj.com/adult4teen/category/fantasy/.
- *Booklist*: With a long history of noting adult titles with teen appeal, the librarians' favorite *Booklist* and its online companion are one of the best resources for finding adult fantasy with strong YA appeal. Look for YA notes at the end of adult book reviews.
- Herald, Diana Tixier and Bonnie Kunzel, *Fluent in Fantasy*, 2nd edition. Part of Library Unlimited's Genreflecting series, this volume annotates more than 2,000 titles in a variety of subgenres. While it is a bit dated, many of the authors writing in 2007 are still active today, and this can serve as a good tool for updating fantasy collection. Herald is a noted teen librarian so her recommendations for teen-appropriate titles are spot on.
- Zellers, Jessica. "Fantasy" in *Integrated Advisory*, Jessica E. Moyer, ed. Libraries Unlimited, 2011. In addition to a thorough overview of the genre, Jessica selects titles in every section that have especially strong teen appeal. The multimedia approach is particularly good for working with teens who enjoy fantasy stories across formats.

Collection Development

Collection development librarians looking to expand their collections should consider making connections to popular fantasy TV series. *Once Upon a Time* is one of the best, as it borrows heavily from a wide range of fantasy and fairy tales, from Snow White to King Arthur, Disney's Sorcerer's *Apprentice* to *Rumpelstiltskin* and even modern heroines like Merida from *Brave*. NBC's *Grimm* is a good second choice. Fantasy video games are another good connection for teen fantasy fans, make sure to have classics like *Skyrim*, *Final Fantasy*, and *Fable* that are noted for their player-driven plots and characters. Other formats like graphic novels cannot be ignored; teens excited to read adult books like *American Gods* are going to want to check out Neil Gaiman's Sandman series. Finally, it is a good practice to get audio versions of the most popular adult titles. Busy teens often have more time to listen than read and the quality of modern audiobook productions will be appreciated by teens raised on the magical voice of Jim Dale.

The Literature

Traditional Fantasy: Epics and Quests

Pseudo-medieval settings and fully created fantasy worlds are the hallmark of traditional fantasy, yet they have moved far beyond the Tolkien-inspired doorstops of the 1990s and thus have increased appeal to today's teen readers.

Freeman, Pamela. *Blood Ties*, The Castings Trilogy. 2007.
When the Domains were invaded hundreds of year ago, the original inhabitants were forced into a marginal and migratory lifestyle. But the past has not been forgotten, and the stories of Ash, Bramble, and Saker gradually weave together into a compelling story of revenge and redemption. Multiple young adult characters and accessible world building make this a good starting place for new readers, but a unique enough take on epic fantasy to draw in experienced readers. (print, ebook)

Jemisin, N. K. *Hundred Thousand Kingdoms*, The Inheritance Trilogy. 2010.
What would it be like if the gods not only were present on Earth, but living as prisoners of war in the royal palace? How do you keep all powerful creatures captive and submissive? Yeine Darr must confront these challenges along with her newly found vicious and bloodthirsty cousins when she accepts her legacy as heir to the throne of the Hundred Thousand Kingdoms. Yeine is dark skinned, as is African American author, N. K. Jemisen, making this one of the few epic fantasy series with overtly non-white protagonists, increasing its appeal to multicultural teen readers. (print, digital, audio)

Lackey, Mercedes. *Foundation*, Heralds of Valdemar: The Collegium. 2008.
Lackey's Valdemar series has been an entry point for teen readers since the first books were published in the 1980s. Now new readers are welcomed to her world with this new five-part subseries, which can be read on its own or as an introduction to the fantasy world of Valdemar and the legendary

College of Heralds. Magpie, a mysterious orphan who spent his life as a slave in a gem mine, escapes when he is chosen by one of the magical Companion horses and carried away to the capital. Magpie's ignorance of the world outside the mine, plus the college setting, makes this particularly appealing to teens and an excellent choice for fans of Tamora Pierce's Beka Cooper series. (print, ebook, audio)

Miller, Karen. *The Innocent Mage*, 2007, and *The Awakened Mage*, 2008, Kingmaker, Kingbreaker. 2012.
Pragmatic Asher plans to spend a year in the capital solely to earn enough money to buy a boat for his father, but fate has a different destiny in mind for the plainspoken young man. Teens will be intrigued by the world Miller creates; weather magic and the Wall keep the kingdom safe but at the cost of the independence of the indigenous Doranen. Asher's decidedly unheroic attitude will appeal to readers looking for something a little out of the ordinary.

Rawn, Melanie. *Touchstone*, Glass Thorns. 2012.
Wizards, elves, goblins, and humans have been interbreeding for so long that there are few purebreds of any race, and the diluted magic is deemed useful only for theater. Touchstone is an aspiring group of young men, who are determined to be both the best debut players and put their own spin on the traditional stories. Cade, Jeska, Rafe, and Mieka each evolve and grow throughout the series as they struggle with both fame and adult responsibilities. Theater-loving teens will be intrigued by the main plotlines, while epic fantasy readers will enjoy the political subplots and well-developed fantasy world. (print, digital)

Sagara, Michelle. *Cast in Shadow*, Chronicles of Elantra. 2005.
Kaylin is the youngest member of the Hawks, the police force of the city of Elantra, but one of the most dedicated since she fled the dangerous fiefs at the tender age of 13. Now the same mysterious marks that cover her arms are appearing on the bodies of child murder victims, triggering fear, magic, and a desperate race to save the children of Elantra. A mix of crime and fantasy, plus Kaylin's own coming-of-age story, along with several nonhuman races living together in a complex fantasy world will engage readers through all 10 titles in this ongoing series. (print, digital, audio)

Sanderson, Brandon. *Mistborn: The Final Empire*, Mistborn. 2006.
Before Sanderson became famous for completing the *Wheel of Time*, he wrote an inventive epic fantasy trilogy about a world subjugated under the strict laws of the capital, where most of the population is considered disposable slaves. Recruited by master criminal and rebel leader Kel, teenage Vin learns to master her own special powers while struggling to understand her place in a dangerous and desperate world. Plenty of action, interspersed with high-society machinations, makes for a fast pace with lots of appeal for teen readers. (ebook, print, audio)

Sullivan, Michael. Riyria Chronicles and Riyria Revelations. 2011.
Aspiring teen writers will be intrigued by Sullivan's successful self-publications and eventual print contracts with Hachette book group, while fantasy fans will appreciate this lighter take on the traditional epic fantasy. Hadrian is a highly skilled mercenary and his partner, Royce, is an even more skilled thief, and they are happy with their uneventful lives. When they

are framed for the king's murder, both must face their complicated pasts and attempt to save their country. (print, digital, audio Audible)

Grimdark

Traditional fantasy has tended to have lovable heroes accompanied by a band intrepid and loyal friends who all seem to manage to defy the odds and endure terrible odds to see their quest to its finale. In recent years authors have turned this trope upside down, instead writing about antiheroes in dark, violent worlds where shades of gray predominate and few characters are truly good. Teens with a rebel streak and/or a taste for post-apocalyptic stories such as *Hunger Games* are a prime audience, as are male readers of all ages.

Abercrombie, Joe. *Half a King***, Shattered Sea. 2014.**
What happens when the despised and handicapped younger son ends up inheriting a leadership role he never expected? Known for dark and violent fantasies, this is the perfect place for teen readers to be introduced to Abercrombie's revenge-filled take on epic fantasy, as he chronicles the story of Prince Yarvi and his desperate attempts to return home and regain his father's throne.

Bledsoe, Alex. *The Sword-Edged Blonde,* **Eddie LaCrosse. 2007.**
Eddie LaCrosse is happy to work as a sword for hire and never thinks about his past in these noir influenced takes on traditional stories. Ever wonder about the real story behind King Arthur and the Knights of the Round Table? Eddie tells all in *Dark Jenny*. Readers who prefer to start from the beginning can learn the full story of Eddie's tragic beginnings in *The Sword-Edged Blonde*, when his past catches up to him in an attempt to rescue a princess. (ebook, print, audio)

Dalglish, David. *Dance of Cloaks***, Shadowdance. 2013.**
Grimdark tales are more likely to be set in the gritty world of the city than the more genteel rural settings of traditional fantasy. The five books that make up this series were originally self-published, a hook for aspiring teen writers, and are all set in the city of Veldaren, one completely controlled by a criminal mastermind and dreaded assassin, Thren. While his son killed his first man at the age of 8, by the time shy Aaron is in his teens he is no longer sure he wants to follow in the family business. (print, ebook)

Lawrence, Mark. *Prince of Fools***, Prince Jalan. 2014.**
Lawrence's second trilogy features a cowardly protagonist Prince Jalan who is more concerned with saving his own skin than doing anything for others. When he reluctantly ventures away from home, he is caught up in a snare of treachery and deception that may be more than even Jalan can successfully run from. Set in the same dark post-nuclear world as Lawrence's debut Thorns series, this slightly less violent series stands well on its own and is a good starting place for teen readers. (ebook, print, audio)

Lynch, Scott. *Lies of Locke Lamora***, Gentleman Bastards. 2007–**
The Gentleman Bastards are the premier thieves of Camorra, but no one outside their group knows that they are the masterminds behind most outrageous cons and heists plaguing the city. Led by orphan and genius Locke Lamora, the group of teenage con artists soon finds themselves over their heads in plots that risk the very foundation of their world. The devil-may-care

attitude of Locke and company will appeal to rebellious teens everywhere and the Renaissance-era Venice-inspired setting will draw in fantasy readers looking for something new. (print, digital, audio)

McClellan, Brian. *Promise of Blood*, Powder Mage. 2013–2015.
McClellan's debut is a classic of flintlock fantasy, where traditional mages war against those who gain their strength and power from black powder. Twenty-four-year-old Taniel Two Shot is widely acclaimed for his ability to shoot and direct two bullets in a single shot, but he is jaded and worn-out by near-constant campaigns. Only after his equally famous father, Field Marshal Tamas leads a coup, does Taniel agree to take up arms one final time. But first he has to hunt and kill his best friend, the only surviving royal mage. The mix of guns, magic, and meddling gods, plus plenty of action and a grim overtone make this perfect for any reader craving a change of pace. (print, ebook)

Staveley, Brian. *Emperor's Blades*, Chronicle of the Unhewn Throne. 2014–
With the death of the emperor of the Unhewn Throne, his children take up their duties and serve the kingdom. With the eldest son training with elite warrior monks in the remote mountains, and the second son training as a member of an elite military force that fights from the back of giant hawks, only his daughter Adare (now minister of trade) is home in the capital to keep the kingdom together while her brothers struggle to survive long enough to take up their duties. Between the young adult protagonists, the fast pace, and death-defying antics, this is a perfect read for any teen fantasy fan. (print, ebook)

Weeks, Brent. *The Way of Shadows*, Night Angel. 2008.
Raised in the slums, orphan Azoth's only hope at a new life is to convince the city's master assassin to take him on as an apprentice and embrace a new identity as Kylar. But is he tough enough to kill and survive life in the criminal underworld? Gritty and violent, yet with some light at the end of the tunnel, this is a perfect readalike for teens who enjoy the Alex Award-winning *Lies of Locke Lamora*. (print, ebook, audio)

Women Authors and Characters

Despite the grimdark subgenre being dominated by male authors and characters, there has not been a lack in female fantasy and there are plenty of titles to appeal to both male and female readers. This section highlights a few of the newer and outstanding female authors, as well as some female characters with strong teen appeal.

Barker, Emily Croy. *The Thinking Woman's Guide to Real Magic.* 2013.
Nora just wanted some time alone after being dumped by her boyfriend, but when she wanders off she has no idea that she will slip into an alternate world whose beautiful veneer hides a dark and dangerous underbelly. Nora's previous life as a frustrated graduate student makes this an easy suggestion for older teens, and perfect for fans of alt world stories like *Fire and Hemlock* by Diana Wynne Jones. (print, ebook, audio)

Bujold, Lois McMaster. *Beguilement*, The Sharing Knife. **2006.**

Bujold's four-part epic is both a forbidden romance and an exploration of her uniquely hazardous fantasy world. Fawn is a pregnant runaway who kills a vicious malice with Dag's magical sharing knife, saving their lives but not the life of her unborn baby. Farm girl Fawn and Dag, a Lakewalker and ranger, should never have met, let alone fallen in love, making theirs a unique partnership. Teens will appreciate how Fawn learns from her mistakes, but never allows them to dictate her life while all fantasy fans will be intrigued by Bujold's fantasy world. (print, ebook, audio)

Hobb, Robin. Liveship Traders Trilogy, 1999–2003, and Rain Wild Chronicles, 2010–2013.

Oldest daughter Althea longs to captain her family's liveship but it is considered ill luck and few support her mission to rescue the family's missing ship. Althea's quest for belonging will ring true with teen readers, as will the story of the damaged and possibly insane liveship, *Paragone*. Even the most spoiled and bratty characters, like Althea's niece Malta, eventually mature and shoulder the responsibilities necessary for saving the family's home and business. Set several years later, the *Rainwild Chronicles* moves away from the coast into the depths of the hazardous Rain Wilds and features an all-new set of young adult characters searching for a place to belong. (print, audiobook, ebook)

Johansen, Erika. *Queen of the Tearling*. **2014.**

Johansen's debut has quickly become a favorite among fantasy readers jaded by the usual stories of plucky heroines and princesses. Tough and resilient Kelsea knows she will someday inherit the throne, but she also knows that no one will want to marry the plump and homely daughter of a failed queen, even if she carries the fabled Tearling jewel. The mix between a science fictional future and a magical world where jewels give visions are just one of the unique appeals of this series. (ebook, print, audio)

Maguire, Gregory. *Wicked: The Life and Times of the Wicked Witch of the West*, The Wicked Years. **1995.**

Teens may know Elphaba from the award-winning musical, but they will not really know her until they delve in Maguire's complex exploration of good and evil. From Elphaba's birth to missionaries in the Quadling swamps, through her years at the university, and final weeks at the western fortress of Kiamo Ko, teens will be fascinated with this nuanced view of one of the most famous wicked witches ever to grace the page or the screen. Elphaba's not the only strong woman in Oz, her sister Nessarose and best friend Glenda wield great power far beyond the glimpses provided in Baum's original works. (print, ebook, audio)

Martin, George R. R., and Gardner Dozois, eds. *Dangerous Women*. **2013.**

With contributions from dozens of best-selling and award-winning authors, this anthology is notable for its incredible variety of female-centered stories. There is something for everyone, from a Western gunfighter to dragon-flying princesses. Many of the stories can be used as entry points, making this a good introduction for many well-known authors. (print, ebook, audio)

Pratchett, Terry. Discworld. 1983–2015.
From the witches of Lancre using headology to crown kings and ensure the safety of the kingdom to Lady Sybil Ramkin, richest person in the city of Ankh-Morpork, wife of Guard Captain Samuel Vimes, and rescuer of homeless swamp dragons, teens will be thrilled with the diversity of female characters. Whether they are women like Sgt. Angua who is more concerned with being a werewolf than a female in a male-dominated profession or Cheery Little-bottom who bucks dwarf cultural norms and insists on wearing lipstick, there is something for every reader in this expansive series. (print, ebook, audio)

Snyder, Maria V. *Poison Study*. Study Series. 2005–2015.
What's the easier choice? Death by execution tomorrow, or a life as poison taster to the commander? Yelena chooses life, only to discover that training as a poison taster may kill her before she even begins work. Snyder's world development with a military dictator government and a light dose of magic plus fascinating and complex characters have made her a must read for fantasy fans of all ages. (print, ebook, audio)

Historical Fantasy and Steampunk

One of the hottest new trends in fantasy are steampunk-based stories that often incorporate historical settings (Victorian England is popular) along with fantasy staples like vampires, werewolves, magicians, and enterprising young women. The slightly more realistic settings can appeal to teens who are not ready for the fully realized second worlds of more traditional fantasy, as well as to those with an interest in historical stories. With any steampunk, teens interested in the creative costuming and gadget making side of steampunk culture are likely to enjoy these stories.

Carriger, Gail. *Soulless*. The Parasol Protectorate. 2009.
Alexia Tarabotti is more than your average blue stocking Victorian-era spinster; for one she has a terribly embarrassing lack of soul, not to mention an unladylike appetite for treacle tart and a penchant for killing ill-mannered vampires. Carriger's steampunk Victorian-era fantasy series is fast and fun reading, filled with fascinating characters (Alexia's best friend Ivy is obsessed with hats, and her gossiping pal, Lord Akeldama, is a truly ancient vampire), and a plethora of inventive steampunk devices. Alexia's journey of self-discovery will appeal to teens trying to find their own place in the world, while the light levels of steampunk make this perfect for new readers. (print, audiobook, ebook, manga)

Cato, Beth. *The Clockwork Dagger: A Novel*. Clockwork Dagger. 2014.
Cato's first novel also kicked off a trilogy that became an unexpected hit with readers and librarians and has since spawned several novellas and short stories set in the same world. Orphan Octavia Leander has finally graduated and is off to use her healing powers to save cities devastated by the long-running war. But before she even arrives, a series of incidents on her airship make her realize there is far more going on than she ever knew as a sheltered student. With a darker tone and more serious themes, this is the perfect readalike for teen fans of *Queen of the Tearling*. (print, ebook)

Clarke, Susanna. *Jonathan Strange & Mr Norrell*. 2004.
Jonathan Strange and Mr Norrell. A perfect choice for teens who like their fantasy thick and detailed; the footnotes will draw in teens with an

interest in history and research, and the unique magical systems will keep fantasy fans turning the pages. (print, ebook, audiobook)

Griffith, Clay and Susan Griffith. *The Shadow Revolution: Crown & Key.* Crown & Key. 2015.

Similar in style of Robert Downey Jr.'s *Sherlock Holmes*, this fast-paced Victorian action adventure story has all the elements readers have come to expect in a steampunk fantasy. From gadgets to ghouls, magician and playboy Simon Archer will try to tackle anything if he has the help of alchemist and contentedly single Kate Anstruther and their new friend, self-described monster hunter Malcolm MacFarlane. Kate's younger sister is one of the several younger characters that will garner the sympathy of teen reader; make sure to suggest this to teens who like their fantasy liberally laced with fight scenes. (print, ebook)

Monk, Devon. *Dead Iron.* The Age of Steam. 2011.

Moving away from the more typical British settings, Monk's series is set in an alt version of the American west where werewolves are real and men, machines, and magic all populate and battle across a gritty western America. More like Cherie Priest's *Boneshaker*, this is a good choice for teens interested in male characters and a more action-oriented plot. (print, ebook)

Pape, Cindy Spencer. *Steam and Sorcery.* The Gaslight Chronicles. 2011.

With clever, alliterative titles for each new entry, Pape's Gaslight Chronicles tells the adventures of the Knights of the Round Table in nineteenth-century Britain as they help rescue accused witches, damaged barons, and even a terrified photographer. With nearly as much magic as science, these are a classic blend that will appeal to teens looking for a lighter read while still having fun with airships and aviators. (print, ebook)

Schwarz, Liesel. *A Clockwork Heart.* The Chronicles of Light and Shadow. 2013.

Taya loves her job as an Icarus, a winged messenger who travels freely among castles in the city of Ondinium, but her life becomes complicated after a midair rescue entangles her into the highest levels of politics and power. The purely fantasy world is enhanced with steampunk elements, including the Great Machine, the computer that runs the world and helps create and maintain technology like Taya's wings. A good choice for teens who prefer their stories firmly in the realms of fantasy. (print, ebook, audiobook)

Schwarz, Liesel. *A Conspiracy of Alchemists.* Chronicles of Light and Shadow. 2013.

Elle wants nothing more than to work as a pilot, but flying her dirigible costs money and occasionally means taking on jobs that are more than a little bit shady. Dedicated to science and machinery, at first Elle is confused by the mysterious Mr. Marsh and his quest to stop the Alchemists. But Elle is always up for an adventure and she gets far more than she anticipated as she delves into the brewing war between Alchemy and Warlocks. Elle's strong character and independent attitude make this a great suggestion for teen girls who like their steampunk with a strong dose of romance. (print, ebook, audiobook)

Urban Fantasy

For the last 15 years, some of the most popular fantasy series have not been the traditional second-world settings of magic, but stories set in a recognizable here and now. Urban fantasy relies far less on setting than traditional stories, often only lightly sketching in the background with an assumption that the known setting is already familiar to readers. Instead urban fantasy stories tend to be faster paced and less complex, in some ways drawing more from mystery series formats than those of traditional fantasy. The more real setting, quick pace, and more modern characters make these stories popular with a wide range of teen readers.

Cole, Myke. *Control Point*. **Shadow Ops. 2012.**

Lt. Britton has dedicated his career to taking down unauthorized magic users, which makes it particularly difficult when he manifests one of the more unusual powers. Promptly conscripted, Britton is sent off to fight in an alternate dimension, where shells rain down at all hours of the day and night, and few of the enlisted actually want to fight for the U.S. government. Author Cole currently serves in the Reserves and has completed tours as a contractor in Iraq; the accuracy of military life and weaponry is a highlight and will be especially to teen readers interested in a military career.

Correia, Larry. *The Monster Hunters*. **Monster Hunter. 2012.**

What if monsters were real? Well then, someone would need to hunt them down and protect humanity. And that is exactly the job offer Owen receives when he wakes up in the hospital after having tossed his clearly not right boss out of a 14th-story window. Lighter on plot and character development, this four-book series has a plethora of action and fight sequences (plus an impending Armageddon) that will keep readers rapidly turning the pages. A good choice for gamers. (print, ebook)

Drake, Jocelynn. Asylum Tales. 2012–

Gage Powell is a warlock on the run; he managed to escape the tyranny and sadistic training of the Ivory Towers, but now he is forced to hide both himself and his powers. Gage sets himself up as a tattoo artist who can do a little bit more provided he can get the right magical ingredients, staffs his shop with fellow outcasts; Bronx is a troll with a surprisingly deft hand for ink work and Trixie the elf is also hiding her past. Especially good for teen boys as this is one of the few urban fantasy series to feature multiple male characters.

Hearne, Kevin. The Iron Druid Chronicles. 2011–

For nearly 2,000 years, Atticus O'Sullivan has been the only living druid and he has taken great pains to stay hidden from the gods, especially Aengus Og of the Tuatha De Danann who would very much like to take back his magical sword. Masquerading as a 20-something hippie, Atticus runs an occult bookstore in Arizona along with his Irish wolfhound Oberon, to whom he is telepathically bound, when events conspire to cause Atticus to break cover and set off a chain reaction that will resonate across the human and godly planes. One of the most humorous urban fantasy series, Atticus' sharp wit is set off by his conversations with Oberon, who above all is a dog and mostly interested in sausages and biting bad guys.

Lackey, Mercedes, et al. *Invasion*. **Secret World Chronicle. 2011.**

Inspired by a role-playing game and developed into a podcast, the Secret World Chronicles explore an alternate world where metahumans started to appear in the 1920s and super heroes have become real. Which is a good thing when the Thulians invade Earth; turns out these aliens captured quite a few Nazis in the last months of World War II and now alien Nazi war machines are set on destroying humanity and only the metahumans have any chance of stopping them. Written by multiple authors, each chapter is from a different character point of view that creates a particularly well-developed world and a diversity of characters. (print, ebook)

McGuire, Seanan. *Discount Armageddon*. InCryptid. **2012.**
Verity Price may be a member of the most famous monster protecting family on Earth (and one of the most wanted) but she is not willing to let that stop her dreams of becoming a professional ballroom dancer. Which is how she ends up spending a year in New York City working as a waitress at a supernatural strip club at night and dancing by day. But destiny is hard to escape and Verity cannot ignore when cryptids (what others would call monsters) in her city start to go missing. Creative and humorous this series is perfect for teens struggling with family and identity, or anyone who wonders what it would be like to live with a colony of extremely religious talking mice. (print, ebook, audio)

McGuire, Seanan. *Rosemary and Rue*. October Daye. **2009–**
Toby Daye has struggled for years with her half-human, half-fae heritage, but things get really difficult when she is turned into a carp and tossed into the ponds at the Japanese Gardens for 14 years. By the time she escapes, she is forced to build a whole new life that involved embracing her fae heritage and becoming a PI. McGuire creates a world where the fae are as deeply entrenched in the Bay Area as humanity and deftly mixes in a diverse range of characters and creatures from multiple mythologies. Toby's struggles to fit in will resonate with teen readers.

Price, Kalayna. *Grave Witch*, Alex Craft. **2010–**
Alex has been friends with Death for years because she is one of the rare grave witches who can see and talk to the dead. Which makes working as a consultant for the police a perfect addition to her PI agency, that is, until she gets involved in two high-profile murder cases that put her own life at risk. Alex struggles with her place in the world, a difficult family history, and an attraction to the lead detective who is hiding secret of his own. (print, ebook)

Conclusion: Trends in Fantasy

If any genre can be said to exploding in popularity, it is surely fantasy. Urban fantasy and steampunk have greatly expanded beyond the traditional genre stories of epics and quests, and the diversity in characters and settings is also changing. Readers of all ages love fantasy in its many forms, a quick look at popular TV shows and movies makes it clear that fantasy thrives. As long as the genre continues to grow and reflect the diversity of the modern world it will be popular. Keep an eye out for new expansions in the genre like the recent growth in fantasy-based steampunk stories as these new developments are even more likely to attract teen readers.

4

Horror

Kelly Fann

Introduction to the Genre

Definition

Of the mainstream fiction genres, horror is often the easiest to define and yet often causes much consternation by those unfamiliar with it. As identified in Douglas Winter, "Horror is not a genre, like the mystery or science fiction or western. . . . Horror is an emotion" (*Prime Evil*, 1982). Knowing that horror is an emotional genre much like romance, which requires emotional responses of love and passion, the main requirement for horror is that it elicits an emotional response of fear or dread.

With no formulaic requirements beyond invoking fear in the reader and the avoidance of a complete happy ending (those are reserved for romance novels), horror novels cover a wide spectrum of subgenres, themes, and trends; and they typically invoke the supernatural. Supernatural elements allow for the unexplainable. Readers cannot easily dismiss the horror through rational means; the phenomena become undefinable with unearthly monsters and extraordinary threats. Just having a supernatural element in a novel does not mean it is horror; there also has to be a growing sense of dread, the jolts of action should be unexpected and menacing, and the ending should be at least somewhat vague with the sense that the evil may not have been completely defeated.

It is important to remember that what elicits horror is specific to the individual reader. The plot contained within the horror novel brings nightmares to life and serves the purpose of frightening readers and forcing them to confront their fears in a safe environment. Determining which fears pair up with which novel, however, can sometimes be a tricky task, which is where the librarian role comes into play.

Appeals

Brian K. Vaughan states in his introduction to the third volume of Joe Hill's <u>Locke and Key</u> series, "Readers love fantasy, but we *need* horror.

Smart horror. Truthful horror. Horror that helps us make sense of a cruelly senseless world" (Vaughan, 2010). Teens are at an age when they are trying to make sense of world where the realities of life are hitting closer to home. By the time they hit their teenage years, young adults are facing any number of frightening life experiences—bullying, depression, learning disabilities, domestic issues, gang warfare, abuse, rape, racism, suicide, and so much more. While literature serves as a means of escape from real-world horrors, horror novels provide a safe haven for teens and adults alike to face their fears and explore supernaturally frightening events within a safe environment.

In terms of the standard appeal factors as outlined by Saricks, certainly the story line, which can take readers on an adrenaline-fueled ride, figures in; as does setting, which is often immersive (e.g., haunted houses, graveyards, lagoons). Characters—and especially the type of monster (e.g., vampires, zombies, werewolves, ghosts)—also often represent reader preferences.

Teens reading horror novels is not a new trend and in all reality, many teenage horror fans have been reading scary stories since childhood. The Goosebumps series continues to stand the test of time with an avid fan base having garnered a 2015 blockbuster hit movie popular among all ages. Alvin Schwartz's Scary Stories to Tell in the Dark series remains popular since the first volume was published in 1981 and often ends up on the American Library Association's Top 100 Challenged Book list, indicating kids continue scrambling to read these terrifying tales. And of course, do not forget Mike Thaler's 1948 classic, *The Librarian from the Black Lagoon* and Jon Stone's 1971 classic, *The Monster at the End of This Book*, which add in a bit of humor to make the scary subjects easier to face. Kids have been reading scary tales for years as a safe way to face their fears. Teens are no different and will eventually look beyond the standard young adult horror novels that often focus on cookie-cutter characters with a bit of paranormal action for more sophisticated, and scarier horror novels. Adult horror novels can fill the needs of teen readers looking for heart-pounding suspense and page after page of high-powered action with grittier subtext and a wider range of themes and plotlines.

Horror novels not only allow teens to experience their terrors and fears in a safe atmosphere but also afford them the opportunity to question how ordinary people handle themselves in extraordinary situations. Teens can escape the real world and venture into a world of nightmares and then compare themselves to the protagonist and ponder what they would do if placed in a similar situation. The adrenaline seekers also love horror novels just as they would a roller coaster: it is scary looking down from the very top of that first drop, but once the ride gets going and the thrill escalates, you come to the end with your heart pounding and feeling completely alive—just like when you finish a great horror novel.

Working with Readers

When working with horror fiction, the first thing to know is that the newest, hottest horror novel is not always the best choice for teen readers. Great horror novels stand the test of time just as human fears do: ghosts, hauntings, possessions, zombies, ghouls, human and animal monsters, psychological terrors, Satanism, post-apocalyptic wastelands, witchcraft, and so on. Horror novels have broached these themes for decades and will continue to do so, which allows librarians to look at the classics to find the perfect scary fit for readers. In order to discover what might serve to scare the reader, conduct a readers' advisory (RA) interview just as you would for any other "what do I read next" scenario. Ask the patron what scares him or her or to describe the scariest part of a book previously read and enjoyed. If your reader is new to the horror genre, ask about television or movie tastes or suggest short story compilations for uncertain readers.

Be sure to ask patrons how they feel about gore, violence, sex, and foul language as horror novels range from the completely blood/violence/sex/foul-language free to being completely rife with it on nearly every page. Also, keep in mind with short stories that an awful lot of action and suspense is packed into just a few short pages—it can be overwhelming to the unprepared reader. And some readers prefer "psychological horror" to the more visceral types of horror—some of Stephen King's work fits into this category (e.g., *Roadwork*); Ray Bradbury, Dean Koontz, Joyce Carol Oates, Elizabeth Massie (*Sineater*) also fall into this category.

If the patron has previously enjoyed mysteries, thrillers, science fiction, or fantasy, horror could be a great next step as these genres will sometimes include horror elements to their story lines. A way to find out if horror is a good choice is to ask if the patron enjoys thrillers of any kind, is comfortable reading about blood, guts, and gore, prefers action-driven plots over character depth, and appreciates fantasy or paranormal elements. If you get a yes to those options, you have a potential horror lover in your presence.

When it comes to introducing teen readers to adult horror novels, Stephen King reigns supreme. His 1983 novel *Christine* is timeless in portraying a teenager's love of his first car despite all of its flaws. Of course, what happens when the car decides it loves you back and will do anything (aka kill) to keep you? And then there's King's classic 1974 novel *Carrie*, which depicts the uber extreme of what happens when the bullied chooses to exact revenge on her bullies, in this case, during prom. Other classic titles that continue to be popular with teens include *Rebecca* by Daphne du Maurier (1938), *The Thief of Always* by Clive Barker (1992), and *Fear Nothing* by Dean Koontz (1998). Look to the movies to see what horror films are hitting the big screen, and you will likely find them based on a previously written novel. These made-into-movie novels may be a big win for your teen horror audience.

Tools and Resources

The following lists offer you places to learn more about and keep current on the horror genre.

Websites and Blogs, General

The Horror Fiction Review: http://thehorrorfictionreview.blogspot.com
This blog originated as a print fanzine but is now available only in electronic format. Reviews are by fans of horror and titles chosen are those of high quality with most of the B or C rated titles left out.

Horror Writers Association: http://www.horror.org/
The Horror Writers Association is a nonprofit organization that aims to promote dark literature. It is the oldest and most respected professional organization of horror writers and publishers.

MonsterLibrarian: http://www.monsterlibrarian.com
MonsterLibrarian.com was created to support public, academic, and school libraries in horror readers advisory and collection development

practices. Many of the reviewers are librarians, and all reviews come with disclaimers for sex, violence, and language.

***RA for All: Horror*:** http://raforallhorror.blogspot.com/
Maintained and updated by librarian and horror guru Becky Siegel Spratford, RA for All: Horror is a great way to stay on top of trends, hot titles, up-and-coming authors.

Websites, Horror Award Winners

***Black Quill Awards*:** http://www.darkscribemagazine.com/announcements/
Black Quill Awards are given out by *Dark Scribe Magazine* annually in seven categories of dark genre literature, which include horror, suspense, and thrillers.

***Bram Stoker Awards*:** http://www.horror.org/awards/stokers.htm
The Bram Stoker Awards are handed out annually by the Horror Writers Association for superior achievement in horror writing and cover 11 categories: novel, first novel, short fiction, long fiction, young adult, fiction collection, poetry collection, anthology, screenplay, graphic novel, and nonfiction.

***Shirley Jackson Awards*:** http://www.shirleyjacksonawards.org/
The Shirley Jackson Awards recognize outstanding achievement in psychological suspense, horror, and dark fantastic literature. Awards are given in the categories of novel, novella, novelette, short story, single-author collection, and edited anthology.

Databases

NoveList or ***Fiction Catalog*:** use these library database tools as the horror genre is found throughout both of these sources.

Print Resources

Fonseca, Anthony J. and June Michelle Pulliam. *Hooked on Horror III: A Guide to Reading Interests* (Libraries Unlimited Genreflecting Advisory Series, 2009).
Orr, Cynthia and Diana Tixier Herald. *Genreflecting*, 7th edition (Libraries Unlimited Genreflecting Advisory series, 2013).
Saricks, Joyce G. *The Readers' Advisory Guide to Genre Fiction*, 2nd edition (American Library Association, 2009).
Spratford, Becky Siegel. *The Readers' Advisory Guide to Horror*, 2nd edition (American Library Association, 2012).
Wells, P. *The Horror Genre: From Beelzebub to Blair Witch* (Short Cuts Series, 2001). This is a film genre title that can be used to explore readers watching tastes to better match with reading tastes.

Collection Development

Classic titles such as *Frankenstein, Dracula, The Haunting of Hill House, The Fall of the House of Usher*, and *Rebecca* serve as a strong foundation of your horror collection, as these are reads enjoyed by teens and adults alike. When focusing on adult titles for teen readers, be sure to build a robust selection of core authors, such as Stephen King, Dean Koontz, Clive Barker,

Ramsey Campbell, H. P. Lovecraft, Ray Bradbury, and Poppy Z. Brite among others. Make sure the covers of these titles are fresh and up-to-date; old and dated covers will immediately turn off teen readers as being uncool. Up-and-coming authors accessible to teen readers will help round out the fundamental collection, and these new release titles can be found using the standard collection development print and electronic resources. In the case of horror, pay special attention to October issues, which will often focus on the horror genre.

As with any other genre, if a movie or television show based on a book is coming out, be sure to have the book on hand. For example, consider the American version of *The Ring* (2002). Koji Suzuki's 1991 novel *Ring* became the basis of a Japanese television film, then television series, then a full-length feature film, followed by a South Korean remake and finally the American remake. Once the American version came out, libraries were scrambling to have Suzuki's original novel on the shelf. Keeping tabs on movies and television shows is a must for librarians. When the first movie trailer for *Horns* was shown during Comi-Con in San Diego, California, in 2014, most libraries immediately saw their holds list grow for Joe Hill's 2010 novel on which the movie was based. The holds list is likely to continue well past the movie's release date in October.

Current horror television shows based on horror novels include *Rosemary's Baby*, *The Strain*, *The Walking Dead*, *Wayward Pines*, and *Sleepy Hollow*. Teens are watching these shows on prime time and once they discover the shows are based on books, they will be looking for the books in the library. If your library circulates television shows, be sure to have these new titles alongside the classics such as *Dark Shadows*, *Night Gallery*, *Twilight Zone*, *Tales from the Crypt*, *The Outer Limits* (the 1960s and the 1990s versions), *Fright Night*, *Kolchak: The Night Stalker*, *Freddy's Nightmares*, *Tales from the Darkside*, and *Friday's Curse* (originally titled *Friday the 13th*).

When developing a horror collection, include video games popular with teen patrons. Horror video games have a fantastic group of followers and titles include *Dead Space*, *Dead Rising*, *Alan Wake*, *Call of Duty: World at War—Zombie Verruckt*, *Condemned: Criminal Origins*, the *Silent Hill series*, *F.E.A.R. 2: Project Origin*, *Left 4 Dead*, and the *Resident Evil* franchise.

The Literature

What follows is a list of core horror titles, organized by popular themes. To best serve readers, familiarize yourself with these subgenres, as well as specific authors and titles.

Apocalyptic and Post-Apocalyptic

Apocalyptic and post-apocalyptic novels are all about setting, in this case, a world in chaos where the end is nigh, on its way, or already here. What is left of civilization is a band of survivors coping with or trying to survive after an epic disaster such as a nuclear war, global pandemic, or another type of cataclysmic event. This gritty subgenre sets a violent stage where the absolute worst fears are realized, and yet survival is possible and a glimmer of hope can shine through an otherwise dark and unsettling environment. Teens can visualize an inescapable society and apply the idea of "what if?" to their current lifestyle. This particular subgenre can also be found in the science fiction genre. What separates horror from science fiction post-apocalyptic novels is the permeating threat. In horror post-apocalyptic novels, the survivors are not concerned so much with rebuilding but merely living and not being eaten, overrun by the undead, infested by a parasitic animal, or otherwise maimed by the monster in question.

Aguirre-Sacasa, Roberto. *Escape from Riverdale.* <u>Afterlife with Archie.</u> **2014.**
Sabrina, the Teenage Witch has screwed up big time and caused the zombie apocalypse in the beloved fictional town of Riverdale. Gritty and full of pulp horror elements, the classic comic has taken a horrific twist. This graphic novel series has pop culture references at every turn, but keep in mind that the wholesome element of classic Archie is nowhere to be found. (print only)

Bell, Alden. *The Reapers Are the Angels.* <u>Reapers.</u> **2010.**
America as we know it is finished and the streets are infested with zombies. Fifteen-year-old Temple knows only the life of kill or be killed and is now on the run through a world full of violence to seek salvation and sanctuary. Teen girls will find a character worth connecting with in Temple. (print, ebook, audiobook)

Crouch, Blake. *Pines.* <u>Wayward Pines.</u> **2012.**
Ethan Burke is seemingly trapped in Wayward Pines, Idaho, and no matter how many attempts he makes, he cannot escape the town's boundaries. Nothing gets in, nothing gets out and given the one road out of town winds right back into town, Burke knows something is very, very wrong in Wayward Pines. If Burke keeps up his investigation attempts, those in power will find a way to stop him for good. *Wayward Pines* is now a hit television series on Fox. (print, ebook, audiobook)

Everson, John. *Violet Eyes.* **2013.**
After a group of partiers find a remote island once used as a testing ground for genetic warfare, everything that could go wrong does and only one survivor makes his way back to the mainland. Upon his return, flies and spiders begin overtaking his town and they are oh so very hungry. Another pulpy horror novel that has plenty of gross-out scenes and a bit of gratuitous sex. (print, ebook, audiobook)

Kenyon, Nate. *Sparrow Rock.* **2010.**
When a nuclear holocaust takes out nearly everything on the planet, a group of teenage friends happen to be hanging out in a bomb shelter. While it seems logical to stay put, the bomb shelter does not exactly keep everything from getting inside and there are some hungry beings looking for a way into the shelter for a delicious feast. Teens will appreciate the friendship bonds that come to light as the group fights for survival. (print, ebook)

Kirkman, Robert. *The Walking Dead: Book One.* <u>The Walking Dead.</u> **2004.**
This graphic novel series and now hit television series details the daily life of what a zombie apocalypse would entail over passing months and years. Chances are likely that your teen graphic novel readers have already found this series, but for those who enjoy horror and have yet to delve into graphic novels, *The Walking Dead* is a great place to start. (print only)

Lapham, David. *The Strain.* The Strain. **2012.**
An airplane has landed at JFK airport and goes completely dark prompting the CDC to explore the situation. It comes to light that this vampiric plague is of biblical proportions and threatens to wipe out the world in a matter of months. A great deal of blood, guts, and gore are contained within this graphic novel representation of Guillermo Del Toro's trilogy. (print only)

Malerman, Josh. *Bird Box.* **2014.**
The world has gone mad and the only way to survive is to stay indoors; go outside with your eyes open and you will kill others along with yourself. But how long can you survive by staying inside day after day, year after year without ever being able to look out the window? This novel forces the reader to call into question how they could potentially survive in a world when not all of the five senses can be used. (print, ebook, audiobook)

Hauntings

Haunted stories contain spirits, specters, ghosts or poltergeists, haunted houses, buildings, land parcels, modes of transportation, or other unseen paranormal activity manifestations. These tales follow a traditional storytelling pattern through the creation of an easily identified normal world that quickly unravels in a series of violent or terrifying events. This subgenre is typically character driven, oftentimes with the inanimate object being one of the characters. There is varying degrees of gore, violence, and sex so it is important to know where on the scale a particular novel falls. Teens appreciate this subgenre for the growing sense of dread and the element of the "unseen" horror by witnessing ordinary people deal with extraordinary threats and being able to place themselves (safely) in that same situation to reflect on how they would handle the threat.

Boyne, John. *This House Is Haunted.* **2013.**
A truly gothic horror novel set in the 1860s where the young governess, Eliza Caine is charged with taking care of two children in an increasingly malevolent house that tries desperately to remove her in any way possible. With little violence, virtually no gore or foul language, and a bit of under the radar humor, this is a great introductory novel for teens looking to explore adult horror. (print, ebook, audiobook)

Clegg, Douglas. *Neverland.* **2010.**
A classic H. P. Lovecraftian tale set off the coast of Georgia at Gull Island where kids turn an abandoned shack into a clubhouse and the specter called "Lucy" becomes their false god requiring the appropriate sacrifices that false gods always seem to command. The games of children can take a darker turn as teens who read *Lord of the Flies* (Golding, 1954) will remember. Teens looking for something similar to *Lord of the Flies* with a darker, more sinister edge need look no further than *Neverland*. (print, ebook, audiobook)

Cottam, F. G. *The House of Lost Souls.* **2009.**
With elements reminiscent of Shirley Jackson, London's haunted Fisher House is prepared to cause three philosophy students to lose their mind. This is your supernatural, haunted house chock full of ghosts, tale and teens who enjoy the notion of haunted psych wards or hospitals will enjoy this in

epic proportions. For teens who read Madeleine Roux's *Asylum* (2013) and yearn for something similar but darker and more adult, direct them to *The House of Lost Souls*. (print, ebook)

Hill, Joe. *Heart-Shaped Box*. 2000.
    Living the life of a rock-and-roll star does not come without its share of setbacks, in this case, the over-indulgent purchase of a haunted suit. Aging rocker Judas Coyne will have to pay penance for his past careless actions now that he has taken in the suit laced with a vengeance-driven spirit. With music references at every turn, the pop culture, music-loving teens will be glued to the pages. This title is also incredibly creepy in audiobook format. (print, ebook, audiobook)

Hill, Joe. *Welcome to Lovecraft*. Locke & Key. 2008.
    Welcome to the New England mansion, Keyhouse, where supernatural doorways contain the power to transform all those who cross their threshold, but not every transformation is welcome or without evil. High school, family issues, dating life, new schools, and a haunting legacy intermixed with amazing illustrations make this graphic novel series a favorite among teens and adults alike. (print only)

O'Nan, Stewart. *The Night Country*. 2004.
    A car full of teenagers has crashed on Halloween night killing three of the five occupants and one year later, these three ghosts tell the tale. With an ending completely ruthless and unforgiving, this horror novel is not so much full of gore, but rather raw emotion. This horror novel takes on the hard-hitting subject of teen driving by incorporating the loss of friends in a horrific crash and the guilt that accompanies such a trauma without an ounce of sympathy. (print, ebook, audiobook)

Otsuichi. *Zoo*. 2009.
    This collection of Japanese horror stories integrates science fiction elements for a collection rife with death, destruction, and decay. Many of the stories are told from a teenager's point of view with varying levels of gore. These tales will work for teens who are not quite sure they want to read horror as the stories fit a variety of genres including mystery, science fiction, bizarro, thriller, as well as horror. (print only)

Oyeyemi, Helen. *White Is for Witching*. 2009.
    Twins Miranda and Eliot suffer their mother's death quite differently with Miranda fading away into the mysteries of their rather less-than-ordinary house. The house is its own character and it desperately desires to possess and control those it considers its own and it needs Miranda to be its vessel of hatred. This is a great novel for teens who like an air of lyricism, gothic beauty and sadness, broken fairy tales, and blurred lines of reality in their novels. (print, ebook)

Rogers, Ian. *Every House Is Haunted*. 2012.
    A collection of 21 short stories full of apparitions, spooky old houses, witchcraft, and a smattering of other-worldly disconnects. This short story collection is full of dread and suspense without being overly violent or gory making it a good choice for a teen reader looking for a variety of scary tales. (print, ebook, audiobook)

Searles, John. *Help for the Haunted.* **2013.**

Sylvie Mason's parents help those haunted by the paranormal, that is, until they are brutally murdered inside a church where Sylvie served as the only witness to the crime. This novel works well in audiobook format with the perfectly pitched teenager voice performed by Emma Galvin. (print, ebook, audiobook)

Sokoloft, Alexandra. *The Harrowing.* **(2011).**

Thanksgiving break sends most of the college students home for the holiday; however, for those left behind, the seemingly innocuous act of raising an evil spirit begins to wreak havoc in the 100-year-old residence hall. A great forward look at college life to come! (print, ebook)

Suzuki, Koji. *Dark Water.* **2006.**

Dark Water is a collection of seven short stories, the first of which has been adapted to a film of the same name. The running theme for all the stories is water with a smattering of hauntings. As with all Suzuki novels, gore cannot be found within the pages. Instead, he develops such a strong sense of dread and foreboding that the absence of gore and overt violence is not at all missed. Suzuki's portrayal of teen protagonists is spot on, which makes the characters easily accessible for teen readers looking for adult horror novels. (print only)

Suzuki, Koji. *The Ring.* The Ring Series. **2003, translated from the 1991 Japanese title** *Ringu.*

Sadako Yamamura has been murdered and now she is out for revenge: by hijacking airwaves and cursing anyone who watches a VHS tape of her twistedly dark visions. While the technology is dated for teens, the premise of technological elements being taken over by the supernatural is still relevant. This novel does portray images of rape and murder. (print only)

Paranormal Creatures

Paranormal horror novels encompass all that cannot be explained by scientific reason, and paranormal creatures include the vast variety of monsters, demons, zombies, vampires, werewolves, mutant creatures, mythic creatures, ghouls, and other terrifying animals. Titles in this subgenre can vary in format from graphic novels, full-length novels, short stories, and novellas. For teen horror readers, a strong element of danger is necessary and paranormal creatures place the protagonist(s) in highly horrific and dangerous situations with just a slight glimmer of hope of escape and survival. The added bonus of titles often being gory and violent appeal to those looking for a more visceral read.

Brown, Ryan. *Play Dead.* **2010.**

All but one member of the Killington High School's football team has died in a bus crash on their way to the district championship game. Survivor Cole Logan finds a way to resurrect his teammates, but unless they win the championship game, they are all destined for hell. As a coming-of-age tale with high school Texas football as the setting, zombies as the paranormal element, and great comedic elements, *Play Dead* could be a big hit for your male teenagers. (print, ebook, audiobook from Audible and Brilliance Audio read by MacLeod Andrews)

Burns, Charles. *Black Hole.* **2005.**

Suburban Seattle teenagers of 1970s are facing a plague transmitted through sexual contact causing exterior genetic mutations and subsequent alienation and class stratification within the high school. And then the murders start. A supremely dark and visceral graphic novel, teens are exposed to the perils of high school from sex, to bullying, to being completely ostracized. (print only)

Gallaher, David. *High Moon.* High Moon. **2009.**

Western meets horror in this graphic novel series teeming with werewolves and other creatures of darkness that the heroes all named Macgregor must battle to save the village of Blest creating a violent, gritty, and emotionally jarring storyline. For teens tired of the traditional superheroes or for those looking for something a bit darker, this graphic novel series will serve to flip the hero genre on its head. (print only)

Hudspeth, E. B. *The Resurrectionist: The Lost Work of Dr. Spencer Black.* **2013.**

A fictional biography of Dr. Spencer Black traces his life from a childhood spent exhuming bodies to his medical training and carnival travels finishing with his mysterious disappearance. Alongside the fictional biography is Dr. Spencer Black's detailed pictorial representation of the anatomy of mythological beasts that subsequently details his descent into madness. The graphical details will enthrall teen readers as will the beautifully detailed biographical outline of the enamoring madman. (print, ebook)

King, Stephen and Joe Hill. *In the Tall Grass.* **2012.**

Two siblings take a break at a rest stop and hear a child crying off in the tall grass behind the rest area. Believing the child has gotten lost in the grass, they attempt to rescue him; however, they are quickly plunged into a claustrophobic, psychological hell from which they literally cannot escape and find their way out of the grass. The familial connections will resonate with teen readers as will the long distance road trip that has taken a turn for the worse. (ebook, audiobook)

Langan, Sarah. *The Missing.* **2007.**

When a grade-school teacher treks her students to Bedford for a field trip, she unknowingly exposes them all to a virus that transforms them into highly intelligent, insatiable, and terrifying creatures. Kids can be somewhat creepy in their own right, so for teens, this title could be doubly frightening. (print, ebook)

Mellick III, Carlton. *Apeshit.* **2008.**

A cabin in the woods, a weekend of partying, a group of teenagers, what could go wrong? Add in a murderous psycho that just will not die and you have the makings of every fantastic horror film in written form. This title will work well with teens who love the iconic 1980s slasher films like *Friday the 13th* and *A Nightmare on Elm Street* as well as the more recent *Saw* and *Hostel* franchises. (print, ebook)

Nevill, Adam. *The Ritual.* **2011.**

Camping in the wilderness never seemed so bleak, until a group of college buddies think it is a great idea to go on an excursion in the Scandinavian forest and wind up lost, hungry, and hunted by an evil stalking them through the woods. This is the kind of novel one is tempted to recommend to someone embarking on a hiking trip in the Rockies. *The Ritual* is high intensity with an amazing adrenaline rush from page one to the very last paragraph. Be warned, there is some rather foul language throughout. (print, ebook, audiobook)

Niles, Steve. *30 Days of Night.* <u>30 Days of Night</u>. **2012.**
When Barrow, Alaska, plunges into its annual 30 days of darkness, vampires are ready and waiting. Without sunlight to ward them off, this pack of vampires is ready for 30 days of a buffet-style feast for the residents of Barrow. This graphic novel series is rife with violence and gore throughout. (print only)

Smith, Scott. *The Ruins.* **2006.**
A Mayan ruin excursion goes terribly wrong for a group of travelers when they discover that once they enter the sacred ground, they can never leave. Teens will be able to easily identify with the protagonists in this novel and subsequently be able to envision themselves in the fictional situation. (print, ebook, audiobook)

Snyder, Scott. *American Vampire.* <u>American Vampire</u>. **2011.**
The first volume of American Vampire is cowritten by Scott Snyder and Stephen King and features the original American Vampire, Skinner Sweet, who is set to take on the European old world vampires. This is a great teen selection for those who want the polar opposite of *Twilight*. This graphic novel series is full of violence and raw, foul language. (print only)

Snyder, Scott, Scott Tuft, and Attila Futaki. *Severed.* **2012.**
It is 1916 and Jack Garron has run away from home in search of his father; however, the Nightmare that stalks and eats children has decided Jack is next on his menu. This graphic novel puts into question the idea of running away and one of the more horrific repercussions of undertaking that action. (print only)

Conclusion: Trends in Horror

Horror is back in the upswing again as can be seen from the rise in horror-themed television shows such as *American Horror Story*, *The Walking Dead*, *Z Nation*, *Salem*, and *Penny Dreadful.* In addition, the availability of and interest in horror movies continue to rise with movies now hitting the big screen throughout the year instead of only during the typical months of September through November. Even December is no longer immune to the horror movie as *Krampus* takes the big screen in 2015 alongside other holiday flicks. As viewing tastes lean toward horror, so too do reading tastes and publishers are pushing out more and more titles into the mainstream. In addition, the availability of horror graphic novels continues to increase with the success of *The Walking Dead* offering graphic novel fans a wide variety of horror subgenres from which to choose.

Other trends include the use of paranormal creatures. While zombies in literature are still very prevalent, this trend finally seems to be waning giving rise to other maniacal beasts of terror. Vampires no longer glitter and are back to being fear-inducing baddies again. Genetic mutations, biomedical, and scientific horror tap into the rapidly changing technological world by creating horrific environments within our everyday technology reliance.

Horror elements are also trickling over into other genres such as urban fantasy, thrillers, science fiction, and paranormal romance; however, the distinction is still very clear in what constitutes a true horror novel: fear. That being said, readers of these other genres become exposed to horror elements that may open the doors to generating a new segment of horror genre readers. Sci-fi fans of John Scalzi cross lines between teens and adults, and those who loved his horror-mystery-science fiction genre-blending novel *Lock In* (2014) may be prime candidates for the horror genre. For those who love fantasy with a darker edge, John R. Little's *Soul Mates* (2015) melds magic with suspense and adrenaline with sorrow. And in the not-to-be-missed category, there is *Welcome to Night Vale* (2015), an epically creepy podcast turn novel by Joseph Fink and Jeffrey Cranor. Teens have already found the podcast, now you just need to give them the *Twilight Zone*-like novel to go with it.

The love of horror is no longer relegated to the outcasts or misfits as previous stereotypes often dictated. Instead, horror is embraced and sought after by a growing number of readers, listeners, and viewers. The genre has hit mainstream and librarians need to be at the ready-to-arm patrons of all ages with a dreadfully frightening read to feed their horror need.

5

Nonfiction

Kristi Chadwick

Introduction to the Genre

Definition

When dealing with readers' advisory, many librarians go straight to genre fiction, as that is what a majority of people that librarians meet through the course of the day enjoy. Nonfiction readers' advisory can seem like foreign territory. However, the similarities between the two major types of writing can make readers' advisory transactions as simple—or as difficult—as they usually are. According to Dictionary.com, nonfiction is "prose writing that is based on facts, real events, and real people ..." Neal Wyatt breaks nonfiction down into two kinds of books: nonnarrative, which explains the process of how something is accomplished, such as how-to books, cookbooks, and other instructional texts, and narrative, which gives a story-like feel to the prose. Selection criteria for adult nonfiction should include factors such as organization of material, reliability and accuracy, currency of topic and information, and table of contents or comprehensive indexing that will help all library users, adults and teens find the specific information they are seeking within the book.

Teens are already using the nonfiction section, particularly for information and research. But as we also know, nonfiction collections are used for much more than research and information seeking; many readers seek out nonfiction for recreational reading. It is this category of adult nonfiction we will examine more closely.

Appeals

Appeal factors are not as easy to type with nonfiction as they are with fiction. Appeal factors (Joyce Saricks) or "doorways" (Nancy Pearl) for nonfiction revolve around three other elements, as explained by Wyatt: type, narrative, and subject. In nonfiction, subject is of utmost importance, as it is the main reason that teens will be searching for these titles. Each book is a teachable moment by the author, and how much the author knows on a particular subject is key to nonfiction. Some subjects are rooted in the past, such as World War I, the Holocaust, and the Trail of Tears, and the subject is not going to change as the events have already happened. Other subjects are based on currency, especially in the sciences, and as new information comes to light, new nonfiction works are introduced.

Narrative nonfiction relies on voice; this is the main element to bring readers into the subject. Authors of narrative nonfiction use language to create a mood and setting that can be understood, even if the subject is not generally one they deal with. Books with a high narrative content are going to engage a reader similarly as fiction; memoirs are a good example of high narrative titles.

Type deals with the way the information is expressed in a nonfiction title. Memoirs, letters, and textbooks are all different types of nonfiction. When librarians are performing readers' advisory services, they will need to evaluate what type of nonfiction the teen is looking for. Those who are looking for quick facts may need a reference text, or works with detailed table of contents or indexes; teen patrons looking for easier access into nonfiction subjects may find that narrative, heavily illustrated, or nonfiction graphic novels are excellent crossover entry points to adult nonfiction.

Working with Readers

The readers' advisory interview should reveal the reasons why teens are looking for nonfiction and allow the librarian to suggest crossover titles. Are teens coming in for reference and research topics? By understanding a particular project or assignment, topical works of varying depths can be recommended. For teens looking for recreational reading, the directions that readers' advisory take, can be aligned with a specific subject or with a particular fiction genre.

A teen's interests, hobbies, or even popular culture hooks can create nonfiction recommendations. Those who are already reading young adult (YA) fiction that revolves around a particular topic may be easily introduced to adult nonfiction around that same topic. Ensuring that the titles are highly narrative or illustrated will create the best transition across genres. When creating nonfiction matches based on appeal factors (Saricks) or doorways (Pearl) due to genre-reading habits, crossover suggestions can cast a wider net. Teens who are interested in recent dystopian YA may want to explore natural sciences or historical works on war aftermath. Those who have read a large amount of historical YA fiction can choose from American and international history narratives or personal memoirs of world leaders and "regular" people. The point in suggesting crossover nonfiction is not to stop teens from reading fictional works, but expand their reading tastes beyond the one area in the library.

Tools and Resources

Finding adult nonfiction titles for teens may require some additional work by library staff; however, there are tools available to ease into finding a good base of benchmark titles. Librarians who are already skilled in searching for nonfiction suggestions for adults can use the same resources for teen readers. Professional print resources include Wyatt's *The Reader's Advisory Guide to Nonfiction, The Real Story: A Guide to Nonfiction Reading Interests* by Sarah Statz Cords, and some subject guides in memoirs, women's nonfiction, and food literature from Libraries Unlimited. *Booklist* title reviews will include a listing on adult titles if it seems to be a good crossover or have YA appeal. Each year Young Adult Library Services Association (YALSA) presents the Alex Awards, a top 10 list of adult titles that will have appeal to teens, and the Outstanding Books for the College Bound, which are title lists by academic discipline. Each of these will regularly give a selection of adult nonfiction titles that are recommended as good picks for teen readers.

The Literature

When categorizing nonfiction, there are many different directions you can take—narrative versus nonnarrative, topical, graphical. For the purpose of this selection of titles, we will use three main categories that highlight some of the larger trends in current YA reading tastes: historical, adventure, and popular culture. This will give a broad expanse of topics and styles within each category, serving both librarians and readers searching for an appropriate crossover.

Historical

Looking into the past to enjoy the present is a pastime for readers of all ages. When guiding young adults to historical fair, identify whether it is the actual time period, setting of the story, or even characters that are the driving appeal.

Brown, Daniel James. *The Boys in the Boat: Nine Americans and Their Epic Quest for Gold at the 1936 Berlin Olympics*. 2013.
In 1936, nine young men from the University of Washington stunned the world as they took home gold in front of Adolph Hitler at the World Olympics in Berlin. Centering around Joe Rantz, this book shows that responsibility and family can be created through work and sports. A mash-up of the boys' own memories, stories, and diaries, it highlights for teens that their struggles for independence and a sense of home are not uncommon. (print, audiobook, ebook)

Capote, Truman. *In Cold Blood*. 1965; reprint 1994.
Delving into the brutal 1959 murder of the Clutter family in Holcomb, Kansas, Capote brings to life the family, the town in the aftermath of the deaths, through to the trial. Referred to as a classic in narrative nonfiction, teens who are interested in historical accuracy and crime dramas will be drawn into this book. (print, audiobook, ebook)

Hillenbrand, Laura. *Seabiscuit: An American Legend*. 2002.
Which teen girl did not have a love for horses? A trio of men take a crooked-legged racehorse to the greatest of heights in 1938. Seabiscuit became a household name during that year, and had more press than other world topics. Teens who enjoy horses will be taken by the details of the racing lifestyle, and the "overcoming the odds" theme will be a popular one. (print, audiobook, ebook)

Larson, Erik. *The Devil in the White City: Murder, Magic, and Mayhem at the Fair That Changed America*. 2004.
The 1893 Chicago World's Fair becomes the backdrop for two men—one who dazzles the fair with his genius, the other who strikes fear there by his

multiple murders. Rich in historical details and scenes, teens who seek out strong world building will imagine the magical look of the World's Fair, and those who crave mystery will find the search for H. H. Holmes one that keeps them turning the pages. (print, audiobook. ebook)

Sides, Hampton. *In The Kingdom of Ice: The Grand and Terrible Polar Voyage of the USS Jeannette.* **2014.**
    Funded by the owner of the *New York Herald*, in 1879 the *USS Jeannette* set sail from San Francisco to explore the top of the North Pole. When the ship becomes trapped in ice and destroyed, the surviving crew must cross the endless winter above Siberia and fight to survive and come home. Historical facts become a thrilling adventure in the hands of a teen. (print, audiobook, ebook)

Skloot, Rebecca. *The Immortal Life of Henrietta Lacks.* **2011.**
    Detailing the life of the woman whom scientists knew as HeLa, Lack's cells—removed without her knowledge—are used 60 years after her death to investigate polio and cancer, cloning and gene mapping—all without permission even from her surviving family. This book not only commemorates the life of this African American woman but also delves into harder topics of bioethics and scientific property. Teens who want to know the people along with the scientific details will get both topics in large doses. (print, audiobook, ebook)

Yousafzai, Malala and Christina Lamb. *I Am Malala: The Girl Who Stood Up for Education and Was Shot by the Taliban.* **2013.**
    When the Taliban took over Malala's Pakistani home valley, she advocated to continue her education, and it almost cost her her life. The story of her recovery and continued humanitarian work is already inspirational and has placed her in the history books as the youngest person to win the Nobel Peace Prize in 2014. Teens who are looking for global women's issues will find Yousafzai's tale one that they can relate to as a contemporary, and one that will be told for many years to come. (print, audiobook, ebook)

Adventure

    For many readers, adventure books are a way to explore a terrain that is not their own, without any hardship to them beyond turning the pages. Description and reflection are two major components of personal adventure accounts, allowing teen readers to see inside the adventurer's head along the way. Detail is of vital importance: the more finely detailed, the more the teen will be immersed into the setting and narrative to evoke a deeper reading experience. This becomes an entry point for many high fantasy, series readers, or even those who enjoy the darker look at current topics, such as kidnapping or abuse. Similar to their fictional counterparts, adventure books cover high stakes; mental, physical, and emotional limits are tested with both success and failure at the end. Challenges are made, whether by the adventurers themselves or another counterpart, and the journey may be fraught with obstacles to be overcome, inside and out. Teens who are searching for these books may want to have the visceral experience of the adventure, truly enjoy a "disaster book," or are looking for a more reflective journey.

Abagnale, Frank. *Catch Me If You Can.* **2000.**
    Fraud and forgery may seem more like white-collar crimes, but when one man can not only pass as some of the most trusted people in life, but then

cash out on it—to the tune of $2.5 million—by the age of 21, this is no simple case. Telling his own story of racing, and being chased, across the globe, Abagnale details his life of crime and its ultimate end. When redemption comes for full disclosure, this becomes a true story of lessons learned. Combining adventure, crime, and coming full circle, the personal touch of this crime memoir will strike a chord in teens who want to believe that bad times can get better. (print, audiobook, ebook)

Bryson, Bill. *A Walk in the Woods: Rediscovering America on the Appalachian Trail*. 1998; reprint 2006.

Bryson lives near the Appalachian Trail and decides to discover the interest others have in it while traveling with his friend Katz. The toll is immediate: physical burdens, waning camaraderie, and lack of preparation all contribute to a not-so-successful hike. Bryson combines the serious facts of local wildlife and communities with a humorous prose, making this narrative easily accessible. (print, audiobook, ebook)

Dugard, Jaycee. *A Stolen Life*. 2012.

In 1991, 11-year-old Jaycee Dugard disappeared from her school bus stop near her home. Held by her captors for over 18 years, Dugard was abused and eventually bore two children. The discovery of her, alive, is thought of as near miraculous, but it is her written story that tells the truth behind those hard years. Emotionally raw and with rough details, teens who find survival or overcoming near-impossible odds will find this book appealing. (print, audiobook, ebook)

Hillenbrand, Laura. *Unbroken: A World War II Story of Survival, Resilience, and Redemption*. 2014.

Having proven his skills in running at the Olympics, Louis Zamperini took to the skies as an airman during World War II. But in 1943, when his plane crashes into the Pacific Ocean, Zamperini will discover his true strength as he fights to survive floating on a raft on unending waters. Teens who enjoy a true battle of survival will enjoy this tale, with great storytelling, and crossing into historical and sports territories additional bonuses. (print, audiobook, ebook)

Junger, Sebastian. *The Perfect Storm: A True Story of Men against the Sea*. 1997; reprint 2009.

In October 1991, the "storm of the century" hit the North American eastern seaboard, caused by a rare combination of weather factors. Detailing the history of fishing and the final tale of the *Andrea Gail*, Junger combines a number of witness accounts, radio transcriptions, and survivors' stories to highlight what may have actually happened to the six men on board. Vivid prose and images will accentuate this adventure tale for teens. (print, audiobook, ebook)

Krakauer, Jon. *Into the Wild*. 1997.

Krakauer traces the steps of Christopher McCandless, who left his home in Virginia and moved west, abandoning most of his possessions along the way. Winding up in Alaska with extremely limited resources, McCandless survived the snowy conditions for nearly 100 days before dying due to some type of malnutrition. This hard look at a journey for "enlightenment" can serve as inspiration, and warning, to teens struggling to fit in with their own surroundings. (print, audiobook, ebook)

Krakauer, Jon. *Into Thin Air: A Personal Account of the Mt. Everest Disaster.* **1999.**

In March 1996, Krakauer was part of one of three expeditions heading up Mt. Everest, only to be caught in a hurricane-force storm that resulted in the highest death toll during the peak's history. Evoking the journey up the largest mountain in the world, Krakauer's personal narrative is balanced by historical accounts of other expeditions. (print, audiobook, ebook)

Kurson, Robert. *Shadow Divers: The True Adventure of Two Americans Who Risked Everything to Solve One of the Last Mysteries of World War II.* **2005.**

When two deep-wreck divers come across a German U-boat off the coast of New Jersey, the mystery of how it came there became one that would overcome their lives. With scuba diving continuing to be a popular sport, the stories of the riskier dives take on a life of their own. Teens looking for an "armchair thrill" and understanding how wreck recovery works will find this title a good match. (print, audiobook, ebook)

Lansing, Alfred. *Endurance: Shackleton's Incredible Voyage.* **1959; reprint 1999.**

Recounting the failed 1914 Imperial Trans-Antarctic Expedition, where Shackleton's ship became trapped in ice and the efforts for survival the following two years. Teens who search out survival stories in history can be given this book. Already a popular assigned title for high-school history classes, those who want more information about some of the transcontinental journeys will find this book satisfying. (print, audiobook, ebook)

Strayed, Cheryl. *Wild: From Lost to Found on the Pacific Crest Trail.* **2012.**

With 1,100 miles stretching before her, Cheryl Strayed recounts her physical and emotional journey through California and Oregon. Teens may be drawn to this due to the 2014 movie release, but the troubled past, death of Strayed' mother, and essential "coming of age" tale will hook readers who want the visceral experience. (print, audiobook, ebook)

Popular Culture

Popular culture may be considered a "catch-all" phrase; readers who are reading fiction based on what is happening in their world now, or looking at topics from a perspective of learning, may find that diving into popular culture titles are worthwhile. People will always want to know "how things work," and the growth of television shows, or entire networks, dedicated to current topics of food, travel, sports, and science only highlight the popularity. While this topic can provide the fastest possibility of outdated material (for instance, yearly trends and fads, anything referring to Pluto as a planet), it is one that has some material that can come "back in" depending on the tastes of the current population. Popular culture writings that are made accessible to lay people are great for teens for both their information and narratives.

Almond, Steve. *Against Football: One Fan's Reluctant Manifesto.* **2014.**

After watching this beloved sport for almost 40 years, Almond chronicles the reasons why he will not engage as a spectator any longer. A combination of personal critique and factual analysis, teens will be drawn into the witty, acerbic tone of Almond's writing, and those who are actually questioning the influence of the sport will find it just as intriguing. (print, ebook)

Bissinger, H. G. *Friday Night Lights: A Town, a Team, and a Dream*. 2000.
From September through December in Odessa, Texas, the Permian Panthers bring a town together for the love of football, when every other month social, racial, and economic tensions threaten to keep them all apart. Teens who have played football will understand the devotion for the team, while those who know the popular television series of the same name can look deeper into the town that inspired it. (print, ebook)

Fey, Tina. *Bossypants*. 2013.
When young, dreaming about what you will be when you grow up is common. Fey not only shares her childhood dream of being a comedian but also many tales of years growing up, joining *Saturday Night Live*, and moving through motherhood, not so much with dignity and grace but always with a sense of humor. Fey's self-deprecating prose and messy life will give readers an appreciation of modern famousness. (print, audiobook, ebook)

Friedberg, Susanne. *Fresh: A Perishable History*. 2010.
Friedberg delves into the histories of six foods that people can find when they open their refrigerator. A look at mass consumption and changes in attitudes around food, this underscores the actual cost of keeping food "fresh." Richly detailed but clearly written, teens who actually want to know more about food will find this book accessible and smart. (print, ebook)

Hawking, Stephen. *A Brief History of Time: And Other Essays*. 1998.
Hawking's book is considered to be one of the landmark volumes in science writing. Exploring topics on black holes, quarks, and the Big Bang, scientific detail is written in a clear and understandable prose from one of the greatest science minds of the world. Teens who are looking for more details into astronomy, or a look at a man whose own physical impairments are overshadowed by his mental agility may want to read this book. (print, audiobook, ebook)

Kingsolver, Barbara et al. *Animal, Vegetable, Miracle: A Year of Food Life*. 2008.
Famous for her fictional works, Kingsolver describes the journey of moving her family to the rural Appalachians where they decide to eat only what they can source locally or grow themselves. With fowl exploits and laments about bananas, this book is one of the main tomes for the locavore movement. Humorous days are interspersed with more details on agriculture and recipes by family members. (print, audiobook, ebook)

Powell, Julie. *Julie & Julia: 365 Days, 524 Recipes, and 1 Tiny Apartment Kitchen*. 2005; reprint 2009.
Bored with her life in Queens, Powell recounts how she took her mother's copy of Julia Child's *Mastering the Art of French Cooking* and attempted to master all 524 recipes it contained in the span of a year. Inspiring a 2009 movie, teens with a bend toward popular culture and "bloggers made big" will find Powell's writing amusing. (print, audiobook, ebook)

Roach, Mary. *Gulp: Adventures on the Alimentary Canal.* **2013.**

From entering the mouth, all the way through the digestive track, Roach covers all of the questions one was afraid to ask about taste, digestion, and how holy water can be administered rectally by an exorcist. Besides the odd-ball questions and gross factor, teens will enjoy understanding how this particular system works in wondrous, humorous detail. (print, audiobook, ebook)

Ruhlman, Michael. *The Making of a Chef: Mastering Heat at the Culinary Institute.* **2009.**

Ruhlman joins the 1996 class at the Culinary Institute of America in Hyde Park, New York, to participate in the culinary classes, learning not only the fundamental skills but also about the people behind the stoves and tables. This draws not only on the appeal of food but of cooking techniques, which are incredibly detailed, and any teen who looks to culinary school as an option will enjoy the overview. (print, audiobook, ebook)

Sagan, Carl. *Cosmos.* **1980; reprint 2013.**

Based on Sagan's 13-part television series of the same name, this work goes further into science and civilization and how they developed together. With Neil deGrasse Tyson now taking *Cosmos* back to television, teens who want to see where it all began should be handed this book. Those with an interest in astronomy or the historical figures in science will find this book engaging too. (print, ebook)

Conclusion: Trends in Nonfiction

The future is always ahead of us, and topics that appear in nonfiction works will continue to appear on libraries' shelves. Be aware of anniversaries of historical events such as the upcoming World War I anniversary, as these tend to increase demand and probably publication of works that will be useful for teens. Essays will continue to be another popular entry subject for teens, with their balance of memoir and world criticisms. Popular culture always feeds nonfiction, and teens nostalgic for their subject hooks keep coming back.

Factual information and accessibility continue to be two key factors in providing successful readers' advisory to teens with adult crossover titles. As teens age, their desire to continue reading may be left in the hands of those librarians who were able to balance the need for the truth with the need to read.

References

Cords, Sarah Statz. *The Real Story: A Guide to Nonfiction Reading Interests.* Westport, CT: Libraries Unlimited, 2006.

Wyatt, Neal. *The Readers' Advisory Guide to Nonfiction.* Chicago, IL: American Library Association, 2007.

6

Romance

Ilene Appelbaum Lefkowitz and C. L. Quillen

Introduction to the Genre

Definition

Romance novels focus on the developing relationship between two people. The love story drives the plot and the book ends with a happily ever after (HEA) or more commonly over the last two decades—a happy for now (HFN). In romance novels, just like contemporary life, readers know that the characters they left gazing into each other's eyes making plans for a wedding or a baby may face challenges or tragedies that will impact on their happily ever after.

Romance novels focus on the growth of the characters. In most cases, there is something in the main characters' lives, which they must learn or understand about themselves in order to develop a successful relationship with their partner. Readers enjoy reading these kinds of stories because they can relate. We are all learning and growing each day and that growth impacts on our romantic relationships and emotions. Romances provide a strong emotional connection with the characters. In our fractured society, this is a welcome diversion.

With over $1 billion in sales, romance novels account for 13 percent of all books purchased each year. The popularity of this genre warrants the Readers' Advisor's attention.

Appeals

Romance is an ideal genre to be used as a crossover with teen readers. Teens are just beginning to learn about love and romance. They want to know what first love and relationships are really like. They talk to their friends about their experiences, but seeing it described in print validates their experience in a different way and reassures them that they are just like everyone else. Romance books provide readers with an escape from their lives and a peek into someone else's life. In a romance novel, the heroine and the hero grow as characters both separately and together as a couple. Watching this growth within the characters can be a very positive modeling of behavior in relationships. Of course, it can also show teens what not to do in a relationship. Reading romance offers them the chance to explore social and moral limits without engaging in risky behaviors in the real world. Teens today live in a chaotic and often stressful world. They crave stability and boundaries. Romances offer both in their standard formula of boy gets girl, boy loses girl, boy gets girl and guaranteed happy ending.

The diversity of the genre is also an appeal to today's teens. Romance books feature characters of all races, all religions, all walks of life: rich, poor, sick, and healthy, in all manner of settings and time periods. This means that teens will be able to find someone who they can identify with or that they can aspire to be like when they get older.

As long as romance books have been published, teens have been reading them. Prior to the 1970s, there were not a large number of dedicated teen books being published. Starting in the 1970s, books have been written specifically for young adults featuring teen characters and the types of situations and experiences that they are going through. Each passing year has seen a rise in the number of young adult books and in the quality of the writing.

So, why read adult romances if there are so many available specifically for them? Why not? Adult romances give teens a glimpse at what is to come; and many teens eagerly anticipate the time when they become adults—moving out on their own, falling in love, being in a relationship, and perhaps even starting a family of their own. Romance allows them to dream about times to come. This is especially true of the rising genre of New Adult books (see Chapter 7 for more on this emerging genre).

New Adult takes off just where teen books end. They feature protagonists between 18 and 25, striking out on their own for the first time. Whether it is in college, a first job, or the military, they are experiencing life in a manner completely different from a typical teen novel. New Adult books tend to be edgier, addressing difficult issues, but the characters are still close enough in age and experience that teens can relate to them or know that they will be dealing with the same issues in only a few short years. New Adult books are also more sexually explicit than teen books. For this reason alone, teens want to read them!

Working with Readers

While the majority of romance readers are female, there are males that read romances. The RWA cites that approximately 16 percent of romance readership is male. For males looking to read romances, there are more books coming out with multiple points of view, including the male point of view. For male teens looking for heterosexual romances try books by John Green, if they are looking for teen romances or M. L. Buchman, for adult romances. Both authors are male and write from dual point of views. Publishers such as Riptide and Bold Strokes are producing books for lesbian, gay, bisexual, transgender (LGBT) audiences in a wide variety of genres including romance, both in print and ebook.

One of the keys to providing Readers' Advisory for teens wanting to read romance books is the RA interview. Asking the reader not only what they like to read, but what TV shows they watch, and which movies they have enjoyed will help you to put together a clearer picture of their reading interests. In dealing with teens and romance, it is essential to assess their comfort level with sexuality and explicitness. Do they want to read a romance that is sweet, and either has no sex or is not descriptive, or are they looking for something more explicit?

As a starting point, try using the genre of their favorite TV shows to suggest book titles. Popular fantasy TV shows lead to suggesting paranormal romances; crime dramas lead to suggesting romantic suspense.

Most important, respect what readers say and their opinions. Teens can be hesitant about approaching a librarian because they expect that their needs will be judged. Teens are used to being treated with less respect than adults and librarians have to go out of their way to make sure that teens feel welcome. Teens who ask for a book that is "just like" one that they recently read are usually not looking for a book with a similar plot, they are looking for a book that makes them feel the way the mentioned book did. When you make recommendations to teens, make sure that you use a lot of adjectives and descriptive language to make sure that you are on the same page with your suggestions. Teens know what they want but do not always have the vocabulary to describe it.

Tools and Resources

The following list of resources will help you learn more about the romance genre and working with teens in readers' advisory services, and offer guidance in developing your collection.

All about Romance: http://likesbooks.com/
Filled with thousands of reviews, articles, thematic lists, and readalike lists, this is a great starting place for romance readers of all ages.

Booth, Heather. *Serving Teens through Readers Advisory*. Chicago, IL: American Library Association, 2007.
Beginning by providing information about teen reading habits and how they differ from that of adults, Booth sets the stage for Readers' Advisors who do not have a background in working with teens. She breaks down the RA interview and how to negotiate with teens who may be less than forthcoming with their answers.

Dear Author: http://dearauthor.com/
"For Readers by Readers." The site reviews a wide variety of romance books ranging from contemporary books to ebooks and just about every subgenre of romances imaginable. Featuring an extensive "If You Like" section, recommended reads, and a top 100 list.

Heroes and Heartbreakers: http://www.heroesandheartbreakers.com/
Here you will find book reviews, cover reveals, articles, booklists, film and TV recaps, and original short stories.

Quillen, C. L., and Lefkowitz, Ilene. *Read On ... Romance*. Englewood, CO: Libraries Unlimited, 2014.
This book breaks the romance genre into five major appeal areas: story, character, mood, language, and setting. Within each appeal area, there are thematic lists ranging from romances featuring food and chefs to romances set in hospitals. Teen books are included throughout the book and are clearly noted.

Ramsdell, Kristin. *Romance Fiction: A Guide to the Genre*. Englewood, CO: Libraries Unlimited, 2013.

Arranged thematically, this guide incorporates important classics and older titles as well as newer titles in many categories. Award winners are noted, and titles are appropriate for teens.

Romance Writers of America: http://www.rwa.org/
If you are looking for publishing information about the genre, this is the place to go. Award lists, best-seller lists, contests, local and national conference information, and more can be found.

RT Book Reviews: http://www.rtbookreviews.com/
The site has reviews, author interviews, cover reveals, top picks, and reader discussions. There is a separate section dedicated to Young Adult books.

Smart Bitches, Trashy Books: http://smartbitchestrashybooks.com/
This site offers book reviews, cover reveals, and discussions about everything related to the genre.

Collection Development

Romances account for 13 percent of sales of adult fiction each year. The majority of romances sold are in either e-format or paperbacks. Less than 10 percent of romance sales are for hardcover books. While this means that librarians can get more bang for their budgets, it also means that romances go out of print much more quickly and are rarely reprinted. In addition, paperbacks tend to show their wear and tear faster making it necessary to visually check the shelves for books that are in disrepair. Books that are in poor physical shape are less likely to be taken out and should probably be weeded from the collection.

Librarians who are actively working to build or maintain a romance collection need to advocate for a library subscription to *RT Book Reviews* (RTBR). While all of the professional journals (*Booklist, Publisher's Weekly, Library Journal*, etc.) cover romance, the number of books reviewed each month is a small fraction of the number reviewed in RTBR. RTBR also has a monthly listing of new books in series, which is very important because the majority of romance readers are series readers and want to read all of the books in order, as they are published.

Displays boost circulation and romances provide lots of opportunities for display, as so many of them have multiple common themes. There are small town romances, romances featuring pets, holiday romances, romances with strong secondary characters. (For more ideas for displays, see Quillen and Lefkowitz's *Read On . . . Romance.*) Displays of romances can be tricky due to cover images. Many romances still have suggestive covers, so finding enough adult romances that will appeal to teens, but that will not make them blush if they are displayed in the teen section can be challenging. For ideas on creating library displays, try browsing Pinterest. There are a number of library display idea boards to use as inspiration for your own romance displays.

Romance is a genre that blends easily with almost all other genres. Romantic suspense is one of the more popular genre blends. Popular authors in this category are Alison Brennan, Karen Robards, Elizabeth Lowell, Suzanne Brockmann, and Anne Stuart. Steampunk is a genre that has been on the rise blending elements of fantasy, science fiction, and historical fiction.

Add in romance and you have a somewhat new genre blend of steampunk romance. Popular authors in this category include Bec McMaster, Beth Ciotta, Kristen Callihan, and Kate Cross.

A fun way to explore genre blending is with Megan McArdle's website, the Genre Blender (www.blender.genrify.com). Simply choose two genres from the list and click "Blend." A list of blended titles with annotations appears. Given teens' love of technology, this could be a great way to interact with them.

A great way to expand romance for teens is with your library's movies. Romantic movies fill the shelves; there are comedies, dramas, paranormal, and suspense. Teens are often passionate about the movies they like. Asking them about their favorite movies can provide you with insight to suggest several watch-a-likes for them. Do they enjoy romantic comedies? Suggest *Clueless*, *10 Things I Hate About You*, or *The Silver Linings Playbook*. Looking for a classic? Try *Dirty Dancing*, *Gone with the Wind*, or *An Officer and a Gentleman*. For more movie advisory, look at IMDb.com or RottenTomatoes.com.

The Literature

The following titles (and authors) will especially appeal to teen readers. They are organized by popular subgenres that reflect specific romance reading interests, so it is relatively safe to recommend a title within a subgenre to a teen who has enjoyed another title in that section.

Contemporary Romance

Contemporary romances account for approximately 50 percent of the romances published each year. Readers are looking to escape from their real lives into a world that is similar enough to their own to be identifiable, but that offers them something that may be lacking from their own lives. Contemporary romances are set in the present or the very near past and reflect contemporary attitudes and norms. Contemporary romances appeal to teen readers because they can relate to them and see themselves in the characters and events of the story.

Carr, Robyn. *Harvest Moon*, Virgin River. 2011.
Sous-chef Kelly Matlock collapses in the kitchen after a particularly stressful day at work. Needing a break, she heads to her sister Jill's organic farm in Virgin River. There she meets widower Lief Holbrook, who has his hands full dealing with his teenage stepdaughter, Courtney. Courtney's story plays a significant part in this novel and teens will feel a connection with her and her issues—her mother dies young and her father does not really want her around. Carr does a great job of portraying a teenager's emotions and describing the complex relationships she has with her stepfather and his new girlfriend. (print, ebook, audio read by Therese Plummer)

Deveraux, Jude. *True Love.* Nantucket Brides Trilogy. 2013.
After breaking up with her boyfriend, aspiring architect Alix Madsen has the chance to spend a year in Nantucket working on her portfolio, planning her BFF's wedding, and lusting after acclaimed architect Jared Montgomery. Meanwhile Alix is staying in a home left to her by Adelaide Kingsley, who hoped she would uncover clues about an ancestor who disappeared more than

200 years ago. Ghosts, mysteries, and reincarnation will keep teens eagerly turning the pages. (print, ebook, audio read by Tavia Gilbert).

Dingman, Carolyn. *Cancel the Wedding.* **2014.**
Olivia seems to have it all, but lately she is having some doubts about her upcoming wedding to Leo. When the chance comes to take a road trip to Georgia to discover why her late mother Janie wanted her ashes to be sprinkled in Huntley, Georgia, the hometown that she never spoke of, Olivia cannot pack her bags fast enough. She brings Logan, her teenage niece. In Georgia, they meet Elliot and his younger brother Graham and work to discover Janie's secrets. Teens will enjoy the secondary romance between Graham and Logan and be fascinated by the mysteries in Janie's previous life. (print, ebook)

Helms, Rhonda. *Scratch.* **2014.**
Casey survived a family tragedy at the age of 13 that left her with terrible scars on her stomach. Now a college student and part-time DJ, she meets and falls for Daniel, another college senior. Casey is instantly attracted to him, but scared because she has closed herself off from everyone for such a long time. A playlist for the book is available on Spotify. Many teens enjoy "problem novels," and the characters in this New Adult novel have many issues to overcome. (print, ebook)

Higgins, Kristan. *Anything for You.* **2015.**
Jessica Dunn grew up on the wrong side of the very small town of Manningsport, New York, with her alcoholic parents and younger brother Davey, who suffers from fetal alcohol syndrome. Nicknamed "Jessica Does" in high school, she has worked hard to create an almost-perfect life since then. She has a great job and a good relationship with Connor O'Rourke, even if they have kept it quiet. Then Connor proposes, but there is no way they can ever get married. Jess is committed to being there for her brother and Davey still blames him for the death of his dog when they were children. (print, ebook)

Pettrey, Dani. *Submerged.* Alaskan Courage. **2012.**
When her beloved aunt dies in a plane crash, Bailey Craig must return to Yancey, Alaska. In the 12 years since she left, Bailey has worked hard to overcome her reputation and rediscover her faith. When divers discover that the crash was no accident, Bailey must work with her former crush, diver Cole McKenna, to discover what really happened before anyone else is killed. Pettrey's debut novel features memorable characters who will get their own stories in later books in the series. Teens will enjoy the blend of love and suspense. (print, ebook, audio read by Christina Moore).

Roberts, Nora. *The Search.* **2010.**
Ten years ago, Fiona Bristow was the only survivor of the Red Scarf Killer. She moved to the Pacific Northwest to rebuild her life and train dogs. When master woodworker Simon Doyle needs help with his adorable, but out-of-control puppy Jaws, he meets Fiona. A copycat killer starts targeting women nearby, and the police suspect Fiona will be next on his list. Romantic suspense and details about dog training will keep teens reading late into the night. (print, ebook, audio read by Tanya Eby)

Scott, Ginger. *This Is Falling.* Falling Series. **2014.**

After surviving a school shooting during her sophomore year of high school that left her best friend dead and her boyfriend brain damaged, Rowe Stanton is trying to figure out how to pick up the pieces and move on with her life. On her first night at college, she meets baseball player Nate Preeter. At first, Rowe cannot believe that Nate could possibly be interested in her, but as their relationship progresses, Rowe has to decide if she can let go of the tragedy that has come to define her. This dual narration and torn-from-the-headlines plot will be of great interest to teen readers. (print, ebook)

Selvig, Lizbeth. *The Rancher and the Rockstar.* **2012.**

Abby Stadler's quiet life on her horse farm in Minnesota becomes a whole lot more interesting when her teenage daughter Kim's Facebook friend Dawson comes to visit. Neither Abby nor Kim knew that Dawson was not really 18 and that he had run away from boarding school in England. When Kim's celebrity crush, rock star Gray Covey, arrives at the farm searching for his son, he was also not expecting to find love. Teenagers Kim and Dawson are a big part of the plot and teens will feel for Kim when her crush falls in love with her mother. (print, ebook)

Wilde, Lori. *The First Love Cookie Club.* Twilight, Texas. **2010.**

Sarah Collier will never forget the humiliation she experienced as a teenager when she tried to stop Travis Walker's Christmas Day wedding. Now a well-known children's author, Sarah returns to Twilight, Texas, after receiving a letter from a sick little girl, who turns out to be Travis's daughter. Teens will empathize with Sarah's experiences as a teenager and cheer on the triumph of true love. (print, ebook)

Historical Romance

Historical romance is a treasured subgenre of romance. Readers enjoy historical romances because it gives them a glimpse into time. Time and place are big appeal factors in historical romance, and the details give the reader a true sense of what the time was like. Historical novels frequently take place during major world events. Historical novels are generally well researched and readers enjoy the accurate period details.

Cabot, Meg. *Ransom My Heart.* **2009.**

For those teens who adored *The Princess Diaries*, this is a sure winner! Written by Meg Cabot and Mia Thermopolis, Princess of Genovia. Finnula Crais is just trying to help her family and especially her sister when she man-naps Hugo to ransom off and pay for her sister's dowry. She never expected to fall in love with her intended victim. Both Finn and Hugo are keeping secrets that threaten to derail their newfound love but in the end, as it should be, true love saves the day. (print, ebook)

Camden, Elizabeth. *Beyond All Dreams.* **2015.**

In 1897, Anna O'Brien is a map librarian for the Library of Congress. Discovering an error in a report about the *USS Culpepper*, the ship that sank with her father and 55 other men on board, she reports it to the Navy, but rather than thanking her, Anna is told the case is closed. She meets Congressman Luke Callahan; he is attracted to her and offers to help solve the mystery. The blend of politics, mystery, and maps in a historical setting will intrigue; both characters deal with family issues that will resonate with contemporary teens. (print, ebook)

Forester, Amanda. *A Winter Wedding.* Marriage Mart. **2014.**
James Lockton, the Duke of Marchford and spy for the Crown, needs a wife. His grandmother's companion, Miss Penelope Rose will soon have nowhere to go. To solve both their problems, James proposes; but after working with his grandmother to matchmake for the ton as Madame X, Pen wants her own love match. Girls will enjoy reading about a strong female character who is not willing to settle. Add to that Christmas traditions, a Peruvian jungle cat, and a lot of comedic moments and readers will spend a few delightful hours laughing until they cry. (print, ebook)

Gohlke, Cathy. *Promise Me This.* **2012.**
Annie Allen is heartbroken when her brother Owen dies aboard the *Titanic*. A stowaway, Michael Dunnagan survives and tries to make good on his promise to Owen that he would take care of his sister. At first contact, Annie is furious that Michael survived. She wants nothing to do with him but as Michael's letters continue to arrive she softens toward him and they develop a deep relationship, until Annie's letters stop with the onset of World War I. Michael is desperate to find her before it is too late. A beautiful, haunting saga that teen readers who adored the movie *Titanic* will savor. (print, ebook)

James, Syrie. *Jane Austen's First Love.* **2014.**
The imagined story behind Jane Austen and her first love, Edward Taylor. The year is 1791, and young ladies are supposed to follow the rules and not ask questions. Jane, 15, is not very good at either. During a family vacation, thankfully the rules ease up, and she is allowed to attend a party where she meets Edward. Despite them not being of the same station, love blooms. A treat for Austen fans of all ages. (print, ebook)

Kelly, Carla. *Borrowed Light.* **2011.**
Returning to Salt Lake City after completing a course at the Fannie Farmer Cooking School in Boston, Julia Darling is uncertain about her engagement and on a whim, answers an ad for a cook/housekeeper for a rancher in Wyoming. She falls for Paul Otto, the ranch's owner, but has concerns about his mysterious past. Julia is struggling with her faith, but could never marry outside the Mormon church. Wyoming in the early 1900s and details about the Mormon church will be of interest to teens who are looking for something a little different than the usual Western romance. (print, ebook)

Klassen, Julie. *The Girl in the Gatehouse.* **2010**
When her family sends her away, Mariah Aubrey takes up residence in a distant relative's gatehouse with only her former nanny as a companion. She plans to live out her life quietly while supporting herself writing novels under a pseudonym. All that changes when the dashing Captain Matthew Bryant rents out the estate. He is fascinated by Mariah, but does not want to get too close once he learns of the scandalous behavior that got her banished. Teens will be intrigued by the slow reveal of Mariah's story. (print, ebook, audio read by Elizabeth Jasicki)

Peterson, Tracie. *The Icecutter's Daughter.* Land of Shining Water. 2013.

In 1896, being the only female in a house of males is not easy but Merrill Krause made a promise to her dying mother that she would take care of her brothers and help with the family ice-cutting business in rural Minnesota. Rurik Jorgenson has come to town to help his uncle. Luckily, Rurik is not afraid of her unruly brothers or her tomboyish ways. Before they can be together, scandal stands in their way. A different time period, tempting descriptions of Swedish pastries, and a sweet love story will have teens hooked. (print, ebook, audiobook from audible read by Stina Nielsen)

Quick, Amanda. *Second Sight.* 2007.

Venetia Milton, spinster, psychic, and main supporter to her collection of relatives is happy to have a job photographing an alchemist's collection of oddities for Gabriel Jones. Giving into passion, the two spend one night together before they are separated by Gabriel's death. Venetia is thrilled when he is not dead but on the run from thieves and enemies. Together they attempt to track down the thieves while falling in love. A quick and fun read for teens who like their history with a touch of magic, witty dialogue, and smart characters. (print, ebook, audiobook from Brilliance read by Anne T. Flosnik)

Willig, Lauren. *The Secret History of the Pink Carnation.* Pink Carnation. 2005.

Harvard graduate student Eloise Kelly travels to London to research the identity of the most notorious nineteenth-century British spy known only as the Pink Carnation. Her research leads her to the private papers of Arabella Selwick-Aderly, a descendent of Richard Selwick aka the Purple Gentian and to the handsome Colin Selwick. The plot moves back and forth between Eloise and Colin's story in the present and a love story surrounding his ancestor Richard. Teens who love both historical and contemporary romances and series will love this one, as Eloise's story continues in the next 11 (to date) books. (print, ebook, Penguin audio read by Kate Reading)

Paranormal Romance

Paranormal romance accounts for 30 percent of all romances read. Paranormal gives readers a chance to escape to a world where anything is possible. Readers can set aside the trials of everyday life and get lost in a fantasy world where there will still be a happy ending. There is a wide range of subgenres within paranormal—vampires, shape-shifters, witches, angels, and demons are but a few.

Allen, Sarah Addison. *Garden Spells.* 2007.

Allen has infused a small town contemporary romance with just enough hints of magic to make it a paranormal romance. Claire has devoted her life to her catering business and not falling in love. Her food is legendary for its ability to affect the diner's emotions. When she is not cooking or fighting with her sister, she is fighting her attraction to her handsome new neighbor. Teen girls who have sisters will relate to the love/hate relationship between Claire and her sister. The idea of being able to influence the emotions of others will capture their interest as well. Allen published a sequel in 2015, *First Frost*, which continues the sister's story. (print, ebook, audiobook from Brilliance Audio, read by Susan Ericksen)

Andrews, Ilona. *Clean Sweep.* <u>The Innkeeper Chronicles</u>. **2013.**
> An online serial that turned into a charming novella. Dina Demille is the innkeeper at a small B&B in a small town in Texas. Her neighbors have no idea the inn is a way station for otherworldly guests. When there is a killer loose in the neighborhood, she reluctantly gets involved in the search, butting heads immediately with her new neighbor and werewolf, Sean Evans. A great suggestion for teens looking for something on the shorter side. (print, ebook, audiobook from Brilliance read by Renee Raudman)

Bretton, Barbara. *Casting Spells*. <u>Sugar Maple</u>. **2011.**
> Chloe Hobbs is a half human who owns a knitting store in sleepy Sugar Maple, Vermont. It used to be a town protected by a charm but that charm is fading. It is up to Chloe to find love and come into her powers to save the town. Cute detective Luke MacKenzie, who comes to town to solve a murder, might just be the answer to her problems. Teens looking to figure out who they are in the face of familial expectations will relate to Chloe's journey. (print, ebook)

Cassidy, Dakota. *The Accidental Werewolf.* <u>Accidentals</u>. **2008.**
> Marty Andrews was not looking for love that night she took her darling teacup poodle for a walk, but love found her in a most unusual way. Cassidy's sarcastic and humorous series opener is a laugh-out-loud look at a young woman trying to find her place in the world. Instead of climbing the corporate ladder, she now must learn about packs and pack politics. A great choice for teen readers. (print, ebook, audiobook from Tantor Media read by Margaret Mitchell)

Cooper, Isabel. *Legend of the Highland Dragon*. **2013.**
> Mina Seymour is working as a secretary in Victorian London. She is concerned about her employer after a strange visit from Laird Stephen MacAlasdair, something about him does not seem right. That something is that he is really a shape-shifting dragon. Now the two of them are embroiled in a battle for their lives as Stephen's old enemies come calling. A good blend of history, mythology, and of course, romance. Teens will appreciate Mina's loyalties to her employer and her no-nonsense attitude. (print, audiobook from Tantor Media read by Derek Perkins, ebook)

Frost, Jeaniene. *Beautiful Ashes*. <u>Broken Destiny</u>. **2014.**
> Ivy's sister is trapped in a parallel dimension. To get her back, Ivy has to face her worst nightmares and team up with Adrian who might be a demon, but he is the one she cannot live without. Teens will empathize with the horrific losses Ivy has been dealt and will cheer her on as she faces one obstacle after another. Finding her sister sounds easy compared with dealing with her conflicted feeling for Adrian. Is he one of the good guys or the bad guys? (print, ebook, audiobook from Blackstone Audio read by Tavia Gilbert)

Grayson, Kristine. *Charming Blue*. **2012.**
> If your teens are fans of *Grimm* or *Once Upon a Time*, then *Charming Blue* is for them. Jodi Walters is a fixer, she can and does fix magical problems. Her latest problem is Bluebeard, now Blue. There is a stalker on the loose, who is terrorizing the magical community who looks like Blue and is even calling himself Blue. To figure out the problem, Jodi meets with Blue who has cleaned up his act and himself to reveal a very attractive man.

Blue wants nothing to do with Jodi despite their growing attraction. He is afraid that she will die if she gets mixed up with him. (book, ebook)

Harper, Molly. *How to Flirt with a Naked Werewolf*. 2011.

As Mo tries to establish her own life away from her overbearing hippie parents, she takes a job at a restaurant in Grundy, Alaska. Finding herself attracted to rude, arrogant Cooper Graham certainly was not on the list. Cooper also happens to be a werewolf. Could he be the werewolf responsible for the recent vicious wolf attacks? Together Mo and Cooper generate enough heat to keep themselves warm during the cold Alaskan winter. It is a laugh-out-loud, lighthearted romance that teens will enjoy for the laughs and for Mo's struggle for independence. (print)

Lamm, Gina. *The Geek Girl and the Scandalous Earl*. 2013.

This time travel/historical romance is a fun, light read. Comic-loving geek Jamie is not exactly thrilled when she somehow tumbles back in time to 1816 London. She lands in the home of the dishonored Earl of Dunnington, Micah Axelby. Attempting to adjust to life without indoor plumbing, TV, and her iPhone is tough, but luckily Micah is there to help her. Teens will easily identify with Jamie's adjustment issues and her feelings of insecurity in this new world. Plus, there is an adorable greyhound who takes a liking to Jamie. (book, ebook)

Conclusion: Trends in Romance

Amish romances continue to grow and to be a very good choice for crossover books; they are an excellent choice for teens who are looking for "clean" romances. Inspirational romances are also a good choice for teens looking for a romance without a lot of sex and the references to religion have become more subtle, in many of them.

Another trend to be aware of is that adult authors are now writing for teens and teen authors are now writing for adults. This may make readers' advisory easier, as teens may be more willing to read authors that they are familiar with.

Blending romance with historical fiction is not new, but an increasingly popular time period of late is that of the Edwardian period and reaching into the 1920s, the Downton Abbey period. Teens are captivated by the upstairs/downstairs storylines, the lavish clothing, the impeccable manners, and the changing roles of women and society. Try these authors to start: Sherri Browning's Thornbrook Park series, Judith Kinghorn's *The Last Summer*, or T. J. Brown's Summerset Abbey series.

One of the biggest trends in romances is ebooks. Avid readers never have to be without a book or seven, and they can access their books on their phone, tablet, dedicated e-reader, or on their computer. The availability of ebooks is also a boon to readers who may not want everyone around them to know what they are reading. With the rise in self-publishing, many new authors are starting out in digital form (E. L. James, Tracey Garvis-Graves) before their books are published in print, and some authors publish some or all of their work exclusively in digital format. While this can be great for readers, all of the issues associated with ebooks makes this more of a challenge for librarians.

Romance with its many subgenres is an ideal crossover genre for teens. As long as one keeps in mind the RA guidelines and is cognizant of the varying levels of sexuality in romance novels, there is no shortage of titles to recommend to teen readers. It is important to remember to not judge teen readers on their choices or their likes and dislikes. There is a romance out there for every reader!

References

Booth, Heather. *Serving Teens through Readers Advisory*. Chicago, IL: American Library Association, 2007.

Quillen, C. L. and Lefkowitz, Ilene. *Read On ... Romance*. Englewood, CO: Libraries Unlimited, 2014.

Romance Writers of America. http://www.rwa.org/.

7

New Adult

Elizabeth Burns and Kelly Jensen

Introduction to the Genre

Definition

In 2009, St. Martin's Press held a contest for manuscripts featuring 18-and-older characters that read like Young Adult (YA) but would best be published and marketed for adults. They called this fiction category "New Adult" (NA). NA, as envisioned by this contest, would especially appeal to readers in the 18–25-year-old range, who were newly emerging in their adulthood; the books would be more mature in scope and content but they would have similar appeal to readers who grew up enjoying young adult novels. Since then, this category has seen tremendous growth, as well as debate about its legitimacy and place as a separate entity from Young Adult and Adult books.

Sexuality, coming-of-age, and relationships have all been a part of YA fiction, but in NA fiction, these issues are explored with more drama and explicitness. If YA fiction asks the question, "Who do I want to be?," then NA fiction asks, "How do I become the person I want to be?" Coming-of-age is a hallmark of YA fiction, but with the emergence of NA literature, the idea of coming-of-age takes on two distinct levels. In YA fiction, there is the emotional preparation for the journey. In NA fiction, it is the journey itself. To put it in a different way, NA fiction takes the coming-of-age journey beyond the dependence of adolescence into the independence of adulthood, with independence marked as the legal age of 18.

NA fiction as a literary category is still in its infancy. Currently, much of it mirrors contemporary romance, with romance and romantic tension playing significant roles in the story. It has some comparisons to what many once called "Chick Lit," a bit of a sexist and belittling label, though NA tends to have a darker edge to it. But as NA grows, entries into this category are shifting to highlighting themes of independence and finding one's way financially and emotionally in the adult world. This is also what keeps it from being a subgenre of romance. NA literature encapsulates an age of experience, rather than being a specific genre.

For the purposes of this book, NA literature is defined as books that feature protagonists who are between 18 and 30. They are adults, but new to adulthood. They are encountering the "firsts" of being out of high school: first full-time job, first time at college, first time away from "home," first apartment, first group of friends not defined by neighborhood or high school, first job, and first career. All of this is without the same level of parental involvement that a typical minor teen experiences.

NA fiction first garnered buzz as a self-publishing phenomenon, with forerunners in 2012 like *Easy* by Tammara Webber, *Wait for You* by Jennifer L. Armentrout, *Losing It* by Cora Carmack, *Slammed* by Colleen Hoover, and *Walking Disaster* by Jamie McGuire building the category's steam. As NA fiction gained traction online, many NA and non-NA literature authors spoke about how they had been discouraged from submitting books with college settings because they did not sell. The success of NA fiction showed there was reader interest, not just an author desire for such books; and self-publishing, with its quick timeline and reader response, was a fertile ground to prove this.

NA books found an audience of ravenous readers, and authors discovered they could publish fan-satisfying stories fast. Big publishing houses followed, acquiring these high-performing books to reach this eager, growing readership. Even as more NA titles hit bookstore shelves and mainstream press because they are now being published through big houses, NA largely remains and evolves in the self-publishing market. Because NA is a category or type of literature rather than a genre, these books are not necessarily being promoted in a specific market.

Some corners of the publishing industry recognize NA fiction as a separate category, but not all do. Thus, the work of distinguishing what is and is not a NA title becomes tricky. In general, you will not find specifically designated NA shelves in bookstores or libraries. Most frequently, these titles are published as adult or romance fiction; and fans of NA books either know they are NA titles or label them as such when the label fits. Titles published before the NA fiction boom that feature the hallmarks of new adult can and do get reclaimed by NA readers. Some publishers have taken the new adult label and created lines of titles specifically for this category, including Zest Books's "Pulp" imprint, dedicated to new adult high-interest nonfiction.

NA's strength within the self-publishing world further complicates its categorization. Many well-known NA authors began their careers self-publishing NA titles, and their paths blazed the way for more to follow. Because of the speed at which self-publishing allows authors to publish, successful authors are able to satiate excited and eager readers much faster than they could through traditional publishing houses. This allows the category to grow quickly, and allows for popular NA series books to cater a bit more to reader demands and interests, which may explain why romance plays such a central role in these books. If readers want romance and will pay for it in another book, authors want to give it to their fans.

Appeals

Many adults enjoy reading YA literature. It is not surprising that these readers would want to see the elements that attracted them to YA fiction in the other books they read, including adult and NA titles. Published for a narrow segment of adult readership, NA literature addresses themes close to the teen experience, blurring the lines between intended and actual audience. Though these books may not feature teen characters nor be written with teens in mind, they appeal to teen readers who are looking ahead to their next phase of maturity. The challenges of navigating early adulthood, the coming-of-age journey, and the gritty elements of growing up, relationships, and sex/sexuality are hallmarks of NA literature, which is why both teens and adults find these books so appealing. NA literature can be edgier and more explicit than even the most provocative YA.

While NA fiction is more than setting, its setting is a perfect example of this category's crossover appeal: high school students curious about what life after graduation will be like; college-age readers wanting to read about people like themselves, not people younger or older; and older readers who remember their younger days and want to revisit them in fiction.

Working with Readers

New Adult is the generally accepted terminology for this category of books, but for librarians that term can be problematic, especially when searching lists and reviews for collection development and readers' advisory. Libraries continue to have "new adult books" that highlight their new books for adults rather than books in the new adult category. With increased usage of the NA label, one will hopefully find the resources they need more easily.

In the meantime, there is currently no Dewey or Library of Congress (LOC) classification to make cataloging and finding NA books easier. With other genres or categories such as science fiction, historical fiction, or young adult, there is generally a starting place, even if it is broad. Libraries need to be proactive in how NA books are cataloged, what booklists are created, to help readers find these books, and to assist library staff in locating NA books their readers want. Library staff who take extra steps in developing a collection and creating a smart and intuitive system will be rewarded with patrons who see the library as a place that respects their tastes in books, "gets" what they are looking for, and provides what they want.

With an evolving category like NA literature, which includes titles on both sides of the YA/Adult divide, it is vital to understand what it is that the reader wants when they say "New Adult." While one element of NA books is the age of the protagonist (aged 18 to 29), a frequent readers' advisory error can be in looking at the age of the main character and stopping there. Questions to consider when offering reader's advisory for NA include:

- Is the reader interested in a college setting or a post-college setting?
- Many NA books have companion books, featuring overlapping characters that are friends, relatives, or neighbors. Is this—a set of books in a shared world—what the reader wants?
- Is the coming-of-age journey what the reader seeks? Do they want a character navigating their new world—a world of college, first apartment, new job, trying to make ends meet?
- If the reader is interested in romance, how are they defining "romance"—what level of "heat" do they want?

As teen librarians know, teens frequently read adult books, including romance books. These adult romances already being read by teens include "spicy" titles—that is, books that contain explicit sexual content. NA books are a good fit for such readers because these readers have shown an interest in books that are more explicit than typical teen books. NA books are also about the world that teens will soon be entering, and that is a world that teens are naturally curious about. NA characters are closer to teens in age, experience, and outlook than most typical adult romances, and that has appeal for teen readers. Because of the content of most NA books, they will most often be in the adult section of the library. Teen readers will realize what that means for content and can decide for themselves whether that is something they want to read. So a good place to begin when recommending NA to readers who are not already familiar with it is to take cues from their interests in romance, college settings, or topics relating to first leaving one's home and entering adulthood.

Tools and Resources

With NA literature rising out of the self-publishing ebook world, the best readers' advisory tools are less traditional. Currently, the blog world is perhaps the most solid resource for NA. Blogs such as NA Alley (http://www.naalley.com) focus exclusively on NA, and romance blogs such as Heroes and Heartbreakers (http://www.heroesandheartbreakers.com/tags/new-adult) often cover NA as well.

Because NA was fostered by the interest of impassioned readers, another resource for staying on top of NA is where those passionate readers talk books: Goodreads. Reader-developed lists for NA (https://www.goodreads.com/shelf/show/new-adult), user books tagged as "new adult" (https://www.goodreads.com/genres/new-adult), and the thriving New Adult Book Club Group (https://www.goodreads.com/group/show/85934-new-adult-book-club) showcase the range of styles, voices, authors, and genres readers consider NA.

Traditional library trade journals are also beginning to pay more attention to New Adult fiction. *Booklist* (August 2014), *The Horn Book Magazine* (January/February 2014), and *Publishers Weekly* (http://www.publishersweekly.com/pw/by-topic/industry-news/publisher-news/article/63285-new-adult-matures.html) have published articles and book lists of the emerging category, while *School Library Journal*, *Library Journal*, and *Publishers Weekly* have offered webinars featuring leading NA authors, many of which are archived online for reference.

Collection Development

The good news about NA literature is that it can be found in most libraries, even if it is not labeled as such or displayed in its own distinct section. Take note on what is in your adult and YA collections: characters who are just beyond the teen years, are set in college or just beyond college, and focus on the challenges with which people in their late teens and early 20s grapple. Themes of independence, ranging from personal to financial, as well as themes of dating, shifting relationships among friends and family, and the discovery of self are key elements of what NA readers want.

These books are not limited to the novel format, either; graphic novels and graphic memoirs offer a treasure trove of new adult themes. As noted earlier, it is possible that NA nonfiction may also emerge, but rather than building an entire NA nonfiction collection, scour what is on hand for those titles that would be of interest to NA readers, including, and especially, memoirs.

The NA category is not just limited to reading. Topics and themes that NA readers enjoy are seen on television and film too. HBO's *Girls* is frequently cited as an example of what NA looks like, exploring the immediate post-college years. *Broad City*, *The New Girl*, and *Supernatural* may also fit the "New Adult" categorization on television, as they center around this particular time in life and the challenges of developing and embracing personal independence. Season 3 of *Glee* and the following seasons may also qualify as NA.

The Literature

The list of titles that follows offer you a starting place for exploring and promoting New Adult literature. Titles are grouped by themes that are popular with NA readers.

College Setting/The College Years

All of these titles are set either in college or in the college years, and while romance may play a part in the story, it is not the focal point. Some of these stories follow 18–25-year-olds who are attending Ivy Leagues, while others follow those in that age group who have chosen an alternate path to college. Teen appeal is high with these titles because the characters are exploring the "what next?" part of their life journey as they transition out of their family homes and graduate from high school. These stories are about the excitement and fear that come with newfound freedom.

Beyer, Ramsey. *Little Fish*. 2013.
Through real-life journals, collages, lists, and drawings, Beyer chronicles her first year away from her small town at an art college in a busy city. This graphic novel hybrid explores the highs and lows of moving across the country for school, and adapting to a new and different environment. The style makes this memoir approachable and appealing. (print, ebook)

Doller, Trish. *Something Like Normal*. 2012.
When Travis returns home on leave from the Marines, he is greeted with his parents' impending divorce, his brother stealing his girlfriend, the grief of his best friend's death, and Harper, a girl demanding an explanation for his past behavior toward her. It is not college, but military service, that makes this title stand out for how it approaches the post-high school years. (print, ebook, audible digital audio read by Anthony Haden Salerno)

Flack, Sophie. *Bunheads*. 2011.
Hannah devotes her life to dance as a member of the prestigious Manhattan Ballet Company, but when she meets Jacob—a musician not part of the company—she begins to wonder whether this competitive, tough life is what she really wants. Aside from the story's setting in an alternative to college, Flack's novel explores personal choice, and what it means to change what felt like one-solid life plans. (print, ebook)

Forman, Gayle. *Just One Day*. Just One Day. 2013.
Allyson took a chance on Willem for one day while traveling in Europe after graduation; now, she is spending her first year in college wishing they could be together. This is not a story about the romantic notions of college. Allyson struggles to fit in and find reason to be there, as she wants nothing more than to travel again and be reunited with Willem. (print, ebook, audible digital audio read by Kathleen McInerney)

Kelly, Tara. *Amplified.* **2011.**

Jasmine gets kicked out of her house because she does not want to go to college, so now she is attempting to make a name for herself in the Santa Cruz music scene. This story about "making it" with no support—financially or emotionally—from your family follows the less-traditional path of choosing career dreams over college. There is no shying away from challenges, but there is plenty of pulse-pounding music. (print, ebook)

Martin, C. K. Kelly. *Come See about Me.* **2012.**

Bastian's death sends Leah into a tailspin and she fails out of college. When she moves into an apartment owned by Bastian's aunt, she isolates from those in her life, but slowly learns how to come around and make a life after loss. This story of grief explores the nontraditional paths outside of college, as well as how new relationships—including sexual ones—can be built again. (print, ebook)

Peterfreund, Diana. *Secret Society Girl.* Secret Society Girl. **2006.**

Amy receives an invitation to Rose & Grave, the country's most powerful and notorious secret society even though she is not rich, connected, or a male, and she is going in headfirst. Secret societies are perennially appealing, as are the lives of the elite. This series features plenty of mystery and plenty of romance too. (print, ebook)

Rowell, Rainbow. *Fangirl.* **2013.**

When fan-fiction writer Cath and her twin sister Wren move into their college dorm, their relationship changes, and Cath must learn how to create new friendships (and maybe romances too). The pop cultural references, the voice, and the challenges of balancing one's past with an uncertain future make this title stand out. (print, ebook, audio read by multiple narrators)

Snadowsky, Daria. *Anatomy of a Single Girl.* Anatomy. **2013.**

Dominique thinks her busy pre-med course load will keep her mind off the breakup from her first true love, but then she meets Guy and finds there may be room for another relationship. Exploring sexuality, the rigors of university study, and what and how relationships are built and broken, readers get to see an entire range of new adult experiences in the college environment. (print, ebook).

Thompson, Alicia. *Psych Major Syndrome.* **2009.**

Leigh, a freshman psychology major at Stiles College, is great at helping her friends solve problems, but solving her own is not her specialty, especially those involving her boyfriend Andrew. Why is spending time with him challenging? Why cannot she commit to more for their relationship? Navigating new terrain at college along with a relationship that is not what it once seemed makes Leigh's transition tough, and maybe she is overthinking it all. (print, ebook)

Romance College Setting

The college and college-age setting is perfect for NA books and readers: characters young enough to be grappling with questions of love, lust, and their future and old enough to act on those feelings and emotions without parents looking over their shoulders. Here are samplings of college-age settings.

Aguirre, Ann. *I Want It That Way.* 2B Trilogy. 2014.

When Nadia is not studying to keep her scholarship, she is working hard at the local day care to pay her bills. She does not have time for herself. Daniel is a young single father, working full time and going to night classes. He does not have time for love. They cannot fight the attraction and end up as friends with benefits. You can guess how that ends up. (print, ebook, audible digital download read by Bailey Carr)

Alva, Sara. *Social Skills.* 2013.

Connor is a wonderful musician who is terribly shy. At college, he slowly begins to make friends. Enter Jared: Connor's opposite, a popular, social football player. Sparks fly when Jared and Connor meet, but Jared is afraid of coming out of the closet. Appeal factors: Connor's growth in self-confidence, the love story, and both young men's journey toward coming out. (print, ebook, audible digital audio read by Andrew Eiden)

Bowen, Sarina. *The Year We Fell Down.* Ivy Years Series. 2014.

Corey Callahan's freshman year at Harkness College is not what she planned. She is not playing on the ice hockey team; she is not in the freshman dorm. Because of an accident the year before, she is in a wheelchair and living in the only handicapped-accessible dorm. Corey is not going to let her protective parents, or a college mostly built before ADA laws, stop her from enjoying all that college has to offer. And of those things may be Adam Hartley, the really hot guy who lives across the hall from her. (print, ebook)

Carmack, Cora. *All Lined Up.* Rusk University. 2014.

For Dallas Cole, college is the time to finally get away from football. But she ends up at school with both her college football player ex and her father, whose first-time college coaching job is at her university. Once again, football threatens to overshadow her own life. Then she meets Carson McClain. She does not know he is on the team. He does not know he has fallen for the coach's daughter. First in a series. (print, ebook, audio read by multiple narrators)

Crownover, Jay. *Rule.* Marked Men. 2012; reprint 2013.

What links the men of the Marked Men series is a tattoo shop, The Marked. *Rule*, the first in the series, is an opposites attract book: Shaw's a straight A pre-med college student, Rule's a rebel with piercings and tattoos. It is not just that they are opposites: She is also his dead twin brother's girl. Angst matters in NA books, and the dynamics from the loss of Rule's twin years earlier provides plenty. While NA is often about independence, this is also about family. Shaw has become a part of Rule's family because of her friendship with his twin, and that family matters to her. (print, ebook, audible digital audio read by multiple narrators)

Glines, Abbi. *Fallen Too Far.* Rosemary Beach. 2012; reprint 2014.

Blaire is a 19-year-old farm girl, who spent the last three years taking care of her sick mother. Rush is 24, the spoiled son of a rock star. They are also step-siblings, sharing a Florida beach house while their parents vacation in Paris. Rush may be a player but he is also gorgeous. It may be a familiar formula—"good girl falls for bad boy, will he change?"—but there is a reason these stories are popular and Glines tells it well: It is hot, sexy, addictive. (print, ebook, audio read by Jennifer Bronstein)

Hoover, Colleen. *Maybe Someday.* Maybe. **2014.**
    Sydney, 22, thinks her life is perfect: college is great, work is wonderful, and she has got a great boyfriend and best friend. Until she finds out her boyfriend is cheating on her. Sydney is drawn to her neighbor, musician Ridge, but there are reasons why a relationship between them is "maybe someday" not now. Angst, dual narrators, and a triangle with three likable characters add to the sexual tension. Original music created for the books is available. (print, ebook, audible digital audio read by multiple narrators)

Lynn, J. *Wait for You.* Wait for You. **2013.**
    Avery has gone to a college as far from home as possible to escape her hometown, what happened to her years ago on one terrible night, and her family. Cam is the handsome guy who lives in her building whom she keeps running into. Avery wants to reinvent herself; does Cam fit into her life? Will Cam wait for Avery to be ready? Can Avery heal enough to be ready for Cam? Emotions, angst, and healing all combine. (print, ebook, audible digital audio read by Sophie Eastlake)

McCarthy, Erin. *True.* True Believers. **2013.** When Rory's friends find out she is a virgin, her roommates hire tattooed Tyler to sleep with her, but do not tell Rory what they have done. Tattoos, piercings, and all around hotness do not mean a boy is bad, and Rory and Tyler fall for each other. Appeal factors are the connection that develops between Rory and Tyler; Tyler's complicated, messy home life and the younger brothers that he feels responsible for add a dimension. (print, ebook)

Park, Jessica. *Flat-Out Life.* Flat-Out Love. **2011.**
    College freshman Julie's housing falls through, so she moves in with family friends, the Watkins and their children: MIT student Matt and teenage Celeste, while the oldest, Finn, is traveling and present in Facebook chats and e-mails. Can someone really fall in love with someone they have never met? And what secrets are in the Watkins family? Going to college is typically about creating a family of friends; but for Julie, it is learning about a family and family dynamics. And it is about falling for two different brothers. (print, ebook [Kindle only], audio read by Julia Whelan)

Sorensen, Jessica. *The Coincidence of Callie and Kayden.* The Coincidence. **2013.**
    Callie reinvents herself at college, glad to leave her past behind. She finds herself running into Kayden, from her hometown, and Mr. Popular to her Miss Outcast. At college, though, they connect, finding more in common than either realized. Both have past pain and trauma they have been hiding from the world. It is a steamy love story where Callie and Kayden are learning to heal and trust. The first in the series ends on a cliff-hanger, and the series follows Callie and Kayden and their friends through multiple volumes, including Seth and Greyson (Book 8, 2015) (print, ebook, audible digital audio read by Leslie Bellair).

Tucker, K. A. *Ten Tiny Breaths.* Ten Tiny Breaths. **2013.**
    Kacey's parents died four years before, and she cannot stand another minute living with her aunt and uncle so she takes her little sister, Livie, and leaves. Kacey, 20, is struggling to make ends meet and to take care of her

15-year-old sister. She is not looking for love. Then she meets sexy Trent, her next-door neighbor. Rebuilding a life, starting over—it does not all happen by going to college, and sometimes people have responsibilities, like a younger sister. (print, ebook, audible digital audio read by Elizabeth Louise)

Webber, Tammara. *Easy.* Contours of the Heart. **2012.**

Jacqueline followed her long-time boyfriend to college, only to be dumped by him in her sophomore year. Shortly after, one of her ex's fraternity brothers attempts to rape her; she is saved by Lucas. Will Lucas be her perfect rebound, or something more? *Easy* has essential NA appeal factors: a college setting offering plenty of independence, a trauma (attempted rape), Jacqueline taking control of her life and love, and a sexy read. Lucas's side of the story is told in the companion book, *Breakable* (2014). (print, ebook, audio read by Tara Sands).

Beyond College and Romance

What about those years immediately following college? What about books that are not contemporary romances and fit instead into other genres? These are the books that feature stories set in the immediate post-college time frame, or they are titles that could fit within other genre designations but are instead being sold and marketed as new adult. These stories grapple with the same questions that those set in college or in contemporary settings do, but through the lens of either entering the "real world" and job market for the first time or entering an entirely new world altogether.

August, Noelle. *Boomerang.* Boomerang. **2014.**

Boomerang.com is a steamy, no-commitments dating site, and when Mia and Ethan hook up with one another and discover they both intern for the website, things become quickly complicated—they are both hoping to score a permanent job with the site. A post-college story of romance and the workplace. (print, ebook, audio read by multiple narrators)

Burgess, Gemma. *Brooklyn Girls.* Brooklyn Girls. **2013.**

The first in a series, four 20-something girls share a brownstone in a hip Brooklyn neighborhood and learn to navigate the highs and lows of post-college life in the big city. Romance, humor, and honesty make this series especially appealing to teens. (print, ebook)

Chase, Nichole. *Suddenly Royal.* Suddenly. **2013.**

Samantha is working on her master's degree in wildlife biology when she finds out she is an heiress! With an estate and a title, she travels to the (fictional) Lilaria to learn more about her inheritance, and meets the handsome, charming, heir to Lilaria. It is a modern fairy tale. Appeal factors: a grown-up main character, and while it is a fantasy (long lost royalty) it is also about dealing with the unexpected (like being long last royalty) and having to change life plans. And, of course, a prince. (print, ebook, audio read by Caitlin Davies)

Evans, Katy. *Real.* Real. **2013.**

Brooke is a recent college graduate, just starting out in sports rehabilitation. Remington is a star in underground fighting circuits. Brooke goes to one of his fights. They notice each other, and sparks fly. The sexual tension and steamy times increase when Brooke is hired to tour with Remy as his personal sports therapist. (print, ebook, audible digital audio download read by Charlotte Penfield)

Harian, Sarah. *The Wicked We Have Done.* Chaos Theory. **2014.**
For NA readers who want something different than contemporary romance. Evalyn, 22, has been accused of murder and is now in an experimental prison with an obstacle course—survive, and it proves she is innocent. She is locked in with nine other prisoners. She hopes to survive; she does not expect to fall in love. (ebook)

Knisley, Lucy. *An Age of License.* **2014.**
When Knisley is invited to speak at a comic convention in Norway, she uses it as an opportunity to travel through Europe, where she hears the phrase *age of license* as one to describe the time frame of figuring yourself and your goals out in your early 20s. This graphic memoir features travel, a foreign romance, and highlights the value of taking risks and making commitments in your life. (print)

Kwok, Jean. *Mambo in Chinatown.* **2014.**
Twenty-two-year-old Charlie grew up in Chinatown, and her entire life has been limited to the neighborhood. When she gets a job as a receptionist in a dance studio and begins to dance—and falls in love with dance—she has to choose between staying true to her cultural roots and spreading her wings and exploring the world beyond her community. (print, ebook, audio read by Angela Lin)

Maas, Sarah J. *A Court of Thorns and Roses.* **2015.**
Maas, author of the popular young adult series Throne of Glass, enters the NA arena with a sexy adventure story. From the book copy: "When nineteen-year-old huntress Feyre kills a wolf in the woods, a beast-like creature arrives to demand retribution for it. Dragged to a treacherous magical land she only knows about from legends, Feyre discovers that her captor is not an animal, but Tamlin-one of the lethal, immortal faeries who once ruled their world." (print, ebook)

McAdams, Molly. *Sharing You.* Sharing You. **2014.**
Kamryn moves to a small town where no one knows her and opens a bakery, where she meets Brody. Brody is married, but the marriage is not a good one. Can they date? Should they date? This series explores the immediate post-college life of moving, finding a job, and figuring out relationships and relationship boundaries. (print, ebook, audio read by multiple narrators)

McHugh, Gail. *Collide.* Collide. **2013.**
College graduate Emily is in New York City for a fresh start. Her mother has just died of cancer and she is in New York City to be with her boyfriend, sweet, caring Dillon—all Emily would want in a man. Until she meets Gavin, a rich, sexy playboy. Emily cannot fight her attraction to Gavin, but Dillon has been there for her. Being a college graduate does not mean a person has all the answers, or their life is all set. (print, ebook, audio read by Mary Kowal)

Parr, Allison. *Rush Me*. New York Leopards. 2013.

First in a series that centers on an NFL team, the New York Leopards. In *Rush Me*, college graduate Rachel accidentally crashes a New York Leopards party, meeting quarterback Ryan. Other people may be impressed but Rachel, hoping to break into publishing, is not. This is not love at first sight; it is friendship that becomes something more. And it is a new adult with all of the sparks and none of the angst. (ebook, audible digital download read by Daniella Rabbani)

Young, Samantha. *On Dublin Street.* On Dublin Street. 2012.

Jocelyn left the United States and moved to Scotland to get a fresh start, but when she moves into a new apartment and meets Braden, he is going to push her until she lets down her guard. This steamy, intense romance is about fresh starts, both in new places and in new relationships. (print, ebook, audible digital audiobook read by Paula Costello)

Conclusion: Trends in New Adult Literature

Ideally, NA fiction will continue to stretch beyond its contemporary romance roots and expand the themes that make it so attractive into additional genres. NA literature should remain primarily the kind of stories that feature 20-somethings in college or of college age with romance at the center. There likely will not be a change in how it is shelved or marketed, but it will remain up to librarians and readers to be aware of books that fit this niche because readers WANT these stories.

While traditionally published authors who have written college-age characters and settings are excited about NA's potential—and many current books are labeled as NA "beyond the romance genre"—the question remains whether NA is a subgenre of romance or a genre of its own. This is not a slam on romance but a question as to the current and future scope of NA fiction.

As of this writing, the uptick in NA fiction being published through traditional publishers has already slowed, though they are and will continue to be published. NA literature will continue being popular in digital platforms, where speed and price point are hugely appealing to readers.

PART II
Teen Books for Adults

8

Thrillers, Suspense, and Adventure

Jennifer Haas Thiele

Introduction to the Genre

Definition

Murder mystery, detective, suspense, horror, supernatural, action, espionage, true crime, war, and adventure are all categorized as thrillers according to the International Thriller Writers Society (International Thriller Writers Association, 2015). This would include (but is not limited to) subjects such as murder mystery, detective, suspense, horror, supernatural, action, espionage, true crime, war, and adventure. Tixier Herald's Genreflecting categorizes suspense and thrillers into the category of adventure, a genre that is perhaps the oldest in existence (Tixier Herald, 2006). However, according to author and readers' advisory expert Joyce Saricks, the suspense, thriller, and adventure genres can be more specifically defined within the overarching category of adrenaline. No matter how you define them, each category has its own unique appeal, with specific elements that distinguish them within the genre.

Appeals

Because the genre of thrillers is extremely large in scope, the appeals are varied. The most distinguishing characteristic of the genre is that the main character is secondary to the plot. Thrillers address varied subjects, often focusing on professional areas like medicine or law. These professions are often infused with danger. Also, the pacing tends to be fast (Tixier Herald, 2006). There are suspenseful elements to thrillers, but the focus is the framework of the scenario that the main character is in. Often, expertise or knowledge is what gets this protagonist out of the situation he or she is in (Saricks, 2009).

With all adrenaline genres, pacing drives the stories with the exception of psychological suspense, which has a more measured pace. Thrillers can be very long and filled with engrossing details of certain professions, yet continue to have fast pacing overall. Topicality is of importance with thrillers, many of them taking place in history, often times during war periods. Fast-paced espionage stories are often popular, with several plot twists to capture the reader's interest. Thrillers often are very cinematic, often being made into movies. Thrillers, unlike adventure stories, often feature strong female protagonists and have characters that have definitive moral codes (often in contrast to the dominant society). However, those who read thrillers are not typically interested in complex characters. The tone in these novels is most times dark (Saricks, 2009).

Suspense is the most challenging category to define, as many genres do contain suspense as part of the story. However, the entire purpose of a suspense novel is to build tension and uneasiness. This uneasiness derives not from the events that happen in the story, but instead from the things that might happen. An individual may have a normal life up to that point, until the danger takes hold (Saricks, 2009). According to Saricks, suspense novels have a characteristic pacing with the action taking place within a narrow time frame, with flashbacks of things that happened before that point. Many of these books have short chapters with cliff-hangers and alternate points of view, increasing the sense of danger. A menacing atmosphere with dark days and oppressive weather helps create a dark mood. A connection between the protagonist and the reader must be established, but the villain is often not identified until the end. At times, the reader can get the perspective of both the protagonist and the villain, adding to the suspense. The stories are characteristically nightmarish, as the protagonist's normal life is often invaded by threats. Unlike thrillers, suspense novels almost exclusively take place in the present day.

Psychological suspense on the other hand, "plays with our minds." These books have the most measured pace of all the genres, and are often mistakenly categorized as suspense, thrillers, or mysteries. Heavily character driven, these novels are often referred to as the "orphan genre" (Saricks, 2009). Psychological suspense has enough significant appeal difference that Saricks does not categorize it into the other adrenaline chapters when examining storyline, tone, frame, characterization style, and pacing. While psychological suspense does not have as much physical action as thrillers and traditional suspense novels, they do have just as many plot twists. The genre can often mimic literary fiction in many ways especially because they are written with elegant language. With an unsettling tone, these books often take place within the confines of the character's mind, which might be unreliable, and sometimes even mentally ill. These character misfits are outcasts from society and are utterly unpredictable. Often the endings are unresolved, which is a similarity the genre shares with literary fiction (Saricks, 2009).

When reading adventure fiction, the reader experiences danger in exotic locations. According to Saricks, these adventures often include treasure hunts, puzzles, and varied obstacles along the way. While at one time these books were declining in popularity, they are currently experiencing a resurgence (Saricks, 2009). In fact, according to Tixier Herald, adventure is one of the most popular genres that exists, with many titles almost guaranteed to be best sellers upon release. Adventure stories have appeal most typical of adrenaline genres. The brisk pacing, forward action, and definitive heroes (often male) make these stories alluring. In fact, Colleen Warner, head librarian of the Popular Culture Library at Bowling Green State University, describes this genre as a type of "male romance" (Tixier Herald, 2006). The focus is often on a dangerous mission, with the setting of particular importance most times being exotic or historic. Like the other genres, the atmosphere is dark and moody, and the language is colorful and filled with jargon (Saricks, 2009).

The adrenaline genres crossover age barriers because of the intensity of the stories. Often, a quick plot captures the attention of the reader, which attracts a young adult (YA) population, where reluctant readers are often fans of the genre. Reluctant readers are not just confined to the YA population, though. Many adults who do not do much leisure reading are also inclined to pick up adrenaline-type books because the stories capture their interest in the first few pages. This genre has been a crossover for some time, as suspense and adventure books have been popular with both adults and children of all ages. Many of the classic adventure stories, such as Rudyard Kipling's *Treasure Island*, fall into this particular genre as their fast pace holds the interest of adults and teens with shorter attention spans. Thrillers like *Jurassic Park* (by Michael Crichton) bring kids and adults into worlds that they might already hold some interest in. The fact that the adrenaline and thriller genres are so cinematic, often result in film tie-ins, which makes the genre even more alluring to the younger generation as well as adult populations.

YA books appeal to adults for many reasons. Meg Wolitzer wrote a piece for the *New York Times* in October 2014, where she examines the reasons adults read YA books. Humorously enough, Wolitzer highlights the issue of adults loving to read about YA problems, while YAs do not necessarily like to read about middle-aged dilemmas. This issue seems to be less prevalent in the adrenaline genres, where the character is often less important than the plot. The crossover appeal here is easier to see in the opposite, where even those adults who cannot relate to YA characters or avoid YA books because of a belief it is for "children," will be more inclined to read books where the characters are likely less developed than the surrounding action and plot.

Working with Readers

The lines between adult and YA fiction can be blurred, but often times the violence and sexual content is stronger in the adult books. For adults who enjoy a violent and descriptive thriller, many of the YA-oriented books are not good crossover selections. This is why it is important when doing a readers' advisory interview to ask questions, such as whether or not the individual is interested in exotic locations, how much detail they are looking for in scenes of crime, if they have a certain area of interest for thrillers based on professional topics (medical versus legal, for example), or if they gravitate toward books that take place during wars and/or involve espionage. Because there is such a strong movie tie-in with the adrenaline genres, it is also important to ask what types of movies the individual enjoys watching. This could give some clues as to books that would fit (Saricks, 2009).

Tools and Resources

There are several websites that thriller lovers may access to find out more about the trends and genres. The International Thriller Writers (ITW) has an updated and easy-to-navigate website for those who are readers, or for librarians doing reader's advisory. NoveList is a good resource for series fiction and readalikes for librarians who may not be familiar with each individual category and appeal. Many of these titles can be located in NoveList and are available for purchase by most major book outlets and distributors—for example, Baker & Taylor, Amazon, and Barnes & Noble. While not all have audiobook components, many do in MP3, CD, and Playaway formats. Some libraries might find it important to have an entire series in a certain format for readers who would like access to the physical materials at the library. For other libraries that have exceptional interlibrary loan systems and/or good access to downloadable ebooks and media, this may not be as important. Also, many libraries are able to direct patrons to free downloadable ebooks with some of the adrenaline classics that are available online through most major book outlets and public libraries.

Collection Development

A big stumbling block for any crossover reader is the physical location of the YA books in the library. Adults generally do not visit the section of the library where many of these selections are held, and even if instructed, they may be averse to going to the teen section, considering the material there to be "children's books." If the titles are interspersed with the adult books, crossover selections will be easier for these individuals to see and select. Creating book displays that combine both adult and YA fiction on particular themes or topics is another way to attract adult readers.

Note that when collecting in this area, there is a great deal of crossover between the genres of suspense, mysteries, crime, thrillers, and adventure stories. These genres are also multifaceted in that they often have dystopian, supernatural, fantasy, or sci-fi elements. If your library has bookstore model shelving, it might be challenging to decide how to distribute the items or how to sticker them. Be aware of your patrons' needs in this manner and be active readers' advisors to facilitate the process.

The Literature

The following titles are those that have been published for adults but will also appeal to teen readers. They are organized by subgenres that are popular with readers.

Suspense

Most suspense books begin when there is a danger that intersects an individual's normal, everyday life. There is a dark atmosphere and the action begins early on, within a narrow time frame, with a strong protagonist. There is a tension/uneasiness that pervades the entire story from early on in the book (Saricks, 2009).

Abbott, Megan. *Dare Me.* 2012.

Addy and Beth are looking forward to leading their cheerleading squad in their senior year of high school. However, a mysterious new coach arrives, turning everyone's plans upside down. As Addy gets drawn into the coach's world, Beth remains outside. When a suspicious suicide occurs, Addy must determine who is responsible, and how it will affect her coach, the squad, and her school. Adults will enjoy this highly dramatic story about teenage girls in the vein of *Heathers* and *Mean Girls*. (print, ebook, and audiobook read by Khristine Hvam)

McNamee, Graham. *Acceleration*. 2003.
Duncan works deep within the basement of the Toronto transit authority's lost and found where he catalogs lost items. It is there that he finds the diary of a serial killer. Duncan reads the diary and tries to stop the man before it is too late. This novel does have elements of a thriller and will appeal to adults who enjoy a faster-paced suspense novel. (print, ebook, and audiobook read by Scott Brick)

Oliver, Lauren. *Panic*. 2014.
Heather lives in the small town of Carp, where there is not much to do. To alleviate boredom, graduating seniors have participated in the risky game of Panic, a game where the stakes are high, but the payoff is higher. Heather finds that she is braver than she believes, but at what cost? The book will appeal to adults, especially those interested in reality and game television with high-stakes results. (print, ebook, and audiobook read by Sarah Drew)

Patterson, James. *The Angel Experiment*. Book 1 in <u>Maximum Ride Series</u>. 2005.
Max Ride and his five friends have no idea why they are running for their lives, they just know that they are meant to either save mankind or destroy it, with the help of their special powers, including flight. Adult fans of Patterson will love this series as well. (print, ebook, and audiobook read by Evan Rachel Wood)

Roux, Madeleine. *Asylum*. Book 1 in <u>Asylum Series</u>. 2013.
For Dan, New Hampshire College Prep summer program is an amazing opportunity. When he arrives, he finds that his dorm is held in an old sanatorium. When he and his friends begin to search the basement, strange things begin to happen and Dan has to figure out what is going on. This book will appeal to adults with the creepy setting and the genuine photographs taken from asylums from earlier time periods that are woven into the story. (print, ebook, and audiobook read by Michael Goldstrom)

Shepard, Sarah. *Pretty Little Liars*. Book 1 in <u>Pretty Little Liars Series</u>. 2006.
When one member of a tight-knit group of friends disappears, the four remaining members begin getting messages from someone who seems to know all of their secrets. Are these notes from the missing friend, or is another sinister situation at play? Another tale of teenage girls, adults will enjoy reading about the social interaction as well as getting the perspective of several characters. (print, ebook, and audiobook read by Cassandra Morris)

Ward, Rachel. *Numbers*. Book 1 in <u>Numbers Series</u>. 2008.
Ever since Jem was a child, she could look at someone and know immediately what day they will die based on the numbers that appear on their face. Because of this power, she avoids relationships. Until she meets a boy named Spyder who witnesses firsthand what Jem's powers can predict. This book has a strong appeal to adults because it touches on bigger issues

like terrorism and prediction. (print, ebook, and audiobook read by Sarah Coomes)

Werlin, Nancy. *Double Helix.* **2004.**
   After Eli graduates from high school, he takes a dream job for a Nobel Prize-winning scientist, Dr. Quincy Wyatt. There he discovers a shocking secret about his family and the activities of the mysterious Wyatt Transgenics. Adult readers will enjoy this book because of current controversial issues that surround genetic engineering and cloning. This book also has elements of a medical thriller to complement the suspense. (print, ebook, and audiobook read by Scott Shina)

Psychological Suspense

   The protagonists in these books might not be sympathetic, and the stories are very moody with the most measured pace than any of the adrenaline genres. The plots are elaborately constructed with multilayered meanings. Style creates mood, and there are unresolved endings (Saricks, 2009).

Alphin, Elaine Marie. *Counterfeit Son.* **2000.**
   Cameron is the son of a serial killer. When his father is killed by the police, he pretends to be one of his father's victims so he could have the home life he always dreamed he could have. But does Cameron even really know who he is? This story will appeal to adults because of the unpredictable twists and turns. (print and ebook)

Bedford, Martin. *Flip.* **2010.**
   A teenager wakes up in other boy's body and begins a life or death race to get to back to his original body. As he slowly investigates the switch, he finds that he is in a race against time to become who he really is meant to be. Adults will be intrigued by some of the bigger topics dealing with the right to die and live. (print, ebook, and audiobook read by Alex Kalajzic)

Cormier, Robert. *I Am the Cheese.* **1977.**
   A young boy tries to recover lost memories in a therapy session and through his own search for his father, but he also knows these memories could put him into grave danger from a world of government corruption and espionage. Mafia- and conspiracy-loving adults will enjoy this title that remains timeless even with an older publication date. There is also a movie tie-in that adults would likely enjoy. (print and ebook)

Hautman, Pete. *Mr. Was.* **1996.**
   Jack Lund discovers a door that takes him back in time to the 1940s. While there, he meets several individuals and witnesses events that will change his life forever. Told through narrative, diaries, and letters, the reader will piece together the events until the end is revealed. Adults will love the puzzle element of this book, as it takes the reader through generations of events. (print and ebook)

Lockhart, E. *We Were Liars.* **2014.**
   A group of friends spend their summers on an island off the coast of Massachusetts. After Cadence has a head trauma while swimming, she tries to piece together the events before. Reviews for this book cite it as a critical

read for those adults who want to explain why they enjoy YA. (print, ebook, and audiobook read by Ariadne Meyers)

Myers, Kate Kae. *The Vanishing Game.* **2012.**
Seventeen-year-old Jocelyn goes to the foster home where she used to live, following clues from her dead twin Jack who died mysteriously. What she finds unlocks the mystery to her childhood and her own memories of the events that unfolded. Myers does an excellent job portraying an unreliable narrator, and this should appeal to adult fans. (print and ebook)

Trueman, Terry. *Stuck in Neutral.* **2000.**
Shawn has cerebral palsy. Although his body is completely paralyzed, his mind is extremely active, remembering every conversation he has ever heard. When Shawn begins to suspect his father is trying to kill him, he struggles to communicate what he wants his father to know. This story appeals to adults because it touches on the larger issues of disability, right to die (or live), and education. (print, ebook, and audiobook read by Johnny Heller)

Vrettos, Adrienne Maria. *Burnout.* **2011.**
After getting treatment for alcohol and drug abuse, Ann wakes up on the subway in Halloween costume, with her hair cut and a sign saying "Help Me." She has no idea how she got there. As she retraces her steps, she pieces together a dangerous night in a race to save her friend's life—and her own. *Burnout* has serious themes of drug use and street-smart teens with a story that is pieced together slowly with recovered memories. (print and ebook)

Thrillers

Thrillers focus on action, plot, and conspiracies, fast paced with sympathetic protagonists. Thrillers often focus on professions and rely on jargon to involve the reader with the story. This technical language does not impact the pace (Saricks, 2009).

Burgess, Melvin. *The Hit.* **2013.**
There is a new drug on the streets of Manchester that gives you the best week of your life. However, the consequence is that you die at the end of it. Adam is miserable and wants to try it. What he finds is more than what he bargained for. This book has some dystopian elements and political themes, which would appeal to adults. (print, ebook, and audiobook read by Samuel Roukin)

Carey, Anna. *Blackbird.* **Book 1 in <u>Blackbird Series</u>. 2014.**
A teen wakes up in the subway, tied to the tracks with a train coming at her head. She has the presence of mind to duck under the speeding vehicle, but has no idea how she got there. She does know, however, that people are trying to kill her and she must outwit those hunting her. A true thriller, adults will enjoy the fast pacing and adrenaline in this title. (print, ebook, and audiobook read by Simona Pahl)

Carter, Ally. *Heist Society.* **Book 1 in <u>Heist Society</u> Series. 2010.**
Katrina wants to leave the family business of art thieving behind, but she gets drawn back in when a mobster's art collection goes missing and her

dad is the assumed suspect. Now she must steal back the art collection to save her father—even though she would much rather have a normal life at the boarding school she came from. Adults who like novels about exciting international crime and espionage will enjoy this book. (print, ebook, and audiobook read by Angela Dawe)

Coben, Harlan. *Shelter.* **Book 1 in Mickey Bolitar Series. 2011.**
Mickey is forced to live with his estranged uncle and switch high schools where he meets a new girlfriend. However, when she disappears, Mickey finds that she is not who she seems to be. For Harlan Coben adult fans, these YA novels will be a crossover hit. (print, ebook, and audiobook read by Nick Podehl)

Gagnon, Michelle. *Don't Turn Around.* **Book 2 in PERSEFoNE Series. 2012.**
Sixteen-year-old Noa is a foster child turned computer hacker. One day, she wakes up on a table with an IV in her arm and has no idea how she got there. Noa is invited to join a secret computer hacker alliance, where she fights a corporation that wants to silence her for what she knows. Those who enjoy the typical jargon or professional thrillers will enjoy this novel. (print, ebook, and audiobook read by Merritt Hicks)

Horowitz, Anthony. *Stormbreaker.* **Book 1 in Alex Rider Adventures. 2000.**
After the death of Alex's guardian uncle, Alex decides to carry on his work as a spy with a British intelligence agency. *Stormbreaker* is the first book in the series, and the book has spawned several manifestations including movies, audio books, and graphic novels. Adults who enjoy the tie-ins will enjoy reading the books. (print, ebook, and audiobook read by Nathaniel Parker)

Plum-Ucci, Carol. *Fire Will Fall.* **Book 2 in Streams of Babel Series. 2010.**
Four teenagers recover from poisoning by terrorists, while operatives track down the terror cell. This is the second book in the series, however, reviews state that it stands alone. Adults who enjoy potential terrorist scenarios and implications, as well as interesting dialogue will enjoy this read. (print, ebook, and audiobook read by full cast)

Zusak, Markus. *I Am the Messenger.* **2002.**
After capturing a bank robber, Ed Kennedy, a 19-year-old cab driver begins to get calls from people who need help through playing cards in the mail. As he receives the cards with addresses on them, he begins to help those in need. However, who is the individual sending the cards, and why are they doing it? This thriller is a little slower paced than a typical thriller, but the serious situations and sophisticated humor are major appeals of the novel. (print, ebook, and audiobook read by Marc Aden Gray)

Adventure

With brisk pacing and with a protagonist on a mission, the stories are action based with danger throughout. Settings are very important with stories set in exotic locales. There is always a hero, often male, who accomplishes the mission. Typically, there is a menacing mood and jargon that can be professional or military (Saracks, 2009).

Bacigalupi, Paolo. *Ship Breaker.* **Book 1 in <u>Ship Breaker Series.</u> 2010.**
Nailer scavenges copper wiring from oil tankers, but when he finds a ship with a great treasure, he has to decide whether to scavenge the ship, or save the girl aboard. This adventure will appeal to adult readers for its unique topic and character interaction. (print, ebook, and audiobook read by Joshua Swanson)

George, Elizabeth. *The Edge of Nowhere.* **Book 1 in <u>Saratoga Woods Series.</u> 2011.**
When abandoned on Whidbey Island, Washington, by her mother, Becca meets a Ugandan orphan with a secret to tell. When he mysteriously falls in the dangerous cliffs of Whidbey Island, Becca must figure out how it happened, and why. Adults will enjoy the setting of the island, which is the key the main events in the book. (print, ebook, and audiobook read by Amy McFadden)

Hiaasen, Carl. *Chomp.* **2012.**
Wahoo Cray lives in a zoo with an animal wrangler father. When their lives get picked up for a reality show, they go on location to the Everglades. After the show's producer goes missing in a storm and search parties vanish, they must figure out a way to get back home with everyone intact. The humor in Hiaasen's books is subtle and sophisticated and will appeal to adults for that reason. (print, ebook, and audiobook read by James Van Der Beek)

Marsden, John. *Tomorrow, When the War Began.* **1993.**
Seven teenagers return from camping to find that their country has been invaded, and they have to survive and fight. As they slowly piece together what happened, they find they must tap into a strength they never knew they had. Adult fans of war, terrorism, and action will enjoy this novel. (print, ebook, and audiobook read by Suzi Dougherty)

Meyer, L. A. *Bloody Jack: Being an Account of the Curious Adventures of Mary "Jacky" Faber, Ship's Boy.* **Book 1 in <u>Bloody Jack Series.</u> 2002.**
After all her immediate family dies from disease, Jackie takes to the streets of London, living with a young group of other survivors. However, Jackie is happy to leave the streets of eighteenth-century London for the high seas to become an excellent sailor. However, "Jacky" disguises the fact that she is a girl and has to keep this secret at all costs. This book will appeal to those who are interested in a historical adventure story with serious themes. (print, ebook, and audiobook read by L. A. Meyer)

Smith, Roland. *Peak.* **2007.**
Fourteen-year-old Peak is arrested for scaling a skyscraper in New York City. Afterward, he is sent to live with his father in Thailand, with the goal of climbing Mount Everest. High-octane adventure fans will love this title. (print, ebook, and audiobook read by Ramon De Ocampo) (print, ebook, and audiobook read by Steve West and Fiona Hardingham)

Stiefvater, Maggie. *The Scorpio Races.* **2011.**
Puck is the first girl to enter the "Scorpio Races," a race to the finish line. Sean is the returning champion. Both will face off with the end result either being life or death. This novel has strong fantasy elements that will appeal to adults who are interested in that genre as well.

Wein, Elizabeth. *Code Name Verity*. Book 1 in <u>Code Name Verity</u> <u>Series</u>. 2012.

"Verity" is arrested by the Gestapo when her plane crashes in Nazi-occupied France. She must face a critical decision—either confess what she knows as a spy, or be executed. War buffs will enjoy this adventure story set during World War II. (print, ebook, and audiobook read by Morven Christie and Lucy Gaskell)

Conclusion: Trends in Thrillers and Adventure Fiction

In all the adrenaline genres, future trends seem to move in the direction of hybrid topics. It is becoming increasingly challenging to find any suspense, adventure, or thriller that does not contain other elements, whether that be supernatural or science fiction. This means not only is there YA and adult crossover, but also genre crossover. While this will make readers' advisory a bit more challenging, it offers many more options for readers. Practicing RA skills and monitoring new publications will prepare a librarian who might be asked for suggestions in the adrenaline genres in future.

References

International Thriller Writer's Association. *About ITW*. 2015. Retrieved from http://thrillerwriters.org/about-itw/.

Saricks, J. *Readers' Advisor Guide to Genre Fiction*. 2nd edition. Chicago, IL: American Library Association, 2009.

Tixier Herald, D. *Genreflecting: A Guide to Popular Reading Interests*. Westport, CT: Libraries Unlimited, 2006.

Wolitzer, M. "Look Homeward, Reader: A Not-So-Young Audience for Young Adult Books." *New York Times*. October 17, 2014. Retrieved from http://www.nytimes.com/2014/10/19/fashion/a-not-so-young-audience-for-young-adult-books.html?_r=0.

9

Science Fiction

Erin Downey Howerton

Introduction to the Genre

Definition

Science fiction and fantasy are often intertwined in readers' minds, as they both deal with the fantastical and speculative worlds that captivate human imagination. If pressed to recall their teen reading, it is not uncommon for today's adults to jumble these two genres together, for their readership is very compatible with one another. Some joke that cover art is the easiest way to tell which genre you are about to read. If the art is mechanical, it is likely to be science fiction. If the art contains elements from nature, it is more likely to be fantasy.[1] To take this idea a bit further, readers might also flip open the cover to examine the endpapers and front matter. If you find a map, you are looking at fantasy; worlds that were built to be known, loved, and defined. The absence of a map indicates the uncharted worlds of science fiction: the unknown, mysterious, and fantastic. Where do readers go from here? Authors who travel into these unmapped voids tell us stories of alien life, broken worlds, altered bodies, and technology to boggle the mind. While writers and scholars have offered many definitions of science fiction over the years, Ray Bradbury has perhaps put forward the best concept that describes the relationship between fantasy and science fiction. In the introduction to *Science Fact / Fiction* by Edmund Farrell, he writes:

> So science fiction, we now see, is interested in more than sciences, more than machines. That *more* is always men and women and children themselves, how they behave, how they hope to behave. Science fiction is apprehensive of future modes of behavior as well as future constructions of metal. Science fiction guesses at sciences before they are sprung out of the brows of thinking men. More, the authors in the field try to guess at machines which are the fruit of these sciences. Then we try to guess at how mankind will react to

these machines, how use them, how grow with them, how be destroyed by them. All, all of it fantastic.[2]

Readers of science fiction are hungry for answers, and captivated by the "what ifs" that occur between the pages. Like Moore's law, the readership increases exponentially over time. Exclusively the province of white, male authors in the 1940s and 1950s, science fiction has grown at an explosive rate and now includes stories by writers of color, plotlines about gay, lesbian, bisexual, transgender, and queer (GLBTQ) characters, and worlds where gender and race take on strange new dimensions. In fact, it may seem as though the science fiction genre did not bother to address teen readership until recent decades, because writers often included youth characters in their stories, and readers were willing to hunt down any title with promise.

Teen readers have historically been willing to read adult titles, and the adult readers of science fiction are certainly willing to suspend disbelief for any book with a fresh new world between the pages. Now, with the mainstream success of teen dystopian tales such as *The Hunger Games* (Collins, 2008), *Divergent* (Roth, 2011), and *The Maze Runner* (Dashner, 2009), adult readers are less likely to differentiate between titles published as teen versus adult science fiction. In addition, these mainstream readers who may not have been initially attracted to the genre find themselves looking for readalikes and exploring other neighborhoods in these galaxies.

Adult readers who have been devoted fans of science fiction for many years will likely have encountered the robots of Isaac Asimov, the off-world adventures of Robert Heinlein and Anne McCaffrey, and the dystopian futures of Aldous Huxley, George Orwell, and Margaret Atwood. They might have traveled through time with Kurt Vonnegut and Marge Piercy, or in the alternate histories of Octavia Butler. Science fiction written with teen protagonists up until the early 1960s were likely published as adult titles, and would have been very accessible and known to adults at that time. However, the publication of Madeleine L'Engle's *A Wrinkle in Time* in 1962 saw a new cleaving of the two readerships through the prominence of their teen protagonists and awards from the field. Another early book that caught the eye of younger readers was the 1970 publication of Sylvia Engdahl's *Enchantress from the Stars*. These two books gained popularity and visibility due to their Newbery nods, and likely encouraged more publishers to take a chance on science fiction that was written for and directly marketed to teens. Other publications with teen protagonists from this era are Robert O'Brien's *Z for Zachariah* in 1974, and *Dragonsong* by Anne McCaffrey, published in 1976. Recently adapted to film in 2015, *Z for Zachariah* continues to quietly win readers over as does *Dragonsong*, which was cited when McCaffrey won the 1999 Margaret A. Edwards Award for lifetime contribution in writing for teens.

It is also remarkable that these four key titles in the teen science fiction canon all feature female protagonists, bravely carving out spaces for themselves in often inhospitable worlds where they struggle, and ultimately prevail. These publications can be linked to second-wave feminist movements and created new precedents for authors looking to tell diverse stories for a similarly diversifying fan base.

Appeals

Joyce Saricks characterizes science fiction as a genre that appeals to the intellect, in the same category as mysteries, psychological suspense, and literary fiction. Diversity in storytelling is a hallmark of science fiction, as there is a wide range of settings, language, pacing, and tone used by writers to convey their tales of other worlds. Many science fiction titles deal in ambiguity, whether moral or factual, and a lack of resolution may attract readers who like to draw their own conclusions. Since science fiction is a genre of the intellect, it is unsurprising that many of the stories must be decoded by the reader. The use of specialized language and invented words by the author not only enhances the sense of world building but also signals to readers that they have entered a strange land. The ambiguity of language can also serve as a great appeal factor to those who enjoy teasing out the meaning from unfamiliar word use. Creative and nonchronological narrative structure is also frequently used and can attract readers who appreciate the richness and variety of this technique in literary fiction as well.

The setting of most science fiction titles is "consistently evocative and visual," according to Saricks. She attributes this characteristic to the origins of modern science fiction titles in radio stories, which demanded that listeners use their imaginations to bring the story to life.[3] Equally compelling can be the characters in these works. Often, readers enjoy long-lasting series where they can spend lots of time with their favorite characters as they go on new adventures. The protagonists of science fiction stories are noted for their diversity of background, experience, and ability. Often, a science fiction protagonist will be an underdog or an outcast who is pitted against an insurmountable challenge, and readers enjoy joining this character in their quest to gain knowledge and ability.

Working with Readers

When talking with prospective readers, emphasize the key traits that science fiction fans look for in a good read. First, talk about bold ideas and philosophy. Utopian and, more frequently, dystopian societies depicted in works of science fiction attract readers who want to contemplate the ramifications of such technology as robot companions, genetic alteration, terraforming alien worlds, and more. They could also be looking for worlds other than Earth—fantastic worlds populated with compelling characters, who must make courageous choices in pursuit of justice, the good life, or the truth. Similarly fascinating are the nomads of galaxies: Space cowboys who take on grand voyages and interstellar travel, sometimes through time itself, in search of adventure and new horizons. In discussing these traits, you will likely get a better idea of what resonates with your readers.

It is also important to confirm what your reader has already read and liked so that you can accurately match them with the right teen book. For those who are fond of sprawling, intense tales with multiple storylines, many characters and an epic scope (i.e., authors like Haruki Murakami and Neal Stephenson) you may want to present YA titles (which tend to be shorter) as novellas; or recommend series that will help them stretch the action and the world building a little longer. There are also many parallels to today's teen science fiction titles and yesterday's required reading in high school, so develop some snappy one-line booktalk hooks like "this is the dystopian *Lord of the Flies* that you wanted to read, but your teacher would never have assigned!"

Tools and Resources

Buker, Derek M. *Science Fiction and Fantasy Readers' Advisory: The Librarian's Guide to Cyborgs, Aliens, and Sorcerers*. Chicago, IL: ALA, 2002.

Crewe, Megan. "Young Adult Science Fiction: A Reading Guide." *Tor.com*, 2009.

Herald, Diana Tixier. *Teen Genreflecting 3: A Guide to Reading Interests*. Santa Barbara, CA: Libraries Unlimited, 2011.

Herald, Diana Tixier. *Strictly Science Fiction: A Guide to Reading Interests*. Santa Barbara, CA: Libraries Unlimited, 2002.

McArdle, Megan M. *The Readers' Advisory Guide to Genre Blends*. ALA, 2015.

Robinson, Jen. "Futuristic, Speculative, Science Fiction, and Dystopian Fiction for Young Adults." *jkrbooks.typepad.com*, 2012.

Welch, Rollie. *A Core Collection for Young Adults*. 2nd edition. New York: Neal-Schuman, 2010.

Awards

Golden Duck Awards (www.goldenduckawards.org)
Andre Norton Award for Young Adult Science Fiction and Fantasy (www.sfwa.org/nebula-awards)

Collection Development

Finding more good YA science fiction is not hard. One of the best sources is a journal called *Voice of Youth Advocates* (VOYA). Their yearly list of Best Science Fiction, Fantasy, and Horror is a wonderful way to find titles that were rated by their reviewers as tops in both writing and potential popularity.[4] Another review journal that provides a yearly "best of" booklist is *Kirkus Reviews*, which highlights their starred titles in December.[5] If you are looking for something in the middle of the year, *Booklist Magazine* puts out a science fiction- and fantasy-themed issue every May, including the Top 10 titles of the past year for teens.[6] Of course, if you are looking for publishers who specialize in teen science fiction titles then definitely check out *Starscape* and *Tor Teen*, imprints of Tor. *Starscape* is aimed at readers in grades 5 and up, while Tor Teen explores topics of interest to grades 8 and up. *Flux*, an imprint of Llewellyn, is another solid choice with many teen science fiction titles.[7]

Online, one may find many resources to connect with new science fiction titles and authors. Tor.com is a frequently updated science fiction blog from the publisher of the same name, featuring new writing, thought pieces, and more. Another blog that has become popular among science fiction readers is io9,[8] a Gawker Media publication. It has an active base of chatty commenters and smart conversation, including a popular online book club and a Books tag for items of interest regarding readers.[9] In the past, a group of commenters participated in Thursday Tales, a thread where they posted original stories and shared their writing. Some of the best of these were anthologized in *We Had Stars Once* (2013). They still share stories weekly online at thursdaytales .kinja.com. One might also cruise to SF Signal,[10] the Hugo award-winning fanzine. It has a robust online presence with lots of critical writing, reviews, and a popular podcast. Notably, its Instagram account features arresting illustrations from both modern and retro science fiction books.[11]

The Literature

The following list offers a sampling of YA science fiction titles that appeal to adult science fiction fans. To help you navigate the terrain, these titles are organized according to themes that correspond to popular reading interests.

The Body Horrific

Medical ethics, genetic engineering, and artificial intelligence all feature in this subgenre of science fiction. While teens identify with the shocking revelations about one's own body (because what is adolescence if not one awkward interaction with one's unpredictable new "growth" after another), adults can recall that experience and recognize their own dependence on technology—who over a certain age does not depend on items like contact lenses or glasses, medical implants, or pharmaceuticals to help us live our modern, daily lives? These tales of cyborgs and clones may keep you up at night wondering if you can ever really know yourself.

Adlington, L. J. *The Diary of Pelly D*. 2005.

A young construction worker on an alien planet uncovers a diary of a privileged young girl whose story takes a turn for the worse when her genetic group is targeted by the powers that be. Adults will quickly see the parallels between this story and the Holocaust, while the setting gives the narrative strange new power in a world where survival hinges on belonging to the right in-group. (print, ebook)

Anderson, M. T. *Feed*. 2002.

A group of teens with neural implants that provide a continuous connection to an Internet-like "Feed" are knocked offline, and protagonist Titus must choose between the soothing surge of reconnection or an alternative proposed by new friend Violet, who is determined to sabotage the Feed's algorithms by acting in unpredictable ways. Adults held prisoner by Facebook's capricious News Feed are the natural audience for this antiauthority tale, told in the timeless voice of a teen who is in it for the LOLs, no matter the century. (print, ebook, audiobook)

Dickinson, Peter. *Eva*. 1990.

A young teen wakes from a coma to discover her consciousness has been transplanted into a chimpanzee, and she must now come to terms with her new body and existence as she no longer feels fully at home with humans. Adult readers will no doubt reflect on the implications that Eva's tale has in current times, where the desired results of an extended lifespan often have unexpected complications. (print, ebook)

Farmer, Nancy. *The House of the Scorpion*. 2002.

Matteo is a clone of the powerful drug lord El Patron, and although he has been spared the intelligence-blunting procedure that his fellow clones were subjected to Matt cannot forget that he is not, strictly speaking, his own person— only a copy kept around for spare parts as El Patron ages and needs revitalization. Adult readers will have a markedly different perspective on this story than teens, and simultaneously fear and identify with the vulnerability of both Matt and El Patron as they attempt to escape their seemingly inevitable fates. Sequel is *The Lord of Opium*. (print, ebook, audiobook)

Halam, Ann. *Dr. Franklin's Island*. 2002.

Three teens crash-land on a remote island and encounter a scientist who finds them to be the perfect blank canvas for his mutation experiments that lead them to become human-animal hybrids. Adults will be just as riveted as teen readers as the plot unfolds and are likely to have read the tale that inspired this one: *The Island of Dr. Moreau* by H. G. Wells. (print, ebook, audiobook)

Lasky, Kathryn. *Star Split.* **1999.**
    In a future where the haves enjoy genetic enhancement and the have-nots go without, Darci grows up believing she is the former when she is actually a clone, and must come to terms with her discovery. Adult readers will identify with Darci's initial struggle to forge her own fate in a world that seemingly sets you on a clockwork path from birth, but the discovery of her clone gives the story a twist that makes it urgent and haunting. (print)

Levitin, Sonia. *The Goodness Gene.* **2005.**
    In the quest to perfect the world following catastrophic collapse, benefi-cent ruler Hayli raises his twin sons to take over for him one day—until one of them discovers that they contain horrific genetic material, and that the carefully orchestrated world of The Goodness hides terrible secrets. Adults who have ever wondered if Hitler's clone would turn out similarly will be hooked by this tale of behind-the-scenes corruption and betrayals. (print, ebook)

Lo, Malinda. *Adaptation.* Adaptation Series. **2012.**
    In a military hospital, Reece awakens to discover she is physically fine, but the world around her has gone into paralysis—strange accidents involv-ing birds, martial law, and a government conspiracy threaten to burst forth at any moment. Adult readers may connect the dots a little faster than teens regarding Reece's treatment near Area 51, but both sets of readers will be in thrall to the chilling atmosphere of fear and civil unrest that runs close to the surface. (print, ebook)

Pearson, Mary. *The Adoration of Jenna Fox.* The Jenna Fox Chronicles. **2008.**
    After a horrific car accident, Jenna has lost her memories and struggles to make sense of her new reality as she discovers that her parents have gone to unthinkable lengths to help her. Adults will identify with the risks that Jenna's family take to preserve what was left of their daughter after the acci-dent, and find thought-provoking moral dilemmas in the bioengineering pos-sibilities that make Jenna's new life possible. (print, ebook)

Reeve, Philip. *Mortal Engines.* Predator Cities **and prequels** *Mortal Engines Quartet.* **2003.**
    Cities have become unmoored from the ground as technology allows them to roam freely, consuming smaller towns for resources while their citi-zens must also struggle for survival. This steampunk invention will be eagerly consumed by adults, who will be just as fascinated by teens at the robotic reanimated corpses, scar- and ink-stained characters who occupy this alternate history of Europe. (print, ebook, audiobook)

Shusterman, Neal. Unwind. The Unwind Dystology. **2007.**
    While all babies are guaranteed to be born, in this dystopia teens can be "unwound" by their parents in a form of retroactive abortion, rendering them into reusable organs and spare parts for adults. Adults will find the three main teen characters and their reasons for being unwound riveting and

surprising, especially the family who believes that it is a supreme expression of their religion. (print, ebook)

Meyer, Marissa. *Cinder.* The Lunar Chronicles. **2012.**
Cyborg Cinder lives in New Beijing, where her mechanical abilities catch the eye of a handsome prince who turns out to need her skills much more than he first expected. Adult readers will enjoy this novel retelling of the Cinderella story, set in a future where the plague threatens life on Earth and the evil Lunar people act as antagonists. (print, ebook, audiobook)

Wells, Robison. *Variant.* Variant. **2011.**
Benson tries to break free of his past at an elite boarding school, but it turns into a raw deal as the students split into factions to survive, academics and adults are in low supply, and the campus is on lockdown as the factions battle for control—and survival. The main plot twist comes later in the book and will surprise adults as much as teens as the school's secret mechanics are revealed. (print, ebook, audiobook)

Werlin, Nancy. *Double Helix.* **2004.**
A job at a genetic research company reveals more about Eli than he ever knew, as his mother suffers from Huntington's disease and his father seethes over Eli's new job and his failure to take the next steps toward college. The past shared between the enigmatic head of Eli's new lab and his parents will engage adult readers, who will be shocked by the hidden secrets and the dramatic conclusion to an epic family drama. (print, ebook, audiobook)

Westerfeld, Scott. *Uglies.* Uglies. **2005.**
Everything is not bubbly for Tally, who eagerly awaits the traditional surgery that makes you pretty on your 16th birthday yet is intrigued by new friend Shay's stories of how being beautiful is not all it is cracked up to be. Adults will smirk knowingly at the addition to the beautification surgeries, but it is easy to remember the insecurities of the teen years that feed the hard choices between popularity and integrity that plague Tally and company. (print, ebook, audiobook)

Broken Planet

Dystopias have always been popular in science fiction—never more so than with teens, who occasionally see the entire world as a dystopia built expressly for them. Tell your adult readers to tap into the mood swings of adolescence and dip their toes into worlds that have been utterly broken by human hands, desolate with desperation in the face of harsh new realities.

Bacigalupi, Paolo. *Ship Breaker.* **2010.**
Catastrophic climate change has reduced Nailer to a subsistence lifestyle, when he encounters a choice between saving a young, wealthy girl or using her to improve his lot and escape his fate. The near-future setting will look eerily familiar to adult readers, who will enjoy the fast-moving plot and the vivid cast of characters. *Has sequel/companion.* (print, ebook, audiobook)

Burgess, Melvin. *Bloodtide.* **2001.**
Rival clans wage bloodthirsty war in the streets of a ravaged London, scarred by genetic manipulation and haunted by legends of Norse myth. With all the violence and gore of the Icelandic saga from which it takes shape,

adult readers will appreciate the mix of science fiction and high fantasy (especially those who enjoy *Game of Thrones*). *Has sequel / companion.* (print, ebook, audiobook)

Cave, Patrick. *Sharp North*. 2006.
　　Miri is given the key to a great secret in the frozen wastelands of Great Britain following severe climate change where a new ruling class clamps down on reproduction among the commoners. Adult readers will chill to this atmospheric thriller that weaves together questions of genetics, power, and politics. *Has sequel / companion.* (print, ebook)

DuPrau, Jeanne. *The City of Ember*. The Books of Ember. 2003.
　　On Lina's 12th birthday, she hopes for a good job assignment but is disappointed when her plans go awry, and she discovers that her family holds the key to a secret that will reveal what is hiding in the darkness beyond their city. The idea of an underground city with families in hiding from some unnamed catastrophe may hit a little close to home for adult readers, who will find Lina's brushes with danger at the hands of the corrupt mayor quite realistic indeed. (print, ebook, audiobook)

Falls, Kat. Dark Life. 2010.
　　Underwater homesteads are at risk of aquatic bandits and evildoers in this tale of teen bravery, discovery, and human adaptability in the face of new realities. Adult readers will appreciate the details of hero Ty's daily life, and the allusions to classic Western tales give the skirmishes with bandits a familiar flavor. *Has sequel / companion.* (print, ebook, audiobook)

Farmer, Nancy. *The Ear, the Eye, and the Arm*. 1994.
　　Twenty-third-century Africa is a place of great danger and intrigue to tween siblings who break free from their safe trappings only to be pursued by detectives with strange gifts courtesy of nuclear accidents. The novel elements of their world will have great appeal to adult readers, while the strong sense of place and detailed characterization will sink readers deep into this unforgettable world. (print, audiobook on cassette)

Hautman, Pete. *Rash*. 2006.
　　When Bo falls afoul of the law in the United Safer States of America, he ends up in a strange spiral of penal camp labor making pizzas for McDonald's, full-contact sports teams, and violence unquelled by doses of sedative drugs. Adults will enjoy the heavy doses of satire, but protagonist Bo is the real draw here with his wry observations of life heavily controlled by the state. (print, ebook, audiobook)

King, A. S. *Glory O'Brien's History of the Future*. 2014.
　　Glory is on the edge of adulthood when she drinks powdered bat with an old friend, and the result is her ability to see into a bleak future where women have been completely disenfranchised while her friend is only able to look into the past. Adults will find the combination of magical realism, surrealism, and time travel fascinating, and the result is an Atwoodian *Handmaid's Tale* for the twenty-first century—powerful and prescient. (Print, ebook, audiobook)

Lloyd, Saci. *The Carbon Diaries: 2015*. 2009.
　　Carbon dioxide rationing crimps Laura's typical teen lifestyle as London clamps down on energy use, nonlocal food, and non-essential travel despite

her desire to keep up with friends and her band. Adult readers will enjoy the diary format, giving a voyeuristic view into Laura's world and her efforts to achieve a new normal. *Has sequel/companion.* (print, ebook, audiobook)

Lowry, Lois. *The Giver.* Giver Quartet. 1993.
Jonas's Life Assignment means learning the truth about the carefully cultivated and ordered world he has lived in for over a decade, where conformity is prized and quietude the ultimate goal. Adults will see the risks inherent in this attempt at a utopian society, and understand Jonas's confusion at learning that strong emotions can provide shape and meaning for a richer life. (print, ebook, audiobook)

Mullin, Mike. *Ashfall.* Ashfall Trilogy. 2011.
When Yellowstone erupts, Alex sets out in search of his family amidst violence, looting, and chaos when he encounters another teen survivor, Darla, and they team up to brave the road in a gritty story of love and survival. The moral quandaries that Alex grapples with will engage adult readers, who would face similar dangers in such a situation, and the setting will appeal to fans of zombie thrillers and other tales of wretched wastelands. (print, ebook)

Pfeffer, Susan Beth. *Life as We Knew It.* The Last Survivors. 2006.
Miranda chronicles life on Earth after a meteor knocks the moon out of its orbit, causing natural disasters and disruption of anything resembling normalcy. Adults will feel the stress of being isolated and trapped in close quarters alongside Miranda and her family, who try to eke out a living together despite a grim long-term prognosis for their community. (print, ebook, audiobook)

Stranger Worlds Than These

Go off-world in tales of strange new life, voyages to promising new planets, and discover aliens among us. Also included here are worlds that we have built; science fiction featuring gaming is always popular with teens and the proliferation of adult gamers in recent decades means a wide audience for these titles.

Gill, David Macinnis. *Black Hole Sun.* Hell's Cross. 2010.
With sharp humor and wit, Durango is a teen on Mars whose assignment is to protect miners from malevolent forces. Durango's hilarious and sassy AI implant (named Mimi) and Gill's fast-paced storyline will have adult readers laughing-out-loud and running to keep up with this team of off-world teens. (print, ebook)

Haarsma, P. J. *The Softwire: Virus on Orbus 1.* Softwire. 2010.
The adults have perished, but 12-year-old survivor Johnny has a mysterious ability to manipulate computers with his mind and must prove that he is not a saboteur as his fellow kid survivors discover that they must pay for their passage via indentured servitude to the aliens on Orbis. Adults who want a fun, quick read will relish this tale of a younger teen challenged to use his new abilities and wiggle out of a jam in his new home. (print, ebook)

Hautman, Pete. *The Obsidian Blade.* The Klaatu Diskos. 2012.
Tucker's dad falls through a shimmering disc hanging near their home's roof, and he returns with a girl from another place and time—and they are

far from the only ones who are using these portals. Hautman twines religion and time travel in a compelling, complex narrative that will appeal to adult readers who will instantly recognize each of the past key events where the diskos appear. (print, ebook)

James, Nick. *Skyship Academy: The Pearl Wars.* Skyship Academy. **2011.**
Surface and Skyship factions of a future Earth are grasping at what seems like their last, best hope: mysterious pearls falling from space that generate much-needed power. Adults will be drawn to the conflict between teens on both sides of the factions, part of a complex socioeconomic conflict that tackles big ideas and the politics of a ravaged Earth. (print, audiobook)

Kostick, Conor. *Epic.* **2007.**
A game dictates your future path on an Earth where there are only winners, who get the resources, and losers who do not. Adults will cheer for Erik as he takes on the system in this spin on video game culture, where real life violence is outlawed and to win the game you must game the system. (print, ebook)

Ness, Patrick. *The Knife of Never Letting Go.* Chaos Walking. **2008.**
The same virus that killed all women on the planet has also made it possible for all men's thoughts to be heard aloud, and Todd must come to terms with what he discovers in the Noise. Adult readers will be spellbound by the roller-coaster journey that Ness creates, and even more so when they arrive at the shocking conclusion. (Print, ebook, audiobook)

Revis, Beth. *Across the Universe.* Across the Universe. **2011.**
Mystery and romance collide on an interstellar journey where Amy is awoken from her cryogenic rest many years too soon, and must unravel the plot to sabotage the ship's mission to colonize a new planet. This slower-paced novel will appeal to adult readers who appreciate the exploration of interpersonal relationships in a sci-fi setting. (print, ebook, audiobook)

Sleator, William. *Interstellar Pig.* Piggy Series. **1984.**
Barney hates the beach, so he is excited while on vacation to encounter friendly neighbors who enjoy playing a board game where the last one holding a pig saves their planet. While adults will see details being telegraphed early on (hint: the neighbors are not human), this classic work of teen science fiction will draw them in if they appreciate realism, tension, and retro fun. (print, ebook, audiobook on cassette)

Sleator, William. *The Last Universe.* **2005.**
A garden maze grown by their scientist uncle leads Susan and her sick brother Gary through multiple universes, where Gary might escape his fate and Susan discovers they may both be doomed. Even if adults do not understand quantum theory, this Schrödinger's garden will lure them in and keep them glued to the page until the twist ending. (print)

Vande Velde, Vivian. *Heir Apparent.* **2003.**
Giannine finds herself stuck in a virtual fantasy game where she must keep her wits about her, because this time if she loses she will die in real life due to actions taken by a protest group who oppose the game. Adults will be

drawn to this one for its depiction of censorship gone awry, and its loving depiction of fantasy role playing game. (print, ebook, audiobook)

Westerfeld, Scott. *Leviathan*. The Leviathan Trilogy. 2009.
Prince Aleksander has had the rug pulled from under him—and now he is on the run as his family has been assassinated, and his own people are after him while a recognizable World War I takes shape in an alternate universe where the Axis has become dependent on steam-powered machines and the Allies are flying their genetically engineered animals as the Darwinist powers breed ever new species to take down the opposing Clanker forces. The charm of such fanciful inventions as "message lizards" is well tempered by the brutal impact of this risky war, which adults with a keen appreciation of military strategy will delight in this revisioning of the Great War. (print, ebook, audiobook)

Williams, Sean. *Twinmaker*. The Twinmaker Trilogy. 2013.
Claire and her best friend use a high-tech transporter to scout parties and hang wherever they wish around the globe, but when an urban legend turns sour Claire discovers a government conspiracy. Fans of Williams's adult titles will gladly make a "lucky jump" into this title, which extends and richly elaborates on the D-mat technology depicted in his other books, an action-packed and riveting thriller with both political and religious resonance. (print, ebook)

Conclusion: Trends in Science Fiction

In general, the same trends that govern adult science fiction also dominate teen titles. There has been a rise in popularity with biomedical titles, where rapid advances in medicine that we see in the news is translated almost immediately to the page with stories of genetic experimentation, decimated populations, natural disasters brought on by human experimentation, and more. The recent developments in space travel and innovation in off-planet exploration means we will see far more titles like *The Martian* by Andy Weir aimed at teens, who are uniquely positioned to realistically imagine the possibilities of deep space travel as a virtue of their youth, having far more years to spare than the average adult reader! And as climate change continues to cause unusual weather patterns, damaging disasters, and more there will certainly be teen science fiction titles that address what young people might do in such situations. There will also be novels that hark back to simpler times, as complex systems are imagined to devolve and with it, our global communications structures. All these themes capture the imagination of science fiction readership.

As long as science fiction readers maintain their desire to read stories that contain novel situations, terrifying scenarios, pulse-pounding action, and the quiet inner workings of the mind as they contemplate the future, there will be a flexible readership that crosses boundaries between teen and adult sections of the library and bookstore to find the next great science fiction title they crave. The readership shares a love of thoughtful plotting, compelling characters, and the desire to ask the big question—*what if?*—as often as they can. And they will continue to do so into the foreseeable (and imagined) future(s).

Notes

1. "Science Fiction," *Teen Genreflecting 3: A Guide to Reading Interests*, LU, 2011, p. 161.
2. "Introduction," *Science Fact / Fiction*, Scott Foresman, 1974.
3. *The Readers' Advisory Guide to Genre Fiction*, 2nd ed., ALA, 2009.
4. http://www.voyamagazine.com/2014/03/21/best-science-fiction-fantasy-horror-2013/.
5. https://www.kirkusreviews.com/lists/best-teen-science-fiction-fantasy-2014/.
6. http://booklistonline.com/.
7. http://www.fluxnow.com/browse_by_category.php?category_id=408.
8. http://io9.gizmodo.com/.
9. http://io9.gizmodo.com/tag/boo-ks.
10. http://www.sfsignal.com/.
11. https://www.instagram.com/sfsignal/.

References

Bradbury, Ray. "Introduction." *Science Fact / Fiction*, pp. 5–6. Ed. Edmund Farrell. New York: Scott Foresman, 1974.

Collins, Suzanne. *The Hunger Games*. Reprint edition. New York: Scholastic Press, 2010.

Dashner, James. *The Maze Runner*. Reprint edition. New York: Delacorte Press, 2010.

Engdahl, Sylvia, and Lois Lowry. *Enchantress from the Stars*. Reissue edition. New York: Firebird, 2003.

Herald, Diana Tixier. "Science Fiction." *Teen Genreflecting 3: A Guide to Reading Interests*. Santa Barbara, CA: Libraries Unlimited, 2011, p. 161.

L'Engle, Madeleine. *A Wrinkle in Time*. Reprint edition. New York: Square Fish, 2007.

McCaffrey, Anne. *Dragonsong*. Repackage edition. New York: Aladdin, 2003.

O'Brien, Robert C. *Z for Zachariah*. New York: Simon Pulse, 1974.

Roth, Veronica. *Divergent*. Reprint edition. New York: Katherine Tegen Books, 2014.

Saricks, Joyce. *The Readers' Advisory Guide to Genre Fiction*. 2nd edition. Chicago, IL: ALA, 2009.

We Had Stars Once: A Thursday Tales Anthology. Ed. Constella Espj. Critical Mass Rocketworks, 2013.

10
Fantasy

Alicia Ahlvers

Introduction to the Genre

Definition

Fantasy at its most elemental is the battle against good and evil by use of magical or supernatural means. Events occur outside the ordinary laws that operate within the universe, magic, or other supernatural elements are key features, and the novels often involve journeys or quests. These stories cannot occur in a real-world setting, nor can they realistically be expected to occur in some far distant future.

Teen fantasy, in particular, is a constantly evolving genre. From the oldest fantasy themes with wizards and epic quests to the newest subgenre with urban settings, fantasy remains popular with teens and, with the surge in popularity of adult readers of teen science fiction, adults are starting to actively seek young adult's (YA) hidden fantasy gems.

The Young Adult Library Services Association (YALSA) of the American Library Association (ALA) categorizes teens, or YAs, as "a person between the ages of twelve and eighteen" so the publishers target audience for these novels is usually geared toward that age group. One aspect that differentiates teen from adult fantasy is that the characters are almost always teens. More important, however, is that these novels have a distinctly teen voice and the teen characters tackle adult issues, all while discovering their unique identity.

Appeals

The teen fantasy genre has changed a great deal since its inception. From its roots in wizards and epic quests to the newest subgenre with urban settings, fantasy remains popular with teens and, with the surge in popularity of teen science fiction, adults have started to discover its unique and creative aspects. Second only to dystopian science fiction literature in terms of popularity, this genre is now spanning all age groups. While there have been children's and YA fantasy novels written for many years, the rise in the popularity of the teen fantasy genre is relatively new in large part thanks to J. K. Rowling, Garth Nix, and Philip Pullman.

While children's fantasy novels have been around for a very long time, teen novels appeal to adults because the themes are more complex, with characters learning how to navigate adult situations and are generally much darker in tone, even to the point of foregoing the happy ending usually found in children's novels.

In addition, all of the appeal factors found in adult fantasy are found in teen fantasy novels including the existence of magic and mythological creatures, epic battles of good versus evil, clearly defined characters who receive magical powers or gifts, beautifully elaborate world building, and long-running series that can give readers enjoyment for years.

Working with Readers

When working with readers, it is important to note that there are many different kinds of fantasy novels. Sword and sorcery sagas have very different elements than an alternative history fantasy, although at their core they are all novels that explore all of the permutations of good and evil. Most fantasy readers enjoy detailed world building; however, preferences for the type of world being built will vary greatly. You cannot expect a fan of epic wizardry multi-book series with very truehearted hero/heroine characters and a strong good versus evil message to necessarily enjoy an urban fantasy novel with a contemporary setting, an unsympathetic antihero, and a world filled with shades of gray instead of clearly defined good guys and bad guys. Therefore, even after you settle on the fantasy genre for a patron, you will have to dig deeper to find out what type of fantasy world they want to immerse themselves in. Ask the patron to describe the last fantasy movie or novel they really enjoyed. Was the novel a thrill-filled ride or did it slowly build toward an epic conclusion? What book did they last read that they did not like? What turned them off about the book? Maybe it was an unsympathetic character or a plot without enough twists and turns. The more complete picture you can form of the patron likes and dislikes, the more successful you will be when recommending titles. In particular, be sure to ask what other teen titles they enjoyed.

Tools and Resources

Seventeen, Teen Vogue, Entertainment Weekly, Justine Magazine, and other teen publications are also a good place to find titles that are hitting it big with teens. Parents often appreciate finding out about titles their children are excited about so they can read along. Early Word (http://www.earlyword.com/category/childrens-and-ya/) has a children's and YA page that reports on the big news in YA publishing. Fan websites such as www.readingteen.net review teen books but reviews are written by and are primarily used by adult readers. These may come and go quickly. Following Twitter YA bloggers and librarians is a good way to find blogs featuring adults talking about teen novels. Science fiction and fantasy sites, such as www.sfbook.com and http://www.tor.com/, have whole sections set aside for reviewing teen titles and adult fantasy websites such as http://www.locusmag.com/ routinely publicize news about YA fantasy novels that are catching the attention of adult readers. Every day new sites like http://www.yabookscentral.com/ spring up that review teen books. Also, pay particular attention to those authors who write for both teen and adult age groups. They often have a large following across genres.

Collection Development

Publishers have a good eye toward the types of fantasy that will appeal to teen and adults so it is important to pay attention to the publicity being generated. Since adults have "found" teen novels, publishers are putting their marketing dollars toward those titles they feel have the greatest cross-over appeal. Ad campaigns in *Library Journal*, *School Library Journal*, *Booklist*, and *Publishers Weekly*, as well as publisher-generated e-mail, are all valuable clues for teasing out those titles that will appeal to adults as well as to teens. Reviews in these journals can also be helpful if you have the time to read them. The YALSA also has a blog, the Hub, that is excellent for keeping up with new trends in YA literature, http://www.yalsa.ala.org/thehub/.

The Literature

Girl Power

While books featuring girls have been around for a long time, today's main characters are a new type of female. She is someone who has quirks and flaws but who embraces her differences and turns those weaknesses into strengths. She exhibits admirable and extraordinary qualities as well and is especially noted for her ability to meet the world head on. She does not have to be blessed with superior physical characteristics like using a bow and arrow (although that is always a bonus) but being capable in her chosen areas of interest is a given. Most important, the qualities she exhibits are not defined by gender but instead typifies the kinds of qualities that lead to a teen growing up to be a good and just leader, no matter the time period or setting. Because they exist in a fantasy world, the characters do not have to adhere to gender norms. Therefore, a large part of the appeal of these titles is seeing girls experience lives that are often very different from the readers in terms of the way they are allowed to overcome adversity.

Ahdieh, Renée. *The Wrath and the Dawn*. The Wrath and the Dawn Series. 2015.
In this dramatic retelling of the *Thousand and One Nights* tales, Shahrzad steps forward to marry the murderous young king who has executed numerous woman of the land, including her best friend. She has vowed to avenge her friend and destroy her husband, Prince Khalid if only she can stay alive past each dawn. Her plan seems to be working until she realizes there is more at stake for her kingdom and the husband she has begun to care for and the price may be her life. Make sure to have a copy of the original to give patrons who come back wanting more.

Aveyard, Victoria. *Red Queen*. Red Queen Series. 2015.
Days away from her conscription into the army, Mare Barrow is offered a job at the Silver Palace, home of the Silvers, rulers with super powers named for the color of their blood. When it is discovered Mare, a Red, has exceptional powers of her own, the king and queen forces her to pretend to be a long-lost Silver in an effort to prevent a civil war. Mare quickly joins the resistance and must face the most difficult decision of her life as she

decides which prince to trust. A sure hit for lovers of science fiction and fantasy stories with strong female characters fighting injustice.

Carson, Rae. *The Girl of Fire and Thorns*. Fire and Thorns Series. 2011.

On her 16th birthday, Princess Elisa is abruptly married to a handsome king from a neighboring country. But Elsa is no ordinary princess but the chosen one. Chosen by god, destined to be special and to accomplish great and heroic things. The problem is that Elisa does not feel special. She is not beautiful. She is surrounded by protectors and often not told everything she needs to know to survive the new world she finds herself inhabiting. And she does not feel worthy of the trust her god has placed in her. But as war looms, Elisa finds that she just might have an inner strength she did not even know she had. Featuring one of the most complex characters in young adult literature, this is a book for those want to watch characters grow and evolve into strong confident heroines.

Cashore, Kristin. *Graceling*. Graceling Realm Series. 2008.

Gracelings have always had special abilities, but none more extraordinary than Katsa, whose ability to kill anyone in any circumstance is legendary. After meeting a charming Graceling prince, she defies her uncle, King Randa, by refusing to be his chief torturer and assassin any longer. Fleeing from her home, she joins Prince Po, in a quest to solve the mystery of his grandfather's kidnapping. What they discover is a Graceling power the two may not be able to defeat. Give this one to readers hungering for characters with superhuman abilities and a thirst for justice.

Maas, Sarah J. *Throne of Glass*. Throne of Glass Series. 2012.

After surviving a year in the most brutal labor prison imaginable, Celaena Sardothien accepts a deal to serve as the crown prince's champion in a competition. If she wins, she becomes the new royal assassin, if she loses, she goes back to prison where conditions ensure she will die a slow and agonizing death. Given her past as an assassin for hire, she assumes she will have no difficulty beating the competition once she regains her health and strength. But when her competitors start dying under mysterious circumstances, winning the competition becomes the least of Celaena's problems. Pair this with *The Hunger Games* book or movie because of its winner-take-all competition.

Meyer, Marissa. *Cinder*. The Lunar Chronicles Series. 2012.

Lihn Cinder, a cyborg, is just trying to survive in a world where she is considered a second-class citizen. When her foster father dies, her foster mother makes her life even more difficult. When her beloved stepsister dies of a deadly plague, her foster mother volunteers Cinder as a test subject to be infected with the same plague. What she discovers changes the course of her life forever and puts her on a collision course with the handsome Prince Kai and the evil Queen Lavinia. Perfect for lovers of reimagined fairytales.

Older, Daniel José. *Shadowshaper*. 2015.

For Sierra Santiago, summer in Brooklyn is all about friends, parties, and street art. But this summer will be different, Sierra will be different. The street art starts to change and her Abuelo starts to tell her about a mysterious supernatural order called Shapeshifters, who seem to be disappearing and Sierra must discover her own hidden abilities in order to save her family, friends, and the neighborhood she loves. Wonderful use of an urban setting and a diverse cast of characters to explore culture, gentrification, urban living, and how mythology evolves.

Pierce, Tamora. *Alanna: The First Adventure*. <u>The Song of the Lioness Series</u>. **1983**.

Alanna has always wanted to be a knight and her twin brother yearns to become a sorcerer but their father has other plans for them. On the day they are shipped off to school, they decide to switch places. Thom will go to the convent to learn magic and Alanna will pretend to be Alan and train at the castle to become a knight. The few who know about the deception are not surprised that Alan(na) thrives, becoming one of the most accomplished of pages. When a magical illness sweeps over the castle, Alanna finally has to embrace the magical healing abilities if she is to save her friend, the prince. The trick will be to serve the kingdom without revealing her secrets. Tamora Pierce is a giant in the world of young adult fantasy and you cannot go wrong recommending any of her titles.

Rutkoski, Marie. *Winner's Curse*. **The Winner's Trilogy Series. 2014.**

In Kestrel's world women have two options, they can join the military or they can marry. In spite of her gift for military strategy, neither of these two options appeal to Kestrel. While out with friends, she impulsively buys a slave, Arin, from the auction block and her entire life changes when she discovers a kindred spirit and the possibility of forbidden love. But Arin has secrets that could destroy the country she loves. The magical elements in this novel are slight so give this to readers who like alternate history fantasy novels.

Snyder, Maria V. *Poison Study*. <u>Study Series</u>. **2005.**

When given the choice of execution for murder or becoming a food taster for the Commander of Ixia, Yelena chooses the chance at life, no matter how risky as opposed to the certainty of death. To keep her under control, she is fed the deadly Butterfly's Dust that requires a daily antidote in order to delay an agonizing death from the poison. Matters go from bad to worse when she starts to develop magical powers and rebels threaten her life. It is difficult to know who to trust and where to turn in the hostile new world. While a good choice for seasoned fantasy readers, you may also want to give this to new readers of fantasy who read and appreciate historical fiction.

Taylor, Laini. *Daughter of Smoke and Bone*. <u>Daughter of Smoke and Bone Series</u>. **2011.**

Set in Prague, Karou, art student and tooth fetcher for the chimera Brimstone, struggles to reconcile her everyday life as a student with her secret life filled with magic and angels. When Akiva, an impossibly beautiful angel, tries to kill her, she becomes caught up in a war between angels and demons. As she finds out more about her past and how she came to be, she must use all of her ingenuity to survive this terrifying new world. Highly unique and creatively constructed, this is an excellent choice for readers who like unusual elements in their fantasy novels.

Urban Fantasy

As the name suggests, urban fantasy is a novel in which magical occurrences take place in an urban setting. The setting must exist in the real world, however, unfamiliar fantastical elements are present. While the majority of urban fantasy is set in the present day, they can take place as far back as the start of the Victorian era with the invention of the steam engine. The major difference between adult and teen urban fantasy is that the main character is newly introduced to the fantastical world around them or they are inexperienced when it comes to dealing with the magic around them. If they are magical, they must seek out others to help them develop their magical gifts and they usually stumble upon a magical adversary as opposed to instigating their adventure. And, as in any compelling teen novel, there is almost always a romance entanglement of some kind.

In 2005, the popularity of YA urban fantasy exploded with the introduction of *Twilight* by Stephenie Meyer. Vampires were soon followed by faeries and werewolves. Most recently, angels and dragons have become all the rage. Maggie Stiefvater's *The Raven Boys* and Julie Kagawa's *Talon* are excellent examples.

The appeal of fantastical elements existing in our world allows the reader to easily imagine themselves as a part of the action. This makes urban fantasy an easy entry point into the world of fantasy and is why you will find such a large and loyal readership always looking for the next new creature to romanticize.

Alameda, Courtney. *Shutter*. 2015.

It is tough being a tetrachromat who sees the auras of the undead but it is even tougher being Micheline Van Helsing, one of the last descendants of the great Van Helsing line. Ever since she was not able to stop her mother from being turned and murdering her two younger brothers, Micheline and her father live in a world filled with silences and blame. She will do anything to return to being the daughter he can be proud of, including going after a ghost so powerful that it has infected her and her crew with a soulchain that will kill them all if the ghost is not stopped in seven days. Filled with references to the greatest horror novels of all time, this will make patrons want to rediscover the characters of Dracula, Frankenstein, and Van Helsing.

Alloway, Kit. *Dreamfire*. Dream Walker Trilogy. 2016.

Some teens get afterschool jobs delivering pizza, Joshlyn Weaver was born into her job as a Dream Walker. Everyone in her family walks the dreamworld, saving the world by battling nightmares before they go too far and keeping the dreamworld balanced. It is dangerous work and many loved ones have died doing work they believe in, and Joshlyn cannot imagine doing anything else with her life. Because she is unusually gifted, on her 16th birthday she is assigned an apprentice. When strange things start happening in the dreamworld, she must be cleverer than those who seek to destroy it or both she and her apprentice may pay the ultimate price. The first book in this series shows all the hallmarks of becoming a teen fantasy classic.

Black, Holly. *Tithe*. Modern Faerie Tales Series. 2002.

Kaye has always lived a nomadic life traveling with her mother's rock band but when her mom is attacked, the two flee to her grandmother's house. Kaye has fond memories of the time she spent there, especially the time spent with her imaginary friends that always felt realer than the life she was leading. It does not really surprise her that her imaginary friends are indeed real and are faeries. What is shocking is when they inform her she is a pixie changeling. Now she must decide if she wants to risk everything, including her life, to help free her friends from a life of slavery in the Unseelie court. This is a dark, gritty novel that readers either love or hate so recommend this to patrons who like unusual and complex novels.

Caine, Rachel. *Glass Houses*. **The Morganville Vampires Series. 2006.**
Claire Danvers is smart; really, really smart with an unfortunate tendency to say what she is thinking, which makes her beloved of teachers but not quite as popular with her classmates. When she graduates early from high school, she is thrilled to be starting fresh. Unfortunately, on the first day of school, she manages to enrage the mayor's daughter, who just happens to be under the protection of vampires and her college career status goes from miserable to downright life threatening. In desperation, she answers an advertisement looking for a roommate and finds a house filled with outcasts, all fighting the Morganville Vampire rule over the town. This is a great choice for those who still love the Twilight Saga series by Stephenie Meyer.

Clare, Cassandra. *City of Bones*. **The Mortal Instruments Series. 2007.**
Clary Fray is out with friends and witnesses a murder by three teenagers with unfamiliar weapons, but strangest of all is the fact that no one else can see the murder or the body. Later on, Clary's mother disappears and then she is attacked by a demon. After meeting Jace, Alec, Isabelle, she finds out that they are Shadowhunters as was her mother and Clary has the same ability to see and fight demons that they do. Now the clock is ticking down in a race to save her mother before the demons can destroy her. Be sure to let patrons know about the television series by the same name.

Hand, Cynthia. *Unearthly*. **Unearthly Series. 2011.**
Clara Gardner is part angel and has just received her purpose, the task she is born to fulfill. When she meets Christian, she recognizes him as important to fulfilling her purpose, and she immediately sets out to get to know him. But interpreting the vision containing her purpose is more complicated that she realized, especially when Tucker suddenly becomes an important part of her life. This is a quintessential example of a teen urban fantasy, complete with love triangle and angels.

Harrison, Kim. *Once Dead, Twice Shy*. **Madison Avery Series. 2009.**
Having a dark reaper kill her is not at all how Madison Avery pictured her prom night ending. The amulet she stole as she died gives her the illusion of having a body, and a light reaper has been assigned to train her to protect herself while the Time Keeper tries to figure out why she survived. When Avery decides to be proactive and barter for her physical body, dangerous secrets are revealed. Readers who like this series will enjoy the MGM television series *Dead like Me* (2003).

Johnson, Maureen. *The Name of the Star*. **Shades of London Series. 2011.**
When Rory's parents are transferred to England to work for a year, she decides that a boarding school sounds like a great way to spend her year. Wexford is located in London and she cannot wait to spend the year exploring the city. The day she arrives she is greeted by a fantastic roommate, a cute boy, and a series of copycat Jack the Ripper murders. After a near-death experience allows her to see ghosts, she realizes that the murderer is a ghost and she may be the only witness. Luckily, the MI5 has a secret branch to deal

with ghostly occurrence and together they race the clock to prevent more murders from taking place. An excellent choice for fantasy readers who are also anglophiles and are addicted to boarding school tales.

Marr, Melissa. *Wicked Lovely.* <u>Wicked Lovely Series</u>. **2007.**
Aislinn sees faeries. Not the charming, benevolent type found in storybooks but the terrifying, cruel creatures of faerie. Her grandmother has taught her the rules for how to keep from attracting their attention but recently something has changed and the Summer King seems to have focused his attention on her, pretending he is human and trying to charm her into becoming his queen. But Aislinn wants to go to college and date Seth and live a normal life and she will go to any lengths to have the life she wants, even if it means battling the terrifying Winter Queen for control of Faerie. Stories set in the world of faerie are always a good choice for those whole like their fantasy dark and twisted.

Schwab, Victoria. *This Savage Song.* <u>Monsters of Verity Series</u>. **2016.**
Gritty, brutal, and with a kind of dark beauty, Kate Harker is desperate to prove to her father that she can be as ruthless as he is. That she can battle monsters and humans and rule over them all. But when she meets August Flynn, all of her preconceptions about good and evil are upended, and she has to decide if August or her father is worthy of her loyalty. Those who like gritty graphic novels like *Sin City* by Frank Miller will be enthralled by this tale.

Stiefvater, Maggie. *Shiver.* <u>The Wolves of Mercy Falls Series</u>. **2009.**
Every time she sees the yellow-eyed wolf, Grace feels a strong sense of connection. There is something almost human about him. When she meets Sam, who has the same eyes as her wolf, she starts to wonder if they are connected and she is right. Sam is a winter werewolf, changing to his human form only in the summer but the time is coming when he will no longer change back to human and Sam wants to be human more than he wants anything, except perhaps Grace. Those who appreciate the rugged werewolf archetype may also appreciate the television series, *Bitten* and *Being Human*.

Epic and Dragons

One of the oldest and most beloved types of fantasy is the epic saga. There is nothing more thrilling to a fantasy reader than a book that includes quests, magic, fantastic worlds, and if at all possible, magical beings. Not all of the books featured in this section include dragons but all include epic adventures and a world rife with magic, used for both good and evil.

Dragons are often depicted as the oldest and most magical of creatures, and their power to destroy is legendary. They often partner with a human but are very particular and only choose a person who exhibits special abilities and a heroic heart. Because they can see the truth of a person, it is an honor to be chosen in this way. In recent years, teen young adult novels have played with the trope and you will see examples here of dragons depicted in a variety of heroic, and not so heroic ways.

Bardugo, Leigh. *Six of Crows.* <u>Six of Crows Series</u>. **2015.**
A master criminal, a thief, a spy, a convict, a gambling sharpshooter, a runaway, and a heartrender have the chance of pulling off the heist of a lifetime assuming they can stay alive long enough to pull it off. Everybody says breaking into the Ice Court cannot be done but Kaz Brekker is not known

as Dirtyhands, the most deadly criminal in Ketterdam, for nothing. This is a perfect tale for those who like their characters dark and complex and their plots full of twists and turns. The author wrote this while listening to "In a Time Lapse" by Ludovico Einaudi and the music really adds to the reading experience.

Goodman, Alison. *Eon: Dragoneye Reborn.* Eon Series. 2010.
For years, Eona has masqueraded as a boy on orders from her master. After 12 years of training, known as Eon, she is competing to become a Dragoneye, a role strictly forbidden to women. When chosen by the Mirror Dragon, Eon enters the aristocracy as one of the most powerful to be gifted with Dragon Magic in 100 years. But something has gone wrong and Eon was not able to fully bond with her dragon. Now she must navigate the dangers of the council and Empire all while hiding the secrets that could kill all those she admires. This is an excellent recommendation for those looking for an East Asian dragon tale.

Hartman, Rachel. *Serephina.* Serephina Series. 2012.
Seraphina's father's instructions were very clear; "Do NOTHING to call attention to yourself." This was not surprising since she has lived her whole life knowing she must never let anyone know that she is half human, half dragon because the consequences could be too terrible to imagine. When she becomes the music tutor for the princess, she draws the attention of Prince Lucien Kiggs. The dashing prince sees far too much and soon she is lying to everyone she knows in order to keep her secrets, including the fact that she may not be the only half dragon in existence. This sweeping tale is especially effective as a spoken word offering and is highly recommended.

Marchetta, Melina. *Finnikin of the Rock.* Lumatere Chronicles Series. 2008.
Evanjalin is perhaps the most annoying person Finnikin of the Rock has ever met. When he and his guardian, Sir Topher, stumble across her she insists the heir to the throne of Lumatere is alive and will break the enchantment that keeps it from being accessible to its people, many who live and die in refugee camps without ever seeing their homeland again. All Finnkin wants to do is to find his people and bring them home again but to do so he must follow Evanjalin on a strange and dangerous journey in the hopes he can make his dream a reality. What sets this fantasy apart is the absolutely enchanting relationship between Finnikin and Evanjalin, and the love they both share for their homeland. Definitely a good choice for fans of the epic fantasy novel.

Nix, Garth. *Sabriel.* Abhorsen Series. 1995.
There are many kinds of magic in Ancelstierre and the Old Kingdom. Free Magic, Charter Magic, and Necromancy all work in different ways. When her father, the Abhorsen, goes missing, Sabriel must enter the Old Kingdom and fight the dead to find him. She has had little experience with the outside world, and must discover the magic within in order to triumph over the evil that threatens her family and her world. With a fully fleshed out magical world and a high-stakes quest, this series is highly recommended for those who love J.R.R. Tolkien.

Paolini, Christopher. *Eragon.* The Inheritance Cycle Series. 2002.
An evil empire. A poor farm boy. A curious blue stone. When Eragon finds a blue stone, he thinks it might be worth enough to get his family

through the harsh winter. Imagine his surprise when the stone turns out to be an egg, and not just any egg, but a dragon egg. Eragon is sure the dragon will be turned over to the empire to be used for evil purposes so he hides the dragon in the woods. When emissaries come in search of the dragon, Eragon's simple life is shattered and he and his new friend must enter a new world filled with danger and intrigue but will they have what it takes to triumph over evil?

Rowling, J. K. *Harry Potter and the Sorcerer's Stone*. <u>Harry Potter Series</u>. 1997.

Harry Potter's life could be going better. He lives with his Aunt Petunia, his Uncle Vernon, and his cousin Dudley who are not excited to have him join their little family. In fact, the only part of the house they are willing to carve out for him is a space under the stairs. Then one day, a giant of a man whisks him away to start a new life at Hogwarts School of Witchcraft and Wizardry and his new life filled with magic begins. Believe it or not, there are still adults who have not read this story so make sure to suggest it to those who like tales of ordinary people who become extraordinary, just like this series. For a twist to this tale, be sure to recommend Rainbow Rowell's *Carry On*.

Tahir, Sabaa. *An Ember in the Ashes*. <u>An Ember in the Ashes Series</u>. 2015.

When Laia's brother is captured and her grandparents kill by soldiers for the Martial Empire, she seeks out the rebels in hopes that they will help her find a way to free him. They agree but only if she agrees to infiltrate the household of one of the most brutal leaders of the empire's military. Elias serves the empire and is slated to graduate from the military academy and go directly into service but he dreams instead of escaping. When he and Laia meet, they must form an alliance in order to fulfill their destiny. Set in a world patterned after ancient Rome, recommend this to anyone who enjoys ancient history, historical fiction, or alternate history fantasy.

Turner, Megan Whalen. *The Thief*. <u>The Queen's Thief Series</u>. 1996.

The King's Mangus needs a thief and Gen fits the bill. Gen needs to get out of prison so the Mangus' offer to release him if he helps him "recover" an artifact for the king to use to make the queen of Anatolia marry him sounds perfectly reasonable to Gen. The adventure they go on is interwoven with stories of the gods. As they get closer to obtaining their prize, Gen must use all of his ingenuity to protect those he holds dear. For those who love the clever banter and charming thief, you may also want to recommend the television series *Buffy the Vampire Slayer*.

Wrede, Patricia. *Dealing with Dragons*. <u>Enchanted Forest Chronicles Series</u>. 1990.

Princess Cimorene did not mean to make life difficult for her parents. She just found fencing, Latin, and magic lessons more interesting than learning how loudly it was permissible to scream when being carried off by a giant. Most of all she longed for adventure, the kind of adventure princes got to have. When she finds her parents are set to marry her off to an exceedingly dull prince, she decides to take matters into her own hands and she sets out to find adventures of her very own. The tone of this is lighthearted and an excellent recommendation for those seeking a bit of humor mixed into their epic question novels.

Conclusion: Trends in Fantasy

Thanks to Rick Riordan, Greek myths have been popular for several years, but recent novels reflect a rise in the use of a variety of myths from other countries, both in historical and in urban fantasy settings. Perhaps this is an offshoot of the push for more diversity in teen novels.

The WeNeedDiverseBooks.com initiative and popular teen actresses with strong feminist messages, such as Emma Watson of *Harry Potter and the Sorcerer's Stone* fame, continue to create additional demand for books with diverse and strong characters. For now, the publishing world seems to be responding. The strength of the trend will depend on continuing pressure on the publishing world to produce these types of tales.

A final trend worth noting is the explosion of LGBTQ characters seen in a variety of stories, with the authors not focused on coming out stories but creating more organic characters mirroring the political and cultural changes occurring in society. A good example is the 2015 Rainbow Rowell fantasy title, *Carry On*, which features a main type character who falls for his roommate, not as a focal point of the story but as a natural romantic element that fits beautifully within the broader tale.

11

Romance and ChickLit

Alicia Ahlvers

Introduction to the Genre

Definition

Romance is the most read, most purchased genre in the world. Indeed, with 13 percent[1] of the fiction market share consisting of adult romance, it is considered one of the linchpins of the publishing world. Even more important, readers often purchase 20–30 books a month, the very definition of a power reader. Readers of romance are daring and have embraced the ebook format and they are more willing than other genre readers to branch out and explore new genres, subgenres, and formats. It is no wonder romance readers were the first to jump on the teen novel bandwagon, embracing dystopian romance long before it was "discovered" by mainstream readers.

To better understand the romance genre, the rules for adult romance are as follows: The novel must have a couple who meet, encounter an obstacle (either real or imagined), and they must work as a couple to overcome the obstacle so they can live happily ever after. It should be noted that none of these criteria is optional. When it comes to teen romance novels, however, the rules change a bit. It is not fun or sexy to read about a teen couple settling down to start a family or to represent their romantic life peaking at age 16. Teen romance instead focuses on the possibilities inherent in growing up using the romance genre to explore the myriad of options available to the central characters. In an adult romance, a sense of romantic completion is the eventual goal. In teen romance, *possibility* is the word to remember. In both cases, you should be left with a sense of hope for the couple in question, even if you are experiencing very different outcomes.

Appeals

Given these differences, why do adults read young adult (YA) romance novels? To understand why adults read teen romance, it is useful to understand why romance in general is so very popular. Romance and ChickLit explore relationships and internal growth in a way that allows the reader to "learn" along with the central characters. Emotional connection can be explored within the safety of the novel and when the novel is finished, a reader can walk away having risked only his or her time and investment in a make-believe world. Readers find comfort in exploring the many ways to deal with conflict within a relationship and the ways romance can encourage or hinder the growth of each individual. This concept is very similar no matter what the target audience might be. Even more important, readers can revisit their own past successes, failures, and experience and create narrative to explain their own life. YA novels, by definition, are books that explore the inner lives of teens. A successful teen novel will show growth of the central characters, explore how they understand themselves, and relate to the world and people around them. Is it any wonder teen novels are of interest to adult readers longing to analyze their lives and relationships?

Working with Readers

Given the high percentage of power readers this genre produces, it is surprising to find that romance readers are still often reviled and ignored within the library field. As libraries struggle to stay relevant, it stands to reason that this market share should instead be a highly coveted target audience and libraries positioned as a reading haven. One way this can be accomplished is by paying attention to the trends within this genre and being ready with multiple recommendations at the drop of a hat. Remember, these readers are often reading up to 30 books a month. Pulling out the same well-worn book recommendation each time a romance reader appears will not cut it for this readership. If you cannot read extensively within the genre, you will need to keep up with reviews, tropes, and trends and nothing is hotter in romance at the moment than the exploding market of YA books and the trends we are currently experiencing.

Tools and Resources

The Romance Writers of America and Romantic Times were some the first to include YA categories for its romance book awards, and sites like All About Romance (www.likesbooks.com), Romantic Times Book Reviews (http://www.rtbookreviews.com), and Smart Bitches, Trashy Books (www.smartbitchestrashybooks.com) routinely include reviews of YA titles. Also important is to keep up with *Entertainment Weekly*, *Teen Vogue*, *Seventeen*, and other magazines teens read for ideas about the current hottest teen romance novels. While romance readers are not the only readers of teen titles, they make up the majority of adult fans and these readers read broadly within the YA framework as opposed to just picking up the current dystopian romance favored by the moviemakers and news outlets. In fact, most of the reviews on these adult review sites focus on contemporary romance and this subgenre has had a strong adult following for years.

Collection Development

While there are a plethora of genres and subgenres in teen romance, when understanding why adult readers might choose novels for the age group it is useful to instead look at the tropes explored in a typical teen romance. According to *Webster's Dictionary*, a "trope is a common or overused theme or device" and is used extensively in romance novels in order to give the characters plausible reasons to create conflict, meet and fall in love, or allow readers to suspend disbelief. Now let's explore some of the popular tropes that define YA romance and will also appeal to many adult readers.

The Literature

A Touch of Nostalgia and Dreaming of Romance

There is something special about one's first love. It is a time of discovery and a time of firsts; a first kiss, a first sexual experience, a first heartbreak. Perhaps more than any other category, this trope appeals to adults because of the sense of nostalgia it evokes. While there can be other relationships, these stories focus on the way the teen years of the main characters are changed or defined by the love relationship. Whether or not an adult experienced what the characters experience in the novel, they can relate to the universal experience of first love and first heartbreak.

Dreaming of romance is similar to what I like to refer to as the *billionaire lover* trope since the adult version appears in the Harlequin serial line in endless variations. The primary feature is larger-than-life characters and/or situations that would be unlikely to occur in most readers' real lives. They are often over the top and are coveted for precisely that reason, to take us out of our practical workday lives to a place we can vicariously experience a fairytale existence. Whether an ordinary girl is being wooed by a movie star or finding out she is really a princess, these stories remind us to dream big and to never rule out the impossible.

While most contemporary romance novels are based in reality and focus on the world as it exists for the reader, larger-than-life romance may also straddle the line between a contemporary and a fantasy romance novel. These titles can also have just a touch of magic to them and it is often left to the reader to decide if the magic is real or imagined by the characters. For the most part these novels are still set in the real world and follow contemporary romance conventions but the romance often has a dreamy mystical feel.

Cabot, Meg. *The Princess Diaries*. Princess Diaries. 2000.

Imagine waking up one day to find that your father is now the crown prince of Genovia and you are the one and only heir to the throne. Mia is NOT happy. Plans for her life included hanging out with her school friends, finding a boyfriend, and not flunking math. Now she has to spend time with her Grand-mère who is determined to turn this free spirit into a princess, all while trying to figure out who likes her for herself and who just wants a royal girlfriend. (print, ebook, audiobook)

Carter, Ally. *I'd Tell You I Love You, But Then I'd Have to Kill You*. Gallagher Girls. 2006.

The Gallagher Academy for Exceptional Young Women is not your ordinary boarding school but is instead an elite (and super cool) school for spies. During a training mission in a nearby town, Cammie Morgan meets a normal boy who seems to like her and suddenly her whole focus is on keeping the truth from him yet still keeping her superspy status intact. Over the top and highly addictive, you will not be able to just read one of these fun and fast-paced tales. (print, ebook, audiobook)

Forman, Gayle. *If I Stay*. 2009.

Mia is the only survivor in an accident that has killed her entire family. In a coma, she finds that she is aware of what is going on around her and it is up to her to decide if she wants to "stay" alive or join her family in death. Because this novel takes the reader through Mia's entire romance and is set in contemporary times, its contemporary status takes precedence over the slight fantasy element that drives the story. (print, ebook, audiobook)

Kenneally, Miranda. *Catching Jordan*. 2011.

Star quarterback, Jordan, is being recruited by college teams and has a good chance of obtaining a scholarship to play football but she also dreams of meeting a boy who will see her as something more than one of the guys. When a new quarterback moves to town, she is faced with an instant attraction and a fear that she will be replaced as the star of the team. The support of her teammates and coach and the sweetness of the boy who eventually wins her heart is not entirely realistic but allows the readers their happily-ever-after ending. (print, ebook)

Levithan, David. *Boy Meets Boy*. 2003.

When David Levithan wrote this novel, he deliberately created an almost utopian town for his young protagonist to inhabit because he was tired of seeing only unhappy, traumatized LGBTQ characters in novels. Our hero Paul is a popular teen and experiences the question all teens face. How do you decide whom to love? At its core, this is a tender love story complete with over-the-top avowals of love, friends, and family who collude in helping Paul to woo his love interest, and the entire cast of characters participating in a crazy and wonderful prom. (print, ebook)

Perkins, Stephanie. *Anna and the French Kiss*. 2010.

Anna is heartbroken when she is sent to Paris to boarding school during her senior year, leaving her friends and her almost boyfriend behind. Meeting fellow classmate Meredith gives Anna hope she can survive school … and then she meets Étienne. He is handsome and smart and they soon become good friends. He would be the perfect guy to help her forget the boy she left behind—if he did not already have a girlfriend. This is the most classic example of a teen romance on the list. The series continues in *Lola and the Boy Next Door* and *Isla and the Happily Ever After*. (print, ebook, audiobook)

Rowell, Rainbow. *Eleanor and Park*. 2013.

Set in 1986, Eleanor is a social misfit who must scavenge for clothing and navigate a hostile home environment in order to manage to stay fed and adequately groomed. Drawn together through their love of music, Park woos her with playlists of his favorite bands and wins her heart by exhibiting a thoughtfulness rarely seen in the portrayal of teen boys. Our hero and heroine struggle with family expectations but each stays true to themselves and each other. The brilliance of this extremely popular novel is the way this unfashionable and withdrawn girl is seen as beautiful through Park's eyes. (print, ebook, audiobook)

Wolitzer, Meg. *Belzhar*. 2014.

When Jam (Jamaica) loses Reeve, the love of her life, she is unable to cope. Fearing for her life, her parents send her to a school for those with "sensitivities." After arriving, she is selected for a highly coveted special topics class that is rumored to change the lives of the participants. Jam starts working on her first assignment and finds that when she is writing she is transported to a place where Reeve is still alive. As events start to spiral out of control, she must decide between preserving her love for Reeve or finding a new love. (print, ebook, audiobook)

The Juliet Effect and Other Dramatic Moments

There are so many ways love can go wrong. In this category, we have the bad boys and girls, star-crossed lovers, a Cinderella life, and for the luckiest of girls, two really hot guys who compete for her heart.

Most of us have had a fantasy or two about falling in love with a bad boy or wild girl, although most adults are too wise to pursue these troubled souls, opting instead for the partner who follows the rules and treats us well. Because, quite frankly, by the time we are into our 20s rescuing and rehabilitating someone still stuck in this cycle begins to sound exhausting instead of appealing. Oh, but if we had only met them when they were young and our love helped them to become who they were meant to be. This fantasy about how the love of the girl or guy next door could change the life of a troubled young (and do not forget hot) love interest is hard to resist. Even better is having two very different people competing for your love, especially if you are that gawky girl or guy who marches to the beat of her own drummer. What could be more seductive than having a worthy love interest see the real you?

Most dramatic and heart-wrenching romance tropes feature two characters from very different worlds who are drawn together by circumstance or chemistry, often in spite of their best efforts to stay away from each other. I like to call this the Juliet effect. While staying true to the romance genre, authors create tension by having characters overcome tremendous odds in order to end up together. Bad boys are the most common character type but by no means the only one. Socioeconomic differences are explored in depth as are religious, ethnic, and even gender issues.

And who can forget the first time their heart was broken? In these stories, not only has the main characters been dumped by their first significant relationship, but it often happens in public and in humiliating ways. Walking in on boyfriends with another girl, being broken up with via text message, being used to make someone else jealous, or just being told they are no longer loved creates situations in which the ability to love again is questioned by the main character. Discovering resilience and learning to trust others again becomes the focal point of these novels and often the biggest obstacle the romantic partners must overcome is the fear of once again being hurt.

Alexander, Kwame. *He Said, She Said.* 2013.

If Claudia has her way, Harvard will be a big part of her future; she does not have time to waste on popular, superficial football star, Omar "T-Diddy" Smalls. When Omar bets his friends he can bed Claudia, he starts doing all kinds of socially aware things he would never normally do. Once the two find a common cause, the sparks start flying and what started out as a bet turns to love. The use of street slang makes this a challenging read but for anyone looking for an edgy African American romance this is just the title to recommend. (print, ebook)

Dessen, Sarah. *The Truth about Forever.* 2004.

Macy's boyfriend is heading off to Brain Camp and he has arranged for her to work his job at a library during summer. Faced with a summer working with two mean girls and a mother still in mourning for Macy's father, she rebels by getting a job with a catering company. The people she meets help her to redefine who she is and how she wants to deal with the people in her life. Sarah Dessen is the reigning queen of teen romance novels and any of her work is worth recommending to readers looking for an angsty romance novel. (print, ebook)

Elkeles, Simone. *Perfect Chemistry.* 2009.
A gang member and prom queen end up as chemistry partners and chemistry of a different sort soon flares between the two. The two also find that their preconceptions about how the other lives their life is very different from reality. Each has problems and each has love in their life. But overcoming the obstacles to being together is an extreme challenge and could lead to the death of the hero and possibly even his family. The escalating tension and the uncertainty of the outcome make this novel a perfect example of the star-crossed lover trope. (print, ebook, audiobook)

McGarry, Katie. *Crash into You.* 2013.
From the outside, Rachel Young's life looks almost perfect. No one knows about her panic attacks or her wildly overprotective family. Rachel's way of coping is to work on her car or sneak out of the house and drive for hours. One night, while driving, she ends up in an illegal drag race where she meets Isaiah. When she is targeted by the criminal who set up the races, Isaiah steps in to protect her and they quickly fall in love but when Isaiah can no longer protect her, can Rachel take care of herself? (print, ebook)

Peters, Julie Anne. *Lies My Girlfriend Told Me.* 2014.
Alix wakes up one morning to the news that her girlfriend, Swanee has died. As Alix grieves, she finds Swanee's phone and takes it as a way to keep her close to her heart and then finds that Swanee was secretly seeing a girl named Liana (L.T.). She arranges to meet Liana and the two are soon drawn together by their shared experiences. But will love be enough this time? Fans enjoy this author's work because the sexual preferences are not central to the story and the focus is instead on the developing romance between Liana and Alix. (print, ebook, audiobook)

Growing Up Can Be Hard to Do: ChickLit

While ChickLit can include a romance or even many romances, the primary focus will always be on the growth of the main female character(s). This genre is essentially the same whether it is an adult or teen novel, only varying in the experience the characters bring to the story. These can be lighthearted tales or complex stories featuring difficult or serious issues that must be navigated in order for the protagonist to thrive or even to survive. Some of the best of these are multi-volume series that follow one or more protagonists through their young adult lives. Readers of character-driven novels tend to gravitate to this type of storytelling because of the exploration of the inner lives of the friends and the way these books help the reader to understand and navigate their own relationships. Ultimately, when deciding if a book is ChickLit or romance, ask how much of the book is spent on a romantic relationship and how much of the book is spent on self-discovery and/or other important relationships. If you have time to read only one teen ChickLit novel, *The Sisterhood of the Traveling Pants* will give you an excellent overview of what to look for in the genre.

Brashares, Ann. *The Sisterhood of the Traveling Pants.* <u>The Sisterhood of the Traveling Pants.</u> **2001.**

Perhaps the quintessential ChickLit book, *Sisterhood* follows four friends over the course of a summer as they push the boundaries of their new-found freedom as well as exploring their established relationships. What sets this apart from romance as well as other ChickLit is that the challenge faced by each friend is completely different and realistic. The following books in the series follow the four into college and beyond, always exploring the variety of situations a young adult must face in order to complete the growing up process. (print, ebook, audiobook)

Hidier, Tanuja Desai. *Born Confused.* **2002.**

Dimple wants to be a photographer and date a hot guy like her best friend's boyfriend. Her parents want her to lead a safe and traditional life. In fact, they start lining up potential "nice Indian" boys for her to meet and the first candidate is exactly as awful as she expected. But when her college-aged cousin invites her to a club she discovers that her "suitable" match is actually a little "unsuitable" in all the best ways. Dimple navigates the often-fraught world of family, cultural identity, friendship, and even romance in this multicultural gem. (print, ebook, audiobook)

McCafferty, Megan. *Sloppy Firsts.* <u>The Jessica Darling Series.</u> **2001.**

The first novels in this series follow Jessica Darling as she navigates the world of high school. She spends her time running track, dealing with her dysfunctional family, navigating the mean girl shark pool and trying to keep her place as valedictorian. When she catches the eye of the local bad boy will he tempt her to throw away everything she has worked so hard to accomplish? While later books in the series take her to college and beyond, the first two in the series are an addictive mix of romance and the excitement of growing up. (print, ebook)

Rennison, Louise. *Angus, Thongs and Full-Frontal Snogging.* <u>Confessions of Georgia Nicolson.</u> **2000.**

No one understands how difficult being 14 is. Georgia's three-year-old sister invades her privacy and may have actually peed in her room, acne has made a dramatic appearance, and summer is almost over. And that is before Robbie the "Sex God" appears on the scene. Set in the pre-cell phone era, this silly and affecting novel will appeal to those in search of a good nostalgic ChickLit. Full of unique slang and inside jokes, Georgia's fans will want to follow her hilarious misadventures through all 10 books. (print, ebook, audiobook)

Conclusion: Trends in Teen Romance

Probably the biggest trend in young adult contemporary romance is the John Green effect, which pits a young person against death or other issues that propel the teens into dealing with very adult issues that cannot be easily fixed or changed. While John Green's most popular novels are not romance, authors have incorporated Green's trademark quirky characters and heart-breaking situations into a more traditional romance format. His contemporary settings are filled with likable teens who are not struggling against difficult home situations but instead are working toward understanding themselves, their relationships, and their place in the universe. This has also given rise to more awkward yet somehow cool male characters who will appeal to boys. There is some sense that the highly popular romantic triangle drawn out over a trilogy or series is on the decline but I would not hold my breath just yet.

A successful teen novel will show growth of the central characters, explore how they understand themselves, and relate to the world and people around them. Given the aforementioned examples, is it any wonder teen novels are of interest to adult readers longing to analyze their lives and relationships?

Note

1. "Romance Industry Statistics," *Romance Writers of America,* accessed December 4, 2015, https://www.rwa.org/p/cm/ld/fid=580.

12
Mainstream Literature

Lucy M. Lockley

Introduction to the Genre

Definition

A definition for mainstream literature that can be equally applied in Young Adult literature is provided by Nancy Pearl and Sarah Statz Cords in *Now Read This III*. They define mainstream fiction as:

> all those novels (and short story collections) that do not conform to any genre classification. . . . [T]hese are primarily books that will appeal to readers through their character development, or prose styles, rather than their conformity to genre conventions.

The authors acknowledge the phrase *mainstream fiction* can be misleading, that many mainstream titles are considered *literary fiction*—a troublesome term itself. Joyce Saricks defines literary fiction, in *The Readers' Advisory Guide to Genre Fiction* (2nd edition), as:

> critically acclaimed, often award-winning, fiction. These books are more often character-centered rather than plot-oriented. They are thought-provoking and often address serious issues. They are not page-turners, per se, although their fans certainly find them engrossing and compelling reading.

Many readers enjoy mainstream titles for the characterizations or writing style. Others may like them because they tell a good story or have beautifully described settings. Mainstream literature is multidimensional, and while a specific book may emphasize one appeal, such as character, over another, such as story, there is generally more than one appeal feature at work in a mainstream title. And in the best, all four appeals will be highly evident.

For this chapter, mainstream literature will be defined as YA books that emphasize character, have a distinct writing style or employ a strong design element, are thought-provoking and encourage discussion, and would attract an adult audience. The books presented are representative of Printz Award winners or Honor Books and other YA titles that, based on reviews, will appeal for various reasons to adult readers.

Appeals

In the "Trends in Mainstream Fiction" section of *Now Read This III*, Cords mentions the increasing popularity of "crossover books"—YA books that adults may enjoy. She says:

> The sharp dialogue and characterization, combined with briskly paced storytelling, which YA authors typically employ to appeal to a demanding youth audience, are often paired with more complex themes and dilemmas sufficient to challenge the most mature readers.

Adults who pursue YA titles will often sit down with any genre: realistic and historical fiction, fantasy, science fiction, or romance. Adults even read mainstream YA books, although there can be a problem in determining exactly what these specific readers may enjoy. Applying Saricks "Appeal Features" approach can be a particularly effective way to identify which traits might attract certain readers. As mainstream fiction can be difficult to categorize, determining whether it is pacing, characterization, story line, frame and setting, tone and mood, or language and style that appeal to a reader can be essential in finding the right titles.

Adults read YA books for a variety of reasons, many of those reasons being similar to why they read mainstream literature. They are (1) avid readers who will read anything, (2) keeping up with their child's school assignments, (3) interested in revisiting the teenage experience or simply wish to be taken away from the complexity of their current everyday life, (4) following their favorite adult author who has ventured into the YA market, or (5) simply curious to know what all the buzz is about with the newest book, movie, or television show, which happens to be based on a popular YA title. Adult readers of YA books are, in other terms, trying to "keep up with the Jones" the same way they might when reading the current adult bestsellers.

Working with Readers

Readers' advisors should keep in mind the popularity of mainstream literature is due in large part to the focus being placed on internal issues. Readers frequently enjoy literature that deals with other people's troubles. They are drawn to books that relate how individuals or groups overcome, accept, or come to terms with personal failings, medical-related difficulties, or social acceptance. This is as true for adult mainstream titles as it is for YA literature. Universal themes such as coming-of-age and intriguing new styles of presentation engage readers of all ages. Adult readers interested in mainstream literature can also be directed to award-winning YA titles, such as Printz Award winners and honor books.

When dealing with adults asking about YA literature, advisors might want to inquire if there are other YA titles the reader has enjoyed or if the reader has a specific purpose for investing time in literature written specifically for youth. With the recent proliferation of television series and feature films based on popular YA titles, graphic novels or comic books, it may be helpful to try and determine if such material has an appeal for the adult reader.

Resources and Tools

There are many professional journals that review YA literature. *Booklist, Kirkus, School Library Journal*, and *Voice of Youth Advocates* (*VOYA*) often highlight YA titles that will appeal to adults. The reviews may include terms such as *literary style* or *lyrical writing*, emphasize *strong characterization* or *well-developed characters*, and suggest the title would be good for book discussion groups or *offer excellent potential for discussion of* ... some contemporary social issue. Readalikes or suggestions *for fans of* ... are often books, films, or television series with a strong adult base, indicating books that have reading appeal beyond the teen audience.

Resources for developing an understanding of YA literature and the relevance to adult readers are available in many forms. Books with annotated lists for discovering mainstream suggestions appealing to adult readers are Tina Frolund's *Genrefied Classics*, Diana Tixier Herald's *Teen Genreflecting 3*, and Nancy Pearl's *Book Crush: For Kids and Teens*. Some tools offering guidance into YA literature that could be applied to serving adult readers are Heather Booth's *Serving Teens through Readers' Advisory* and Michael Cart's *Young Adult Literature: From Romance to Realism*. Chapter 9 in *Integrated Advisory Service* edited by Jessica Moyer gives an overview of "Everything Teen" including a breakdown of the types of readers who enjoy teen stories.

An adult's perspective on teen literature is available from websites such as Love YA Lit at http://http://loveyalit.com/, Mostly YA Lit at http://www .mostlyyalit.com/ and Forever Young Adult at http://foreveryoungadult .com/. The producers of these sites are adults devoted to spreading the word about all forms of teen literature. Mainstream YA titles that adult readers might enjoy can also be found on *Teenreads* at http://http://www.teen reads.com/ as well as on the YALSA Book and Media Awards and Lists for Libraries webpage found at http://www.ala.org/yalsa/booklistsawards/ booklists/.

Reviews in professional journals, print resources, online sites, and literature awards can enhance knowledge of young adult material and provide assistance for working with adults interested in crossing over into the realm of teen titles. These tools provide perspective and are good resources when looking for young adult books that will appeal to adult readers.

Collection Development

To encourage interest in literary YA reading, the Young Adult Library Services Association (YALSA), a division of the American Library Association (ALA), created an annual award that recognizes "a book that exemplifies literary excellence in young adult literature." The "Charge" of the Printz Award Committee is "to select from the previous year's publications the best young adult book ('best' being defined solely in terms of literary merit)." The "Criteria" section of *The Michael L. Printz Award Policies and Procedures* can be found at http://www.ala.org/yalsa/booklistsawards/bookawards/printz award/aboutprintz/criteria.

Writing about the Printz Award in *The Teen Readers' Advisor*, Rosemary Honnold said:

> The main criterion for the award is literary excellence, which can be a subjective and often fairly controversial judgment. Popularity and the message of the book are not crucial elements for winning this award. Interesting discussions usually follow the announcement of the winner, with many librarians elated with the committee's choices, and many disappointed that their favorite titles were not chosen. The Printz committee aims to award titles that appeal to the best readers rather than the average reader, in the hopes of bringing these excellent books to a wider audience. ... While popularity gives readers what they want, literary excellence will challenge readers to think for themselves and invite them to change.

The Literature

The following titles offer a sample of books published for YAs that will also appeal to adult readers. The books are organized by themes that reflect popular reading interests.

Finding Oneself

"Finding oneself" is an expected part of life especially for teenagers and can take many forms. Coming-of-age is the transition from childhood to adulthood and the point at which this occurs can vary. The form of transition varies as well, covering legal age, sexual maturity, religious responsibility, and social accountability. "Finding oneself" also pertains to dealing with adversity. This can mean acknowledging the prospect of dying, recognizing limitations or enduring a disability, accepting a cultural, political, or sexual identity, taking responsibility for actions, dealing with all manner of abuse, and simply finding a place in the world and society. As a topic rife with story possibilities for YA literature, "finding oneself" allows adult readers to explore life changing issues, relive lost youth, delve into history from a different point of view, and try to understand diverse personal, social, or political opinions. The following list of titles include a Printz Award winner, five honor books and other titles that adults may find appealing for a variety of reasons.

Anderson, Laurie Halse. *Speak*. 1999.

Freshman Melinda Sordino has been proclaimed a social pariah for calling the police to an end-of-summer bash. No one knows she was raped during the party and the trauma has left her unable to discuss it. Throughout the year, the callousness of high school life is exposed as Melinda strives to come to terms and learns to speak up for herself. Adults should appreciate the emotional intensity and insight into the issue of teenage rape. (print, ebook, digital audio from Audible, audio from Listening Library, performance by Mandy Siegfried) [Printz Honor book]

A filmed version of *Speak* won the 2004 Woodstock Film Festival Audience Award.

Donnelly, Jennifer. *A Northern Light*. 2003.

Mattie Gokey has a way with words and dreams of becoming a writer; yet, a promise to her dying mother keeps her close to home caring for her family. Her position as waitress at the Glenmore Hotel leads to her holding secret letters for Grace Brown, a guest who mysteriously disappears. Donnelly's gripping, reflective story is based on a 1906 murder in upstate New York. Adult fans of historical fiction, mysteries, and true crime should enjoy this novel inspired by events related in Theodore Dreiser's *An American Tragedy*. (print, ebook, digital audio from Audible, audio from Listening Library, read by Hope Davis) [Printz Honor book]

Green, John. *The Fault in Our Stars*. 2012.

Hazel Lancaster, 16, is still alive three years after being diagnosed with terminal cancer. During group therapy, she meets and is attracted to Augustus 'Gus' Waters, a young man whose cancer is in remission. Their intelligent, witty conversations become filled with desire and although passionately in love with Gus, Hazel is reluctant. She fears the impact on him when the cancer finally takes her life. This emotionally intense novel that pulls no punches should draw adult readers looking for a realistic portrait of life, loss, and death. (print, ebook, digital audio from Audible, audio from Brilliance Audio read by Kate Rudd)

A motion picture adaptation of Green's novel was released in 2014.

Johnson, Angela. *The First Part Last*. 2003.

"But I figure if the world were really right, humans would live life backward and do the first part last." Stark, lyrical sentences in short, alternating "now" and "then" chapters convey the story of 16-year-old Bobby, a single father. After his girlfriend Nia falls into a postpartum coma, Bobby becomes devoted to their infant daughter, Feather, while also trying to preserve friendships and keep up with school. The book should interest adults who like realistic fiction especially for the rare view into teenage parenthood from the father's point-of-view. (print, ebook, digital audio from Audible, audio from Listening Library read by Khalipa Oldjohn with Kole Kristi as Nia) [Printz Award winner]

Lucier, Makiia. *A Death-Struck Year*. 2014.

Spanish influenza infected 500 million people in 1918, killing 50–100 million. Cleo Berry, a 17-year-old schoolgirl, volunteers with the Red Cross as the disease runs rampant through Portland, Oregon. She must come to terms with death, disease, wartime shortages, and the effects of World War I. In light of contemporary outbreaks, this compelling novel should attract adults interested in the possibilities of a major pandemic as well as historical fiction. (print, ebook)

Saenz, Benjamin Alire. *Aristotle and Dante Discover the Secrets of the Universe*. 2012.

This passionate, coming-of-age story follows Ari and Dante as they struggle to live in "a universe of almost-men." Over a year and a half, as their friendship evolves, Ari discovers a family secret, Dante survives a gay-bashing incident, and they come to terms with their budding relationship. Employing spare, poetic language, Saenz relates the complexities of cultural, familial, and sexual identity. This authentic, thought-provoking book should appeal to adults wishing to examine how teens struggle to understand themselves and their place in the world. (print, ebook, digital audio from Audible, audio from Simon & Schuster Audio narrated by Lin-Manuel Miranda) [Printz Honor book]

Silvey, Craig. *Jasper Jones*. 2011.

Thirteen-year-old, bookish Charlie Bucktin and Jasper Jones have nothing in common until the night Jasper knocks on Charlie's window. In 1960's Australia, half-aboriginal Jasper is always blamed for every little indiscretion in their small town and needs help hiding the body of a young girl until the real killer is found. The story focuses on the ugliness of crime, racism, and Charlie's coming-of-age while keeping an impossible secret. Adult readers should be rewarded by this investigation into the truth and lies beneath race and class bigotry and see comparisons to Harper Lee's *To Kill a Mockingbird* and *Huckleberry Finn*. (print, ebook, digital audio from Audible, audio from Listening Library read by Matt Cowlrick) [Printz Honor book]

Vanderpool, Clare. *Navigating Early*. 2013.

After losing his mother, Jack Baker's father abruptly moves him from Kansas to a boy's boarding school in Maine. Jack befriends Early Auden, a strange, exceptional boy who obsesses over the number Pi, creating stories that give significance to the endless of digits. They go off on a wilderness quest leading to Odyssey-like encounters with memorable characters, which mirror Early's stories. Adults should appreciate the intricately plotted, historical drama that combines the mystical with mystery and adventure in a late World War II setting. (print, ebook, digital audio from Audible, audio from Listening Library read by Robbie Daymond with Mark Bramhall and Cassandra Campbell) [Printz Honor book]

Walton, Leslye. *The Strange and Beautiful Sorrows of Ava Lavender*. 2014.

Ava Lavender was born with the wings of a bird yet cannot fly. She longs to understand where she came from and to discover how she fits in the world. She narrates the stories of her great-grandmother, grandmother, and mother leading to her own tale of thwarted love and denial. The Lavender family's tale of doomed love should appeal to adults who enjoy sweeping, coming-of-age stories with elements of magical realism or entrancing narratives such as *Like Water for Chocolate* by Laura Esquivel or Erin Morgenstern's *The Night Circus*. (print, ebook, digital audio from Audible, audio from Candlewick on Brilliance Audio read by Cassandra Campbell)

Quirky, Unique, and Intriguing

"Quirky, unique, and intriguing" can mean many things and be offered through a variety of modes in YA literature. Use of a new, different, or unexpected format or style of presentation can enhance a story and draw readers to a title. The format differences could be a graphic novel, the inclusion of multiple photographs, or the creation of backstories for images incorporated with the text. Styles of presentation might be the use of an uncommon narrator, alternating narrative voices, a contemporary voice matched with one from history, multiple perspectives on the same story, a before and after countdown, or writing the story in reverse—going backward through time. Adults should find "quirky, unique, and intriguing" YA titles interesting due to the variety of formats and styles of presentation. They may be curious to investigate, exercising a willingness to try something different, and thus broaden their reading horizons. There are five Printz Award winners, three Honor books and a series included among the following list of recommendations.

Clarke, Judith. *One Whole and Perfect Day.* **2007.**

Lily sees her lovable, eccentric family as the bane of her existence. She is the reliable caretaker never having time for just herself although she plans to change things soon by falling in love. The story is told with humor and from multiple perspectives, slowly melding each point of view, drawing them all together, offering insight into the lives of Lily and her offbeat family. Clarke's book should appeal to adults looking for a feel-good read about family relationships. (print, digital audio from Audible, audio from Brilliance Audio read by Gretal Montgomery) [Printz Honor book]

Green, John. *Looking for Alaska.* **2005.**

Sixteen-year-old Miles heads off to his first year at an Alabama boarding school citing the final words of the poet Rabelais, "I go to seek a Great Perhaps." Once there he makes friends with Chip, the alluring Alaska, Takumi, and Lara, who lead him into drinking, smoking, and the plotting of great pranks. The chapter-heading countdown foreshadows a climax, which leaves Miles and friends puzzling over whether Alaska committed suicide. Adults should see comparisons to John Knowles's *A Separate Peace* and appreciate the emotionally intense realism of Miles's first year away from home. (print, ebook, digital audio from Audible, audio from Brilliance Audio read by Jeff Woodman) [Printz Award winner]

Lake, Nick. *In Darkness.* **2013.**

"*I am a voice in the dark, calling out for your help.*" So begins an intricately plotted tale of life in the Haiti, a country consigned over time to neglect and violence. The present-day drama of 15-year-old Shorty, a drug-running street kid trapped under rubble from the 2010 earthquake, alternates with a historical retelling of the life of, Toussaint L'Ouverture, a former slave who freed Haiti from French rule in 1804. *In Darkness* should draw adults wishing insight into how Haiti became the world's first black republic or those concerned with the devastation of natural disasters. (print, ebook, digital audio from Audible, audio from Brilliance Audio read by Benjamin L. Darcie) [Printz Award winner]

Partridge, Elizabeth. *John Lennon: All I Want Is the Truth: A Photographic Biography.* **2005.**

Partridge uses photographs, quotes from Lennon and his contemporaries and extensive primary source material to explore the life of the legendary musician. She presents both the sordid and the sublime sides of The Beatles meteoric rise to international fame, always focusing on the music. The book follows John from childhood, through the formation of the band and his life afterward, delving into the influence of Yoko Ono and the impact of his death on the world. Adult fans should enjoy the detailed, photographic reexploration into the creative genius and life of John Lennon and the Fab Four. (print) [Printz Honor book]—nonfiction

Riggs, Ransom. *Miss Peregrine's Home for Peculiar Children.* <u>The Miss Peregrine Series.</u> **2011.**

Using Victorian-era photographs of bizarre images of children, *Miss Peregrine's Home for Peculiar Children* is a complex novel with a gothic feel. Set during World War II, the story centers on 16-year-old Jacob, who suffers a nervous breakdown after his grandfather's violent death. Taken to a remote island orphanage, he meets other "peculiar children" each with an unusual talent. The sequels, *Hollow City* (2013) and *Library of Souls* (2015), continue in London as Jacob and other young mutants use an ability to move through time to escape horrifying monsters and rescue their beloved Miss Peregrine. Adults with a taste for the "peculiar" should be intrigued with the backstory developed for each vintage photograph. (print, ebook, graphic novel, digital audio from Audible, audio from Listening Library read by Jesse Bernstein)

A major motion picture based on the first title in the series is scheduled for release in 2016.

Rowell, Rainbow. *Eleanor and Park*. 2013.

Two misfits take a chance on first love experiencing all the rapturous and sometimes hilarious, joys and pains that can come with teenage romance. The relationship begins when Park, half-Korean with a loving family, grudgingly offers Eleanor, the eccentric new girl with a neglectful mother and abusive stepfather, a seat on the bus. The alternating narrative allows readers to bond with Park and Eleanor over comic books and music, deal with home life issues, and slowly build a consuming love that both understand may not last. The 1980s pop culture references and oddball love story should appeal to adult readers. (print, ebook, digital audio from Audible, audio from Listening Library read by Rebecca Lowman and Sunil Malhotra) [Printz Honor book]

Sedgwick, Marcus. *Midwinter Blood*. 2013.

"*I always prefer a walk that goes in a circle ... Don't you?*" says a mother to her daughter in one of seven interconnected stories tied to a remote Nordic island. Moving backward through time, the brief tales explore a mystery surrounding the tragic romance of Eric and Merle. Although their relationship changes with each story, the two characters are always recognized by variations on their names. Adults who like David Mitchell's *Cloud Atlas*, Audrey Niffenegger's *The Time Traveler's Wife*, or the cult film *The Wicker Man* should consider this transcendental love story. (print, ebook, digital audio from Audible read by Julian Rhind-Tutt) [Printz Award winner]

Yang, Gene Luen. *American Born Chinese*. 2006.

The first graphic novel to win the Michael L. Printz award, Yang's simple line drawings expand the stories of three nonwhite characters, each dealing with aspects of a Chinese stereotype. The use of myth, bright colors, and humor meld together along with the storyline to express sentiments for accepting who you are and dealing with personal fears and insecurities. This is for fans of Toni Morrison's *The Bluest Eye* and adult readers looking to explore an artistic representation of pervasive cross-cultural themes. (graphic novel, ebook) [Printz Award winner]

Zusak, Markus. *The Book Thief*. 2006.

A sarcastic albeit compassionate Death narrates the moving tale of a young girl who grows up in a small village outside Munich in Nazi Germany. Liesel steals her first book at age nine, carrying on amidst the horrors of World War II. Her thievery touches the lives of her stepparents and others who, directly or subtly, encourage her to continue. Adults who appreciate lyrical writing should savor the elegant syntax in Zusak's haunting historical novel. (print, ebook, digital audio from Audible, audio from Listening Library read by Allan Corduner) [Printz Honor book]

A feature film based on the book was released in 2013.

Things Are Not What They Seem

"Things are not what they seem" is a recurring theme upon which many popular YA (and adult) novels are based. The theme centers around the idea that situations, people, and first impressions can be deceiving or misleading, which is often the author's intent. Novels employing this device can have fantasy, supernatural, or paranormal elements. These tales may utilize elements such as making tricky choices, unreliable narrators, mysteries, kidnappings or imprisonment, and falsehood for revenge. YA stories where "things are not what they seem" should appeal to adult readers because of the mystery and suspense brought on by unexpected events or situations, being unsure the narrator is telling the truth, puzzling out some series of events, the necessity for difficult decisions or compromises, or the use of lies for personal gain. Adults may also read such stories to fulfill a desire to escape, even if only for a little while, from their everyday lives. The following list of suggested titles include four Printz Honor books, three award-winning children's or YA books considered suitable for older readers, three series, plus one other book that should be of interest to adult readers for multiple reasons.

Almond, David. *Skellig*. 1999.
"I found him in the garage on a Sunday afternoon." Young Michael, seeking distraction from worrying about his seriously ill baby sister, discovers a wizened old "man" with wings hidden beneath his jacket. The central question of Almond's haunting novel is who or what Skellig is and does he have a connection to Michael's sister. Adults who like magical realism should think about debating the questions posed by this novel and then decide for themselves. (print, ebook, digital audio from Audible, audio from Listening Library read by David Almond), a British TV movie based on the book was broadcast in 2009. [Printz Honor book]

Bray, Libba. *The Diviners*. The Diviners Series. 2012.
A self-styled flapper with a talent for "reading" objects, Evie O'Neill is ecstatic when her parents give her the bum's rush off to New York City. She plans to get dolled up and explore the city's speakeasies, if she can escape her uncle and his "Museum of the Creepy Crawlies." Yet when Unc' Will is called in to investigate a murder, she can hardly wait to help out, leading to a confrontation with the malevolent "Naughty Jack." The series continues in *Lair of Dreams* (2015) with Evie and other Diviners entering the dreamworld to prevent the spread of a mysterious and deadly sleeping sickness. Adults who enjoy series titles, sassy characters, paranormal horror, and historical fiction should consider reading these richly detailed novels. (print, ebook, digital audio from Audible, audio from Listening Library read by January LaVoy)

Christopher, Lucy. *Stolen*. 2010.
Kidnapped from her parents and subsequently drugged, 16-year-old Gemma wakes to find herself alone in the Australian outback with Ty, her handsome, obsessed, 25-year-old captor. Ty intends to "keep her forever" and although the novel is told in the form of a letter from Gemma to Ty, the implied escape does not detract from the complex psychology of the realistic novel. Descriptions of the beautiful landscape provide subtext and symbolism for an evocative story of captivity and the power of relationships. Adult readers should appreciate the chance to discuss the issues of captive/captor

interactions. (print, ebook, digital audio from Audible, audio from Recorded Books read by Emily Gray) [Printz Honor book]

Gaiman, Neil. *Coraline.* **2002**.

A bored, neglected young girl, looking for adventure in her new home finds more than expected through a magical door in a bricked-up closet. Coraline enjoys the attention of some "other parents" until learning that keeping it means abandoning everything in the real world. The mood is sinister and eerie drawing adult fans of horror and should have them wondering what their own children do when they are not around. Adults may also find the comparisons to Lewis Carroll's *Alice in Wonderland* and *Through the Looking Glass* of interest. (print, ebook, graphic novel, digital audio from Audible, audio from Harper Festival narrated by Neil Gaiman)

Hemphill, Stephanie. *Wicked Girls: A Novel of the Salem Witch Trials.* **2013.**

In a quintessential example of things not being what they seem, falsehoods and petty rivalries brought about tragic results. Hemphill offers a fictional account in lyrical verse of the famous witch trials, presenting the accusations and twisted desires of three young women of Salem. *Wicked Girls* offers a poetic twist on real events adults may have explored through Arthur Miller's *The Crucible* or enjoyed by reading *The Physick Book of Deliverance Dane* by Katherine Howe (print, ebook, audio from Recorded Books read by Stephanie Hemphill)

Lowry, Lois. *The Giver.* **Giver Quartet. 1993.**

Jonas lives in a benevolent world with no war, crime, conflict, or choice where everyone is assigned their job, partner, and children. When he is "selected" for the elite position of "The Receiver," everything begins to change. His training with the aging "Giver" opens Jonas's eyes to the "reality" of his world causing him to confront unexpected emotions and difficult decisions about the future. Lowry's "classic" take of how things are not always as they seem should give adults plenty to ponder. (print, ebook, digital audio from Audible, audio from Listening Library performance by Ron Rifkin)

A major motion picture based on the book was released in 2014.

Wein, Elizabeth. *Code Name Verity.* **2012.**

Verity is a spy sometimes called Queenie, Eva, Katharina, or Julia Beaufort-Stuart, and ultimately a prisoner of the Nazi's. She is also friends with Maddie, the Air Transport Auxiliary pilot who flew the plane that crashed and led to Verity's capture. In exchange for mercy, Verity made a deal to tell all she knows, weaving the tale of their friendship into her daily accounts. The story later switches to Maddie's "accident report" detailing her efforts to save Verity. Adult book groups that favor historical fiction and unreliable narrators should contemplate discussing this one for the many plot twists. (print, ebook, large print, digital audio from Audible, audio from Bolinda Audio read by Morven Christie and Lucy Gaskell) Wein penned a companion novel, *Rose under Fire* (2013), dealing with Rose Justice another auxiliary pilot and friend to Maddie. [Printz Honor book]

Wells, Dan. *I Am Not a Serial Killer. John Cleaver Novels.* **2010.**

Fifteen-year-old John Wayne Cleaver has all the diagnosed traits of a serial killer. He does not really want to kill anyone, so John imposes a strict rule to ensure against it. In *I Am Not a Serial Killer*, he investigates a series of grisly murders in his small Middle America town. More "serial" murders occur in the sequels, *Mr. Monster* (2010) and *I Don't Want to Kill You* (2011), with John investigating, learning more about himself and in defiance of his own rules, developing a relationship with a neighborhood girl. Dark humor, suspense, and a paranormal element lend an additional creep factor to the murders. Adult fans of the Jeff Lindsay's Dexter series or those wishing to "ride along" with a struggling, young sociopath in-the-making should enjoy Wells's series. (print, digital audio from Audible, audio from Tantor Audio read by John Allen Nelson)

Zusak, Markus. *I Am the Messenger*. 2002.
Ed is a loser, a taxi driver with no prospects or real place in the world, until the day he foils a bank robbery and begins receiving playing cards with cryptic clues. Oddly, he understands the clues that lead him on a series of missions to save people he has never met. The mysterious individual and the motivations behind Ed's life-altering adventures are not revealed until the last few pages. Adults should appreciate the novel's fast pace and the surprise revelation, which is sure to spark discussion. (print, ebook, digital audio from Audible, audio from Listening Library read by Marc Aden Gray) [Printz Honor book]

Conclusion: Trends in Mainstream Young Adult Literature

With increases in the field of YA publishing and the annual release of new Printz winners and honor books, adult readers should continue to find plenty of young adult literature to peak their interests. Publisher proliferation in YA audio and emedia production plus the growth of self-publishing will provide numerous titles for review and adult consideration. In addition, as new YA authors come on the scene, adult authors cross over into YA writing territory, and teen titles are pursued by Hollywood for translation into film and television series, there seems to be no end in sight to the influx of young adult books for adults to read, enjoy, and discuss.

References

Print

Booth, Heather. *Serving Teens through Readers' Advisory*. Chicago, IL: American Library Association, 2007.
Cart, Michael. *Young Adult Literature: From Romance to Realism*. Chicago, IL: American Library Association, 2010.
Frolund, Tina. *Genrefied Classics: A Guide to Reading Interests in Classic Literature*. Westport, CT: Libraries Unlimited, 2006.
Herald, Diana Tixier. *Teen Genreflecting 3: A Guide to Reading Interests*. Santa Barbara, CA: Libraries Unlimited, 2011.
Honnold, Rosemary. *The Teen Readers' Advisor*. Chapter 4: "Key Books Honors for YA Literature." *The Printz Award*, p. 35. Chicago, IL: Neal-Schuman Publishers Inc, 2006.
Moyer, Jessica E., Ed. *Integrated Advisory Service: Breaking through the Book Boundary to Better Serve Library Users*. Heather Booth and Nicole J. Suarez. Chapter 9: "Everything Teen: Stories of the Teen Years," pp. 292–293. Santa Barbara, CA: Libraries Unlimited, 2010.

Pearl, Nancy. *Book Crush: For Kids and Teens—Recommended Reading for Every Mood, Moment, and Interest*. Seattle, WA: Sasquatch Books, 2007.

Pearl, Nancy and Sarah Statz Cords. *Now Read This III: A Guide to Mainstream Fiction*. Introduction, pp. xi–xii. Santa Barbara, CA: Libraries Unlimited, 2010.

Saricks, Joyce. *The Readers' Advisory Guide to Genre Fiction*. 2nd edition. Chicago, IL: American Library Association, 2009.

Websites and Online

Forever Young Adult: A Site for YA Readers Who Are a Little Less Y and a Bit More A. http://foreveryoungadult.com/. (Accessed December 5, 2015)

Love YA Lit: YA Lit Isn't Just for Teens. http://loveyalit.com/. (Accessed December 5, 2015)

The Michael L. Printz Award Policies and Procedures. Young Adult Library Services Association, American Library Association. http://www.ala.org/yalsa/booklistsawards/bookawards/printzaward/aboutprintz/criteria. (Accessed December 5, 2015)

Mostly YA Lit: Young Adult Reviews from a Teenager Trapped in an Adult's Body. http://www.mostlyyalit.com/. (Accessed December 5, 2015)

Teenreads. The Book Report Network. http://www.teenreads.com/. (Accessed December 5, 2015)

YALSA Book and Media Awards and Lists for Libraries. Young Adult Library Services Association, American Library Association. http://www.ala.org/yalsa/booklistsawards/booklists/. (Accessed December 5, 2015)

13
Nonfiction

Mary Wepking

Introduction to the Genre

Definition

Nonfiction is usually classified in two main divisions: informational books and biographies (including autobiographies and memoirs). Tomlinson and Lynch-Brown (2007) state that nonfiction differs from fiction primarily in its aim. "[T]he emphasis of nonfiction is documented facts about the natural or social world. Its primary purpose is to inform. In contrast, the content of fictional literature is largely, if not wholly, a product of the imagination, and its purpose is to entertain" (p. 100). Young Adult (YA) nonfiction has come a long way since youth collections were filled with series books in library bindings, though, and much of today's YA nonfiction not only informs, but also entertains.

In decades past, a handful of publishers dominated the stacks, with informational and instructional books on every topic from the supernatural to social issues to biographies and history. But today the diversity of subjects covered, quality of writing, and perhaps most notably, the emergence of richly illustrated nonfiction have made the young adult nonfiction stacks a rich source for recreational reading for all ages.

Librarians should expect that the number and quality of YA nonfiction titles will continue to grow, in part due to the widespread adoption of CCSS across the country. "Common Core State Standards mandate that, by fourth grade, students will read a balanced ratio of fifty percent fiction and fifty percent nonfiction for school reading assignments. As students age, this ratio gradually begins to favor nonfiction until, by twelfth grade, they will be expected to read seventy percent nonfiction and thirty percent fiction" (Hunt). CCSS also emphasizes the need for teachers to consider text complexity when connecting young readers and these nonfiction texts. This may result in more teens finding their recreational reading in the adult collection, but it may also elevate the sophistication and literary quality of books published as young adult nonfiction. The net result of this trend is, of course, more crossover in both directions—teens reading adult materials and adults finding rewarding and enjoyable materials in the young adult collection.

Appeals

While it may be easy to classify nonfiction by subject (science, history, art, etc.), in most collections that is already done using the library's classification system. If our aim is to locate the gems in the YA nonfiction collection that will be particularly appealing to adult readers, it may be more useful to think in terms of other appeal factors or "doorways" (Pearl). Adult readers who enjoy character-driven fiction might find some of the biographies in the young adult section of the library particularly appealing. Likewise, those who enjoy story or plot-driven work might enjoy the page-turning narrative nonfiction of Steve Sheinkin or Jim Murphy. For those adult readers who want good writing accompanied by outstanding illustrations and photographs, some of the new visually rich nonfiction in the YA section is worth recommending and featuring in crossover displays. We will use these three categories to take a look at a few dozen nonfiction young adult titles that can easily be recommended to your adult readers.

- Character-driven nonfiction. Whether biography, memoir, or history some nonfiction selections invite readers to connect with a character. With rich detail and sometimes dialogue, writers are able to create vivid and memorable characters. Research provides accuracy, but both pacing and descriptive language can bring the subject/character of a nonfiction work to life.

- Narrative nonfiction. This subcategory has voice, and like good fiction, may also be character-driven. Primarily, narrative nonfiction, whether memoir, history, or adventure, is the type of book that the reader cannot put down. Authors of narrative nonfiction are masterful at creating mood and even suspense, using vivid language, while often giving their readers memorable scenes and imagery. They may not tell a tale entirely chronologically, instead building interest through foreshadowing or flashback. The classic adult text that best represents narrative nonfiction may be Truman Capote's *In Cold Blood*, a spellbinding work of nonfiction that is as well written and plot-driven as some of the best American fiction of the twentieth century. Other notable adult examples include Jon Krakauer's *Into Thin Air*, or some of the work of Erik Larson (*Isaac's Storm*, *Devil in the White City*, etc.). You will find equally readable narrative nonfiction in the young adult collection, with notable examples included in this chapter.

- Illustrated nonfiction. In our multimedia/digital world, both adults and young adults have come to rely on images, sound, and other communication means to convey information, not merely relying on text alone. In the world of young adult literature, an entire visually rich body of nonfiction literature has emerged, with authors such as Susan Campbell Bartoletti, Phillip Hoose, Jim Murphy, Candace Fleming, and others enhancing their research and text with photographs and other images to help convey information. Adult readers seeking an overview of a topic will find illustrated works in YA nonfiction a good fit. Some of the best authors and works are suggested next.

Working with Readers

There are three distinct approaches to guiding adults to teen nonfiction. The first is in the realm of reference work, guiding adults who are seeking specific information or doing research on a topic to both the adult and YA nonfiction stacks. The other two approaches to readers' advisory work for nonfiction should both be employed with adult recreational readers—subject-oriented and genre-matched.

While subject-oriented readers' advisory (RA) might seem like another word for reference work in this area, we are specifically targeting recreational readers, so finding answers to questions or pursuing research is not the motivation to match a reader with a suitable nonfiction work on a specific subject. Rather, when engaging in an RA interview that is focused on a subject, do not forget the many well-written and illustrated nonfiction works in the YA section. Brief but well-researched books, frequently rich with images and photographs, will offer welcome points of view and lively pacing for readers of science, history, the arts, and every other topic under the sun. Some works that should not be overlooked by interested adult readers include Linas Alsenas's *Gay America*, sports writing of Sue Macy, Candace Fleming's biographies, and art books by Jan Greenberg and Sandra Jordan.

Genre-matched RA plays on the doorways of appeal factors of fiction, but expands potential matches to the young adult nonfiction section of the library. If the reader enjoys historical fiction, for example, leading them to nonfiction works on history is a natural fit. Find readable, narrative nonfiction (Steve Sheinkin's *Notorious Benedict Arnold*), illustrated works (Susan Campbell Bartoletti's *They Call Themselves the KKK*), or character-driven works (Deborah Heiligman's *Charles and Emma: Darwin's Leap of Faith*) to expand readers' horizons, while giving them the historical setting and character they are looking for in their recreational reading. Our goal, of course, is not to convert fiction readers to nonfiction readers, but rather to help adults find the gems hiding in the young adult nonfiction collection that will speak to their tastes and interests. If their regular adult fiction reading includes novels with action and suspense, there may be narrative nonfiction choices in the YA collection that might be good choices. Sheinkin's illustrated works come to mind, as do the works of Sally M. Walker. Readers of poetry could also be pointed to YA nonfiction where they will find Stephanie Hemphill's unique verse biography of Sylvia Plath and Naomi Shihab Nye's readable but powerful poems and other crossover works. Readers who love intimate, first-person novels will find satisfaction in some YA biographies and memoirs, and also in well-written narrative nonfiction in which voice, character, and language will create a reading experience not unlike a favorite novel.

Tools and Resources

There is a wide range of resources available to librarians who seek to keep abreast of the best nonfiction young adult materials. Listed next are some of these tools.

- *Reality Rules* (2008) and *Reality Rules II* (2012) both by Elizabeth Fraser, are part of the Genreflecting Advisory series published by

Libraries Unlimited. These are good resources for those with little knowledge of important titles. Although some of the materials included here are more appropriate for upper elementary age readers, there is a good selection of YA materials as well, and the organization by subgenre (true crime, biography and autobiography, and a wide range of subjects) makes these handbooks particularly helpful in readers advisory.

- ***Booklist's 1000 best young adult books since 2000*** (2014) edited by Gillian Engberg and Ian Chipman and published by ALA, is a must-have to support crossover young adult readers advisory in all categories. There is a full section devoted to nonfiction that begins with Engberg's "One-Fifth of the Pie and Growing," a description of YA nonfiction today. Here you will find 200 nonfiction titles published for young adults between 2000 and 2013, in a list that is usefully categorized and fully annotated. Grade level recommendations are included for each title, helping librarians sort the books for young readers from those recommended for high school readers, and helping to identify crossover reads with ease.

- Check the website for the **YALSA Award for Excellence in Nonfiction for Young Adults** (http://www.ala.org/yalsa/nonfiction), which lists not only the winners and finalists for each year since the award was first given in 2010, but also provides the current nomination list. Beyond review journals, this is your go-to source for the current and highly recommended young adult nonfiction.

- Many review journals honor or list top nonfiction materials published each year. One of these is **School Library Journal**, which compiles best-of-the-year lists in many categories, including nonfiction. *VOYA* publishes an annual Nonfiction Honor List, and *Horn Book* announces the prestigious Boston Globe-Horn Book Award for Excellence in Children's Literature, with a separate nonfiction category each spring. Other standard review sources such as *Publishers Weekly*, *Booklist* and more may include best-of lists as well. Read these with an eye toward crossover reading for adults in your library.

Collection Development

Finding young adult nonfiction that will appeal to adult readers requires additional effort by library staff. Keep a close eye on the Youth Media Award winner presented at ALA Midwinter in January of each year. A new award specifically for Young Adult Nonfiction was launched in 2010, and many of these materials might appeal to your adult patrons. Other ALA awards (Printz, Morris) and honors beyond the association (National Book Award for Young People's Literature, Boston Globe Horn Book, and more) might also be given to nonfiction works with crossover appeal.

It is important to recognize that the concept of "crossover" is bidirectional, and that the barrier between YA and adult collections should be porous, with adult readers welcomed into the YA section just as teens are encouraged to find materials of interest in the adult collection, both in fiction and nonfiction.

The Literature

Character-Driven Nonfiction

If you have patrons who enter their books through that character "doorway," seeking to connect or identify with the characters they meet while reading, they may find the believable and relatable characters they are looking for in the young adult nonfiction collection. Here are some of the best selections in recent character-driven YA nonfiction—well researched and information rich, but also vivid and authentic:

Colman, Penny. *Elizabeth Cady Stanton and Susan B. Anthony: A Friendship That Changed the World.* **2011.**

Women's rights and the suffrage movement are thoroughly explored in this joint biography of the leaders of the movement, although the personal lives of Elizabeth Cady Stanton and Susan B. Anthony make this book a good choice for readers looking for well-drawn and relatable characters. Colman treats her subjects chronologically and enlivens the narrative with ample quotes and anecdotes that bring these women to life. Despite their differences in background and diverse life, readers will enjoy this story of a friendship that changed the course of history. (print, ebook)

Fleming, Candace and Ray Fenwick. *The Great and Only Barnum: The Tremendous, Stupendous Life of Showman P.T. Barnum.* **2011.**

This illustrated biography of the fascinating showman P. T. Barnum provides readers with an engaging overview of his life and insight into early twentieth-century American life. Touching on issues of class, race, disability, and character, this book goes beyond the life and exploits of Barnum and offers readers a look at everyday life and amusements. The archival images, clever layout, and visual design all contribute to the success of Fleming's work, one of many nonfiction and biographical books written by this author in recent years. (print, audiobook)

Greenberg, Jan and Sandra Jordan. *Andy Warhol: Prince of Pop.* **2004.**

Unlike the teen audience for whom this book is aimed, adult readers of this brief chronological biography of Andy Warhol may recall his impact on pop culture of the 1950s and 1960s. Readers will be impressed with the honesty in Greenberg and Jordan's treatment of the artist. The book's attractive design, inset of color images of the artist's work, timeline, and bibliography all add substance to this brief biography. Steer interested readers to this pair of authors' youth materials on other artists, too, including Jackson Pollock, Chuck Close, and Vincent Van Gogh. (print)

Heiligman, Deborah. *Charles and Emma: The Darwin's Leap of Faith.* **2009.**

Today's young adult literature is characterized by genre blending, and this intimate joint biography is a perfect example. Readers who enjoy romance, history, science, and even humor will be drawn in by Heiligman's exquisite writing that brings Darwin and his wife Emma Wedgwood to life. Beginning with Charles' scientific reasoning that pointed him toward marriage (he created a list of the pros and cons of marriage, listing "children" on both sides of the chart) and his logical choice of his first cousin Emma to be his wife, readers are treated to an unlikely and very memorable love story. (print, ebook, audiobook)

Hemphill, Stephanie. *Your Own, Sylvia: A Verse Portrait of Sylvia Plath.* **2007.**

An ambitious and remarkably creative work, Hemphill tells the life of Sylvia Plath through original poems composed in a style that mimics Plath's. Although the rich language of the poetry, written in the voices of the poet, her family, teachers and friends, is very effective in giving readers a picture of the poet's short life, Hemphill adds ample footnote to clarify and fill in the details. While the author describes this book as "a work of fiction," her efforts to capture the poet's voice and accurate chronology of her life, all written in poems, will have libraries shelving it in the Dewey 800's. (print, ebook, audiobook)

Hoose, Phillip. *Claudette Colvin: Twice toward Justice.* **2009.**

Hoose, an author of many notable nonfiction titles for young readers, won the National Book Award for Young People's Literature in 2009 for this accessible biography of a little-known civil rights figure. Months before Rosa Parks famously refused to give up her seat on a Montgomery, Alabama, bus to a white passenger, 15-year-old Claudette Colvin did the same. But 15-year-old, unmarried and pregnant Claudette was not the individual the movement needed to bring about change in the segregated South. Her story was lost to history until Hoose, through meticulous research and interviews with Claudette, brought it to life in this illustrated, engaging biography. (print, ebook, audiobook)

Jiang, Ji-li. *Red Scarf Girl: A Memoir of the Cultural Revolution.* **1997.**

Throughout history, there have been cases of children being used for political gain, whether as child soldiers, government supporters or informants (see Hitler Youth below). Ji-li Jiang's memoir of her youth in China, coming-of-age during the Cultural Revolution of Mao Zedong in the 1960s, is an intimate, honest, and authentic story of children turned against their parents and family by a government that turned their zeal into power. Elegantly written with memorable scenes and characters throughout, this is a must-read for young people and adults alike. (print, ebook, audiobook)

McClafferty, Carla Killough. *Something Out of Nothing: Marie Curie and Radium.* **2006.**

Youth biographies in the past could be didactic portraits of heroes and saints, but in the twenty-first century, a more honest approach to history may be found in the YA section of the library. A good example is Carla McClafferty's portrait of Marie Curie. Her life was one of "firsts": first woman in France to earn a PhD, first woman to win a Nobel Prize and first Pole to do so, first woman to teach at the Sorbonne, and so on. Although this biography is brief, McClafferty paints a real picture of this remarkable woman—her many accomplishments as well as her personal and maternal shortcomings. (print)

Myers, Walter Dean. *The Greatest: Muhammad Ali.* **2001.**

This is a brief biography, indeed, but one told by a master of young adult literature and whose work should be introduced to interested adult readers. Myers, who passed away in 2014, was the author of over 100 books for children and teens, ranging from picture books to fiction on mature themes of war and violence. He excelled in nonfiction writing, too, and this biography of Muhammad Ali is a fine example. As is made clear by the book's title, Myers chooses to focus not on Ali's personal life and challenges, but to explore what made him The Greatest: the author looks at Ali as "an American, as a fighter, as a seeker of justice, as someone willing to stand up against the odds ..." (xi). Not comprehensive, but heartfelt, this is a brief, heavily illustrated look at one of Myers' heroes. Fans of Myers should also be pointed to his biography of another icon of the era in *Malcolm X: By Any Means Necessary*. (print, audiobook)

Partridge, Elizabeth. *This Land Was Made for You and Me: The Life and Songs of Woody Guthrie.* **2002.**

Partridge won a Printz Honor for her photo biography of John Lennon, but her work on Woody Guthrie is also to be recommended to adult readers. Organized chronologically from his birth, detailing his tragedy-filled early life and the social and political world in which he lived, all of which inspired his songs, this is a richly illustrated biography for readers from teens on up. The author relied on Guthrie's own writings and the Woody Guthrie Foundation and Archives, plus interviews with his children, with friend and folk legend Pete Seeger, and with many others to create an intimate portrait of one of America's most important singers and songwriters. (print)

Sheinkin, Steve. *The Notorious Benedict Arnold: A True Story of Adventure, Heroism & Treachery.* **2011.**

This award-winning book (YALSA Award for Excellence in Nonfiction 2012 and Boston Globe-Horn Book Award for Nonfiction 2011) could just as easily be categorized as narrative nonfiction since the reading experience equals the pacing and suspense of any adventure or action novel. Sheinkin's debut work, this well-written and carefully researched book offers readers, young and older, an intimate look at one of America's first heroes and villains. Arnold's dual nature brings to mind the scoundrel featured in today's headlines. This is a fast read that is both informative and exciting. (print, ebook, audiobook)

Narrative Nonfiction

This is the nonfiction "page-turner"—the readable, fast-paced book that often surprises recreational readers of fiction. The following selection includes a number of authors who have written multiple works in this subcategory, so keeping these authors on your radar will help you guide your adult readers through the YA stacks. Also, some of these materials could just as easily be categorized as illustrated nonfiction (Marrin, Fleischman, Murphy and Aronson) but are included here since it is their compelling storytelling that make them particularly appealing to adult readers.

Aronson, Marc and Marina Tamar Budhos. *Sugar Changed the World: A Story of Magic, Spice, Slavery, Freedom, and Science.* **2010.**

Marc Aronson is a prolific author of nonfiction for young readers and has produced work on topics ranging from biography to history to science. Adults who have gobbled up the works of today's food writers (Mark Kurlansky, Michael Pollan, etc.) will find Aronson's recent book on the subject of sugar well worth their time. With coauthor Budhos, the history of this important commodity is traced, but more intriguingly, its impact on social and political movements—commerce and trade to slavery and revolution—is explored. The writing is captivating, and the illustrations and photos further the reader's understanding of how sugar changed the world. (print)

Capuzzo, Michael. *Close to Shore: The Terrifying Shark Attacks of 1916.* **2003.**

Popular adult works have occasionally been adapted and released in young adult editions, and that is the case with Capuzzo's exciting book *Close to Shore.* With a new subtitle and frightening cover image (an extreme close up of a shark's razor-sharp teeth), this edition can be offered to adult readers who want a fast-paced, true story enhanced by photos and images not included in the original. Capuzzo's writing is spot-on for this gruesome tale of a rogue great white shark that killed four victims on the New Jersey shore in one month, just at a time when rail travel made the beach accessible to swarms of city dwellers. Suspense is sustained as readers follow the action through the eyes of terrified citizens and ultimately learn the fate of the man-eating shark. (print, audiobook)

Fleischman, John. *Phineas Gage: A Gruesome but True Story about Brain Science.* **2004.**

Although written for quite a young audience (recommended for grades 6 to 10 by most reviews), this fascinating story might have appeal for adults interested in science, anatomy, and history. Phineas Gage was a railroad worker who suffered a disastrous accident when a large iron rod was shot through his skull, entering at his cheekbone and exiting at the top of his head. Amazingly, he was not killed, and in fact, was conscious, speaking and even joking immediately following the accident. What science writer Fleischman explores in this book, though, is not specifically Mr. Gage, but how this accident brought about knowledge of the brain. In fact, libraries classify the book in the 600's with anatomy books, not in history or biography. Plenty of illustrations and excellent pacing enhance this quick read. (print, ebook, audiobook)

Gantos, Jack. *A Hole in My Life.* **2001.**

Newbery Award-winning children's book author Jack Gantos (*Rotten Ralph, Joey Pigza*) reveals a regrettable moment in his early life—his arrest for drug running and sales when he was in his early twenties—in this searing and brutally honest memoir. In a frank and honest narrative, Gantos details his time in Barbados, his agreement to help run a ship loaded with hashish to New York, his arrest, trial, and terrifying time in federal prison. Gantos is looking for inspiration to become a writer, and he found it in this misadventure. The audiobook is not to be missed since it is read by the author, adding authenticity to an already stark tale. (print, ebook, audiobook)

Kuklin, Susan. *No Choirboy: Murder, Violence, and Teenagers on Death Row.* **2008.**

Kulkin interviews four young men on death row who were found guilty of murders while still in their teens. Their stories are told in the first person, adding authenticity and emotion to each tale of trouble and regret. The author also interviewed the family of a victim of violent crime and includes important commentary by noted attorney Bryan Stevenson who has devoted his career to working with inmates on death row. Readers will find a harsh look at the criminal justice and penal systems in our country, especially in terms of the inherent social, class, and race issues that put so many young people of color behind bars. (print, ebook, audiobook)

Marrin, Albert. *Flesh and Blood So Cheap: The Triangle Fire and Its Legacy.* **2011.**

Honored as a National Book Award finalist, this powerful book combines excellent research, compelling writing, and archival photos to tell the tragic

story of the 1911 fire that killed nearly 150 workers. Marrin also delves into living and working conditions of immigrants at the turn of the last century, the fire's impact on worker's rights, and even draws comparisons to the issue of sweatshop labor today.
(print, ebook, audiobook)

Murphy, Jim. *An American Plague: The True and Terrifying Story of the Yellow Fever Epidemic of 1793.* **2003.**

Library copies of this book are typically labeled with a foil sticker to demonstrate its acclaim—winner of the Sibert Award for nonfiction, plus a finalist for both the Newbery and National Book Award. Murphy's history of the 1793 yellow fever epidemic that devastated Philadelphia is a must-read for those interested in medicine, science, social history. Noted author of dozens of books for young readers, this book may be his best work—clearly written, thoroughly researched, engaging, and ultimately thought provoking even today, there is no known cure for yellow fever. (print, audiobook)

Nelson, Pete. *Left for Dead: A Young Man's Search for Justice for the USS Indianapolis.* **2002.**

A story within a story, this is a book for all ages. The *USS Indianapolis* went down in a confrontation with a Japanese submarine in 1945, and the over 800 crew members were adrift in the Pacific for over four days, where shark attacks and death resulted in the loss of all but 317. The captain of the ship was court martialed. More than 50 years after the disaster, a middle school student, Hunter Scott (who also penned the preface to this book) became captivated by the story and through diligent research, plus contact with elderly survivors, righted a wrong by having the captain posthumously exonerated. Nelson ably tells both stories of the loss of the ship and the boy's fight for justice. (print)

Runyon, Brent. *The Burn Journals.* **2004.**

After a particularly bad day at school, which was typical of the many bad days he has endured in his short life, 14-year-old Brent Runyon heads to the bathroom in his house. He puts on his bathrobe and soaks it in gasoline, steps in the shower, and lights a match. Thus begins Brent's journey from his attempted suicide to his long and arduous recovery. The tale is told simply and clearly, with Brent's transformation from suicidal teen to repentant son, brother, and friend both touching and real. Suitable for mature teens, it is also a powerful read for adults who might recall their teen years when small trials seemed to make life unbearable. Ultimately hopeful and upbeat, this is an unforgettable memoir of healing, both physical and emotional. (print, ebook, audiobook)

Sheinkin, Steve. *Bomb: The Race to Build and Steal the World's Most Dangerous Weapon.* **2012.**

The only author to appear twice in this brief list of YA nonfiction suitable for adult readers, Sheinkin gives us an exciting narrative about a pivotal moment in history. He tells his story from the points of view of various players in the race to build the atomic bomb during World War II. From Oppenheimer to a courageous Norwegian resistance fighter to a spy engaged in nefarious work within the United States, the author keeps retelling this story with more detail, richness, and character development than ever before. Visually appealing, and engagingly written, this is a book to hand to reluctant readers, young and old. (print, ebook, audiobook)

Illustrated Nonfiction

A picture is worth a thousand words, which saves a lot of shelf space in contemporary young adult nonfiction collections. These illustrated texts have appeal to young adult readers as well as adults who will find the photos in *Hitler Youth*, the artwork in *A Wreath for Emmett Till*, and the archival images in *Gay America* both informative and emotionally moving. The images in a well-illustrated work do more than supplement the text—they extend a reader's knowledge and understanding of the subject. Extending well beyond history and how-to, other subjects are well served by illustrated texts: art, photography, film, fashion, science, food, sports, crafts, and many more topics throughout the nonfiction collection. Keep in mind, though, that today's digital libraries and online resources might be your best choice in locating visually rich nonfiction materials by subject.

Here are a few YA authors and titles to keep in mind when guiding adults toward illustrated materials in your young adult stacks.

Alsenas, Linas. *Gay America: Struggle for Equality.* 2008.

The first of its kind for young readers, this book gives readers both a written and visual account of the history, treatment, and contributions of gay Americans. As with most nonfiction found in the young adult collection, this is not a comprehensive treatment of the subject, but a well-written narrative, supported by color and black and white images throughout. Told chronologically through individual stories and vignettes, the book is informative and clear. It will lead both teen and adult readers to seek out more information on a number of topics and individuals, and the comprehensive list of resources will point them in the right direction. (print)

Armstrong, Jennifer. *Shipwreck at the Bottom of the World: The Extraordinary True Story of Shackleton and the Endurance.* 1998.

The adventure story in fiction is engaging, but in nonfiction, it is even better. Armstrong tells the story of the British expedition to cross Antarctica, led by Ernest Shackleton. Between 1914 and 1916, he and 27 men found themselves trapped in an icebound ship, then stranded when the ship was destroyed. They camped and somehow survived, hiking and sailing great distances in brutal conditions, until the ultimate rescue of every last man nearly two years after the start of their journey. The book is greatly enhanced by the inclusion of maps as well as archival photos taken by Frank Hurley, the expedition's photographer. (print, audiobook)

Bausum, Ann. *With Courage and Cloth: Winning the Fight for a Woman's Right to Vote.* 2004.

Bausum, another notable author of YA nonfiction with potential appeal to adult audiences, tells the story of the women's suffrage movement through sketches and anecdotes related to both major players and lesser-known voices advocating for the cause. She details the factions that emerged, which split the efforts of the women. She uses the imagery of cloth throughout—these women used their skills with needle and thread to create banners, sashes, and signs, many with the signature purple and gold colors that also embellish this visually rich book. A brief overview, to be sure, but one that looks at the era through both story and character. (print, audiobook)

Blumenthal, Karen. *Bootleg: Murder, Moonshine, and the Lawless Years of Prohibition.* **2011.**

Richly illustrated with archival photos of the era, Blumenthal's brief book on Prohibition intelligently covers the period in retrospect. Acknowledging that the campaign for a dry America had child welfare and shared prosperity as its aims, she details how this failed experiment led to one of the most lawless periods in U.S. history. Exceptional indexing and source notes allow for browsing too. (print, ebook)

Campbell Bartoletti, Susan. *Hitler Youth: Growing Up in Hitler's Shadow.* **2005.**

This powerful book is as much a history as a collective biography, telling the individual tales of a dozen German children who were members of Hitler Youth, excluded from the group, or resistant to the Third Reich. Opening pages feature photos of each child (as available), and most readers will refer back to these pages often as they learn each story. Campbell Bartoletti is a master of this new form (visually rich, masterfully written nonfiction for young audiences), and this book may be her highest achievement. (print, audiobook)

Freedman, Russell. *Kids at Work: Lewis Hine and the Crusade against Child Labor.* **1994.**

Lewis Hine's photographs of child labor, taken between 1908 and 1918, shocked the world. Prolific author Freedman selects from these images to enhance his biographical portrait of Hine. Although not a comprehensive treatment of the photographer's life by any means, this volume is to be recommended to adults interested in photography, history, and social causes. (print)

Macy, Sue. *Wheels of Change: How Women Rode the Bicycle to Freedom (With a Few Flat Tires Along the Way).* **2011.**

Sue Macy is well known for her books on sports and athletes, especially related to women (*A Whole New Ball Game: The Story of the All-American Girls Professional Baseball League*), but in this book, she stretches beyond athletics to make connections to social history. By juxtaposing the invention and growth in popularity of the bicycle with women's suffrage, women's rights, and a general movement toward more freedom for women, she explores two related topics of high interest to readers, young and old. Well written with outstanding illustration, this one is highly recommended. (print, audiobook)

Walker, Sally M. *Blizzard of Glass: The Halifax Explosion of 1917.* **2011.**

A common theme in readable, narrative nonfiction for young people is disasters and catastrophes, and here is a good example. As with most YA nonfiction, it is a very personal account, told through the experiences of children and families affected. *Blizzard of Glass* tells the story of the 1917 collision of a ship carrying explosives and one carrying medical supplies and the resulting explosion that kills over 2,000 people in and around Halifax, Nova Scotia. With archival images, the story is brought to life visually and by its character-driven narration. (print, ebook, audiobook)

Weitzman, David. *Skywalkers: Mohawk Ironworkers Build the City.* **2010.**

Although perhaps not a high-interest read for most teens, Weitzman's account of the 100+-year-old tradition of Mohawk ironworkers is told through engaging text and amazing photos of both triumph and disaster. Readers interested in history, engineering, architecture, American and Canadian Indians, and learning the truth behind the myth of the Mohawk's innate skill and fearlessness in walking the steel beams of skyscrapers will find reward in this outstanding, short book. (print, ebook)

Zimmerman, Dwight Jon. *Saga of the Sioux: An Adaptation from Dee Brown's Bury My Heart at Wounded Knee.* **2011.**

For all those adult readers who read *Bury My Heart at Wounded Knee* years ago, invite them to revisit that classic in this illustrated young adult remake. Limited to the conflict with the Sioux and told through that tribe's point of view, Zimmerman remains true to Brown's message. Additional insight into characters, both Indian and "immigrant," is enhanced through archival images and individual histories. (print, ebook)

Conclusion: Trends in Young Adult Nonfiction

Changes to education standards, most notably CCSS, will most likely spur publishers to continue the trend of producing good, readable, and visually appealing nonfiction for young audiences. In order to connect interested adult readers to these hidden gems in the YA stacks, readers' advisory librarians will want to keep their eyes on YALSA's Nonfiction Award winners each year and scan book review sources such as VOYA and the School Library Journal for suitable new materials to serve a crossover audience. At minimum, an adult reader seeking an overview of a topic (prohibition, Charles Darwin, brain science) may be steered to online or reference sources, but librarians may be missing an opportunity to provide these readers with enjoyable and informative materials found in YA nonfiction.

References

Hunt, Jonathan. "The Amorphous Genre." *Horn Book Magazine* 89(3), 2013: 31–34.

Sullivan, Michael. *Serving Boys through Readers' Advisory*. ALA Readers' Advisory Series. Chicago, IL: American Library Association, 2010.

Tomlinson, Carl M. and Carol Lynch-Brown. *Essentials of Young Adult Literature*. Boston, MA: Pearson, 2007.

14
Graphic Novels

Anna Grace Mickelsen

Introduction to the Genre

Definition

Graphic novels, comics, and manga are narratives conveyed with the aid of sequential illustration. As such, this medium is not a genre but a format that encompasses a wide range of genres—everything from fantasy and romance to nonfiction and history. In the best examples of the format, words and images work seamlessly together to drive the story. *Graphic novel* is the industry term used to describe a book-length bound item and is not strictly limited to fiction or to stand-alone works. Many of the items labeled "graphic novel" on library shelves are collections of previously released single comic issues published in trade paperback form. Graphic works produced in the United States are typically read from front to back, left to right, and top to bottom. Manga, comics, and graphic novels produced in Japan are read from right to left and back to front.

The graphic novel became popular and accepted as a viable publication format in the 1980s. It grew out of developments in long-form comics as well as an active underground movement that formed in response to the artistic restrictions of the Comics Code Authority.[1] In the 1990s, graphic novels took their place as a legitimate form of literary expression. From the 2000s to the present, the graphic novel has been increasingly accepted in the mainstream, extending its reach into libraries and classrooms and even being utilized as a teaching tool through which all types of information (e.g., the *9/11 Commission Report*, *The Cartoon Introduction to Economics*) can be conveyed. The Genreflecting advisory guide *Graphic Novels: A Genre Guide to Comic Books, Manga, and More* divides the format into several categories: superhero, action and adventure, science fiction, fantasy, crime and mysteries, horror, contemporary life, which includes romance and coming-of-age, humor, and nonfiction. These categories indicate the versatility and diversity of the format.

Appeals

Because graphic novels, comics, and manga are formats that include all genres, they will appeal to readers of all ages and interests. Although they have sometimes been perceived as a format for "kids," adult audiences comprise a large part of the market for graphic works.

The primary appeal factor of the format is the increased accessibility of the story offered by the addition of supporting images. Graphic works' unique combination of words and images can aid the development of critical skills and motivate otherwise reluctant readers (e.g., adult learners) to read. A recent study has shown that graphic novel readers may even retain information better than readers of traditional texts.[2]

In addition to accessibility offered by the addition of illustrations, adult readers of graphic works enjoy their participatory format—the graphic novel or manga reader is responsible for linking the story between panels, making connections, and driving the narrative forward. In this way, readers actively work to decode the text and the subtext. Some adult readers may also enjoy the serial aspect of many graphic works.

Working with Readers

Classic titles in the format include *Maus, Persepolis, American Splendor, Love and Rockets, Watchmen, The Sandman, Batman: The Dark Knight Returns, Fun Home, Sailor Moon*, and *Dragon Ball*. Many of these titles are currently used in classroom curricula to enhance students' understanding of different issues. *Maus*, in which Art Spiegelman depicts his father's life during the Holocaust, is often used to make the subject more relatable—something at which graphic works excel. Current adult readers of library-owned graphic works may be people who read comics as children and continue to consume the format, or patrons who are interested in approaching conventional stories from new angles. However, it is also very likely that an adult library patron will be new to the format. Teen graphic novels are an ideal place for some adults to start reading graphic works—once they are convinced that they should.

Possible barriers to entry include patrons saying they "don't know how" to read graphic texts and adults feeling alienated by the covers of teen graphic novels and manga. Some adults may have tried a comic or graphic novel in the past and abandoned the medium because it was too unusual or difficult for them to engage with—or they may never have read comics at all. Some patrons may believe that graphic novels are only superhero stories. A librarian who understands the huge diversity of subject and style afforded by the medium can connect these readers to graphic works that suit their interests.

Because graphic novels, comics, and manga encompass such a wide range of genres, librarians working with young adult crossover titles have a few options. They can ask patrons what type of adult graphic novels they typically read, or they can ask what non-graphic items they typically read. If the patron is a seasoned reader of adult graphic novels, they will likely be interested in teen titles in familiar genres. Some adult patrons who are completely unfamiliar with graphic novels may find teen titles more accessible than adult works, even more so if they are already accustomed to reading and enjoying young adult material.

Stand-alone works are often less intimidating for newcomers than the long series that tend to proliferate in the format. Graphic memoirs and graphic depictions of historical events may provide an access point for patrons who are not traditional fiction readers. Adult readers may be wary of starting with the manga format, which (with its unusual format and tendency toward long series) can be quite daunting, but should be encouraged to try whatever sparks their interest.

Adaptations of other works are one of the easiest ways to encourage readers to try reading a graphic novel. The basic outlines of the story may already be familiar to the patron—either because they read the source material, viewed it as a movie or television show, or simply heard about it as part of general cultural knowledge—giving them an instant access point to the graphic work. Examples of recent graphic adaptations for a teen audience with potential for adult appeal include *Romeo & Juliet*, *A Wrinkle in Time*, *Adventure Time*, *Fahrenheit 451*, and *The Infernal Devices*.

Because of the nature of the format and its fluidity (particularly with regard to traditional superhero characters) between age ranges, adult graphic novel readers may already be familiar with many of the titles intended for a younger audience. The librarian's responsibility for these readers is to keep up with recently published young adult works and find their adult analogues.

To quickly evaluate a graphic novel or manga item for reader's advisory purposes, skim the book and read the back cover; study the first few pages for setting, style, and time period; evaluate character design and colors used by the illustrator; and consider the relationship between words and images. The recently published series *Critical Survey of Graphic Novels* (2013) includes detailed synopses and interpretations of manga, superhero comics, and independent and underground works.

Tools and Resources

Many of the most useful resources available to librarians are located online or in review sources as described next in the section on collection development. Listed here are some particularly useful resources:

Diamond Comics Bookshelf. http://www.diamondbookshelf.com/Home/1/1/20/163. Diamond Comics is a large distributor of comics, graphic novels, and paraphernalia; its website includes reviews, articles, bestseller lists, and core collection lists by age group.

Graphic Novel Reporter. The Book Report Network. http://www.graphicnovelreporter.com/. Website featuring reviews, interviews, news, and other information about graphic novels. The site publishes yearly "Core Lists" of children's, teen, and adult graphic novels and manga recommended for inclusion in library and bookstore collections.

"Great Graphic Novels for Teens." Young Adult Library Services Association. http://www.ala.org/yalsa/great-graphic-novels. The YALSA division of the American Library Association generates a yearly list of recommended graphic novels and illustrated nonfiction for ages 12–18.

Librarians who wish to learn more about the process of interpreting and creating comics can investigate these works by Scott McCloud, which should be available in most large public libraries:

McCloud, Scott. *Understanding Comics: The Invisible Art*. New York: HarperPerennial, 1994.

McCloud, Scott. *Reinventing Comics: How Imagination and Technology Are Revolutionizing an Art Form*. New York: Perennial, 2000.
McCloud, Scott. *Making Comics: Storytelling Secrets of Comics, Manga and Graphic Novels*. New York: Harper, 2006.

No Flying, No Tights. Ed. Robin Brenner. http://noflyingnotights.com/. A well-regarded graphic novel and manga review website run by librarians.

Panels. Riot New Media. http://panels.net/. Website that provides readers' advisory (see the "Comics Recommendation Engine," "Matchmaker," and "Read Harder" features), critical articles, primers on comics and comic characters, and other content.

Collection Development

A library's graphic novel collection should consist of a balanced combination of series and stand-alone titles. Series can be incredibly popular, especially among young adult readers, but sometimes make it difficult for newcomers to find an entry point. Stand-alone titles will likely be more appealing to the casual adult reader venturing into the world of young adult materials. When building or enhancing a graphic collection, consider patron requests and talk directly to patrons who use both the adult and teen graphic collections. Visit local comic book shops and bookstores, if possible, to see what is newly available and discover what is popular in your service area. Consult bestseller lists, such as those provided by the *New York Times*, *Publishers Weekly*, and *Graphic Novel Reporter*.

Reviews for graphic novels and manga are available in professional journals such as *Library Journal, Booklist, Publishers Weekly, School Library Journal, Kirkus*, and *VOYA*. Note the nominees and winners of industry awards such as the Eisner Awards, the Harvey Awards, and the Ignatz Awards, as well as YALSA's yearly Great Graphic Novels for Teens list. Librarians can also request digital review copies of graphic works in advance of publication online through both NetGalley and Edelweiss.

Libraries typically collect bound graphic novels and manga series, although some subscribe to and lend individual comic issues. If your library does not distinguish between collections of graphic novels for teens and adults, consider whether or not it would be worthwhile for your patrons to make that distinction. On a regular basis, review the use of the graphic collection and remember to allocate some funds for replacement of items in series as well as core titles.

Within graphic publishing, as with publishing in general, digital formats are looming larger, with both large and small companies offering digital subscription services. Consider whether your library's audience for graphic works is becoming more digitally oriented when replacing lost, stolen, or missing items. Libraries can subscribe to digital graphic content through platforms and vendors such as OverDrive, Baker & Taylor's Axis 360, Bibliotecha's Cloud Library (formerly 3M), iVerse Media (Comics Plus: Library Edition, available through Boopsie) and the Alexander Press Underground and Independent Comics, Comix, and Graphic Novels database. Hoopla, a streaming media service owned by Midwest Tape, provides patrons at subscribing libraries with access to single issue comics as well as graphic novels from DC, Vertigo, Dark Horse, Image Comics, Boom, and others. Given the uncertainty of the demand and the variety of vendors and publishers involved, it is unlikely that libraries will be able to find just one subscription service that meets all patron needs. Add available graphic content that fits your collection needs within the existing ebook provider to which your library subscribes, and market accordingly.

The Literature

The following lists provide a sampling of graphic novels that were published for young adult audiences but also hold appeal for adult readers. The lists are organized by themes that reflect popular reading interests.

Coming-of-Age

Many young adult books are concerned with growing up and crossing the threshold between childhood and adulthood, and graphic novels are no exception. These stories focus mainly on character development. Whether they are set in high school or beyond, these coming-of-age tales will appeal to adult readers interested in transitions, first times, and coping mechanisms, or simply revisiting their youth.

Brosgol, Vera. *Anya's Ghost*. 2011.
At first, Anya is very happy to have found a new friend in the form of Emily, a local ghost. But then Anya's struggles trying to fit in as a Russian immigrant at an all-American school are exacerbated by Emily and her malevolent agenda. This short, black-and-white rendered stand-alone will appeal to patrons who like mild horror and fish out of water stories. Brosgol's narrative is creepy, dark, and character-driven. Readalikes: *Friends with Boys* by Faith Erin Hicks and The Clique series by Lisi Harrison. (print, ebook)

Gulledge, Laura Lee. *Will & Whit*. 2013.
Sixteen-year-old Wilhemina ("Will") Huxstep is haunted by shadows after the death of her parents. The creative Will makes lamps to combat her fear of the dark, a coping mechanism that fails her when a hurricane ("Whit") causes a blackout in her town. This character-driven story of loss and self-knowledge is illustrated in black and white, with heavily outlined characters and omnipresent, often disturbing, shadows. *Will & Whit* is recommended for adult readers who enjoy narratives of grief and recovery. (print, ebook)

O'Malley, Bryan Lee. Scott Pilgrim. 2004–2010.
Absurdist comic about a 20-something slacker and his quest to defeat Ramona Flowers' seven evil exes. Styled after Japanese manga, the six volumes in this completed series track Scott's progress as he gradually matures and becomes able to sustain an adult relationship. Recently made into a motion picture, *Scott Pilgrim* is popular with both teens and adults. Peppered with humor, pop, and geek culture references, the series was originally released in manga-style black and white, then rereleased in vibrant color. It should resonate especially with fans of Kate Beaton and Fred Chao's *Johnny Hiro*. (print)

Shen, Prudence, illustrated by Faith Erin Hicks. *Nothing Can Possibly Go Wrong*. 2013.
A farcical student body election ensues when the cheerleading squad gets nervous about funding for new uniforms and friends Nate (president of

the Robotics Club) and Charlie (captain of the basketball team) are caught in the middle. This humorous and fresh take on the high school jock versus geek battle resembles the plot of a popular film, featuring underdogs entering competitions, unlikely allies, and wacky hijinks. A wide variety of adult readers will enjoy this plot-driven, compelling story. *Nothing Can Possibly Go Wrong* is illustrated in bold and detailed black and white. (print, ebook)

Shimura, Takako. Wandering Son. 2011–

Manga series about Yoshino, a girl who wants to be a boy, and Shuichi, a boy who wants to be a girl. Shimura's dreamily illustrated black-and-white story is character-driven and moving without being sententious or too angst-filled. The protagonists in this story are young, but their story of self-discovery and their courage when faced with the confusion of sexual development is universal. This graphic interpretation of a trans narrative from both directions will appeal to readers looking for LGBTQ stories. The series is complete in Japan but still being published in the United States. (print)

Tamaki, Mariko, and Jillian Tamaki. *Skim*. 2008.

A high school student and budding Wiccan, Kimberly Keiko Cameron ("Skim") is in the process of discovering who she wants to be and falling in love with one of her female teachers when a local student commits suicide. Cousins Jillian and Mariko Tamaki use Skim's story to explore themes of transition and the changes that love brings. Drawn in black and white in a fluid and expressionistic style, *Skim* is a delicate exploration of identity and authenticity. Recommended for fans of *Ghost World* and *Stitches* or for readers looking for a follow-up to Alison Bechdel's *Fun Home*. Direct readers interested in absurdist high school stories to Mariko Tamaki's *SuperMutant Magic Academy* (2015). (print, ebook)

Takaya, Natsuki. Fruits Basket. 2004–2009.

In this completed manga series, high school students and cousins Yuki and Kyo are part of the wealthy and mysterious Sohma family. When the orphaned Tohru moves in with them, she discovers that many members of the Sohma family have been cursed by the animal spirits of the Chinese zodiac, which manifest when they are ill or hugged by a person of the opposite sex. Tohru may be the outsider who can break the curse. *Fruits Basket* focuses on character development, humor, and coping with difficult situations. Recommended for adult readers who are looking for stories with strong romantic and emotional elements and a wide cast of characters. (print)

Telgemeier, Raina. *Drama*. 2012.

Callie loves working as the set decorator for her middle school's stage productions, but the drama is sometimes more prevalent off the stage than on. Telgemeier's colorful and deceptively simple manga-influenced full-color artwork tells the story of Callie's navigation through a sea of crushes to the successful staging of a musical production. This character-driven and engaging investigation of middle school dramas of all sorts will appeal to a wide range of readers, particularly reluctant ones. (print, ebook)

Vaughan, Brian K., et al. Runaways. 2004–2010.

In this series, six children of supervillains run away and vow to defeat their parents when they discover the truth about their secret identities. The detailed, full-color narrative begins as a coming of age story for the teens involved, then focuses on interpersonal relationships and character development. For fans of superhero books like *House of M* who want a dose of realism, and those who have enjoyed Brian K. Vaughan's work on *Y: The Last Man* and *Saga*. (print)

Wilson, G. Willow, illustrated by Adrian Alphona, colors by Ian Herring. Ms. Marvel. 2014–
Kamala Khan is a Pakistani-American teenager who is already juggling school, friends, bullies, boys, and her Muslim faith when she gains superpowers. Alphona's energetic full-color art complement's Wilson's script perfectly. *Ms. Marvel* will appeal to readers interested in superhero narratives grounded in faith, cultural identity, and current events, as well as those looking for something similar to *Hawkeye, Ultimate Comics: Spider-Man, The Unbeatable Squirrel Girl*, and *Captain Marvel*. (print, ebook)

Yang, Gene Luen. *American Born Chinese*. 2006.
Using humor and Chinese mythology, Yang deftly combines three seemingly unrelated stories into a powerful message about being comfortable with who you are. Illustrated in a bold, full-color style, Yan's narrative is engaging, thoughtful, and funny. Although Yang focuses on multiculturalism and its intersection with the Chinese immigrant experience, this book will appeal to readers from all backgrounds, especially fans of pop culture and slapstick humor. Readalikes: *The Absolutely True Diary of a Part-Time Indian* and *Vietnamerica: A Family's Journey*. (print, ebook)

Strangers in Strange Lands

Fantasy and science fiction settings have always been a standby of comics and graphic novel creators, given the format's ability to depict imaginative scenes. These selections will appeal to longtime adult readers of the speculative genres, as well as those interested in trying science fiction or fantasy in a more accessible graphic format.

Arakawa, Hiromu. Fullmetal Alchemist. 2002–2011.
Completed manga series about two brothers who meddle with the mystical powers of alchemy in an attempt to resurrect their dead mother, leaving one of them maimed and one trapped in a metal suit of armor. Now, in the pursuit of the philosopher's stone to restore their bodies, the brothers find themselves enmeshed in a struggle much greater than their own. The manga was also adapted into two anime series. For patrons interested in steampunk, high-stakes action, family ties, and the intersection of science and religion. Similar titles: *Ghost in the Shell, Mobile Suit Gundam*. (print)

Black, Holly, illustrated by Ted Naifeh. The Good Neighbors. 2008–2010.
Rue Silver's life turns mysterious and threatening when she discovers that her mother is a faerie and her city is a battleground site between the realms. Which side should she join? Black is a popular crossover author for adult readers, and this is her first graphic project. The darkly atmospheric style of Naifeh's black-and-white art works well with Black's prose to create a fast-paced fantasy story with romantic elements. For adults who enjoy young adult fiction like *Vampire Academy* or adult graphic novels like *Hellboy*. (print)

Foglio, Phil and Kaja. Girl Genius. 2001–
    This ongoing webcomic series has made a successful transition to print. The story focuses on Agatha Clay, a brilliant scientist in the making. The action-packed plot mixes steampunk, fantasy, and a strong female lead and is suffused with whimsy supported by bold, colorful illustrations. Two novelizations are also currently available, which may lead readers to the graphic novels. Readalikes: Scott Westerfeld's *Leviathan* trilogy, *Delilah Dirk and the Turkish Lieutenant*, and Alan Moore's *League of Extraordinary Gentlemen*. (print)

Kelly, Joe, illustrated by J. M. Ken Niimura. *I Kill Giants*. 2009.
    Barbara is a giant-killer, but the real enemy she is facing is one that will take all her courage. The reader sees the world from Barbara's perspective as she struggles against monsters that only she can see, pushing everyone away as a result. Niimura peoples Barbara's world with fanciful and threatening objects while giving hints about the truth of her situation. *I Kill Giants* collects all seven issues of this grayscale comic miniseries into one volume. Recommended for adult readers looking for magical realism or stories of coping with tragedy with humorous undertones. Especially for fans of Jeff Lemire and Patrick Ness's *A Monster Calls*. (print, ebook)

Kubo, Tite. Bleach. 2004–
    Long-running manga series featuring the adventures of Ichigo, a high school student who becomes a soul reaper and fights to protect the innocent. This action-heavy black and white manga has a wide cast of characters and a strong coming-of-age theme and is stylistically similar to manga targeted toward an adult audience. The series' explicit violence and bloodshed, rendered primarily through sword battles, might turn off some adult readers and lure others. Readalikes: *Death Note*, *Invincible*. (print)

Medley, Linda. Castle Waiting. 2006–2010.
    A woman takes refuge in a castle sanctuary and is befriended by its various inhabitants. As she becomes accustomed to life at the castle, the stories of other castle dwellers are gradually explored. The black-and-white illustrations ably fit this engaging and escapist narrative that plays with fairy tale and mythological characters. For fans of Robin McKinley and Bill Willingham's Fables series. Also likely to appeal to readers interested in fairytale retellings. (print)

Stevenson, Noelle. *Nimona*. 2015.
    Mysterious shape-shifter Nimona nominates herself to assist the confirmed villain Ballister Blackheart in whatever nefarious schemes he has planned. In the course of their blossoming friendship, things come to a head between Blackheart and his longtime nemesis, Sir Goldenloin, and mounting secrets put the entire country at risk. This full-color work is recommended for fans of Rainbow Rowell's *Fangirl* and *Carry On* and for patrons interested in humorous fantasy. Originally published serially online, *Nimona* is now available as a finished volume. (print, ebook)

Stevenson, Noelle, et al. Lumberjanes. 2015–
    Five intrepid campers confront a series of mysterious and potentially dangerous happenings at Miss Qiunzilla Thiskwin Penniquiqul Thistle Crumpet's Camp for Hard-Core Lady-Types, with the aid of their overly anxious camp counselor. This brightly colored humorous comic focuses on themes

of friendship, teamwork, and inclusion. *Lumberjanes* will appeal to patrons of all ages with a taste for humor, adventure, and supernatural mystery. (print, ebook)

Tan, Shaun. *The Arrival*. 2007.

In this wordless, sepia-toned book, Tan tackles themes of immigration and alienation. Accessible to all ages, *The Arrival* balances one family's experience with that of the universal condition and places the reader in the position of the immigrant by way of its surreal settings. Part picture book and part graphic novel, this detailed stand-alone work will appeal most to those interested in experiencing life from other perspectives and is suggested for fans of *The Invention of Hugo Cabret* or as a potential readalike for *Persepolis*. (print, ebook)

TenNapel, Doug. *Ghostopolis*. 2010.

When Garth Hale accidentally ends up in the world of ghosts, he discovers he has supernatural powers. As he is been diagnosed with a mysterious terminal illness back home, he is not in a great hurry to return. Illustrated in full color with cartoon-like artwork, *Ghostopolis* offers both adult and child main characters for crossover appeal. The narrative is plot-driven, fast-paced, humorous, and scary. Recommended for adults who like ghost stories, Neil Gaiman's *The Graveyard Book* or Kazu Kibuishi's Amulet series. (print, ebook)

Whitley, Jeremy, et al. Princeless. 2012–

Sixteen-year-old Princess Adrienne Ashe has been locked in a tower by her father to await rescue by a suitable prince, as do her six sisters. Impatient, Adrienne saves herself and sets off with the dragon that was set to guard her to save the rest of her sisters as well. For adult fans of *Agent Carter* and *Wonder Woman*, patrons looking for strong African American characters and flipped fairy tales, and those waiting for the next *Ms. Marvel* collection. (print, ebook)

Other Times, Other Sources

Graphic novels, comics, and manga are uniquely suited to the task of adaptation, both from existing works of fiction or nonfiction, or from the fabric of history itself. By combining print and images, authors and illustrators bring stories alive. Historical fiction is traditionally very appealing to adult readers, and graphic adaptations give them the opportunity to access classic texts in new and interesting ways.

Bogaert, H. M. van den, adapted by George O'Connor. *Journey into Mohawk Country*. 2006.

A graphic adaptation of a 1634 journal written by a Dutch trader voyaging into Native American territory. Van den Bogaert traveled through Mohawk and Oneida territory in an attempt to establish trade relations. O'Connor's full-color illustrations add resonance to the seventeenth-century story, especially his interpretation of religion and superstition. Recommended for patrons interested in nonfiction, memoir, and primary sources from U.S. history. (print)

Brown, Don. *Drowned City: Hurricane Katrina & New Orleans*. 2015.

For the 10th anniversary of Hurricane Katrina, Brown produced a full-color account of the disaster that struck the Gulf Coast. Focusing on the struggles of New Orleans, Brown's account provides both individual stories and an overarching look at the tragedy and achievements of the people affected by the storm and its aftermath. Recommended for patrons interested in stories of disaster relief, particularly as a readalike for *Five Days at Memorial: Life and Death in a Storm-Ravaged Hospital*. (print, ebook)

Keenan, Sheila, illustrated by Nathan Fox. *Dogs of War*. **2013.**
A collection of fictional stories about three military service dogs and their activities during World War I, World War II, and Vietnam. Each story includes real historical details from the wars and the history of the military dogs that provided soldiers with physical and emotional support. Keenan's stories spotlight both the animals and their human companions, while Fox's primarily color illustrations portray the solemnity of war. Recommended for dog lovers or fans of narrative nonfiction and history, and stories like *War Horse*. (print)

Kovac, Tommy, illustrated by Sonny Liew. *Wonderland*. **2009.**
This graphic adaptation of *Alice in Wonderland* is the story of Mary Ann, housekeeper of the White Rabbit, and follows her adventures with the Queen of Hearts, Cheshire Cat, and more after Alice's departure from the scene. Originally published as single-issue comics, this collected volume's vibrant color mirrors the absurd and imaginative storyline. Recommended for adult patrons interested in humor, whimsy, and reinterpretations or continuations of classics. Liew's Disney-esque illustrations will appeal to fans of the movie; also consider it as a potential readalike for L. Frank Baum's classic Oz books. (print)

Larson, Hope. *Mercury*. **2010.**
Larson alternates between 1859 and present-day Nova Scotia in this tale of prospecting and betrayal. In 1859, Josey and her family are taken in by a traveler who convinces them to invest in his gold-prospecting scheme. In the present day, Josey's descendant Tara has returned to the area after her house burned down. The entwined stories of Josey's forbidden courtship and Tara's difficult reacclimation yield a bittersweet and emotionally intense character-driven narrative. Touches of magic realism surface in this black-and-white, atmospherically illustrated volume, ideal for fans of *Blankets* or *The War at Ellsmere*. Also appropriate for readers interested in historical fiction or the Salem witch trials. (print, ebook)

Lewis, John, Andrew Aydin, and Nate Powell. *March: Book One*. **2013.**
Lewis, John, Andrew Aydin, and Nate Powell. *March: Book Two*. **2015.**
Congressman John Lewis's story of the civil rights movement takes vibrant life in these nuanced black-and-white volumes. In the first installment, Lewis recounts his childhood in rural Alabama, his first meeting with Martin Luther King, Jr., and the battle against segregation through peaceful sit-ins. The second details the growing civil rights movement, the efforts of the Freedom Riders, and the lead-up to the March on Washington. *March* will appeal to readers who enjoy nonfiction, memoir, and history, and has already been added to school curricula around the country. (print, ebook)

Mori, Kaoru. Emma. 2006–2009.
In this completed manga series set in 1895 London, Emma is a maid who falls in love with William Jones, the oldest son of a wealthy middle-class

family attempting to rise to the level of the gentry. Mori follows the progression of their star-crossed relationship through 10 engaging volumes. Well-researched, historically accurate, and drawn in meticulous black and white, *Emma* is ideal for fans of *Downton Abbey*, *Upstairs Downstairs*, *My Fair Lady*, and other stories of British class relations, as well as readers of historical romance. (print)

Shelley, Mary, adapted by Gris Grimly. *Gris Grimly's Frankenstein, or, The Modern Prometheus*. 2013.

A dark and heavily sinister adaptation of the classic work that features Shelley's full text accompanied by Grimly's macabre illustrations. In a seamless integration between author and artist, the tale of Frankenstein and his monster is lovingly relayed through atmospheric and detailed black-and-white artwork, giving energy and direction to text that might otherwise be difficult for a modern reader to digest. This adaptation is ideal for adult students who are assigned or want to read older works but have had difficulty finding an access point, and also appealing for fans of classic horror. (print, ebook)

Yang, Gene Luen. *Boxers & Saints*. 2013.

This two-volume work concerns the Chinese Boxer Rebellion of 1898 and the individuals involved, focusing on a different main character in each volume. Yang makes able use of a little-known historical setting to create deep character studies and contemplate serious themes of idealism, magical realism, and faith. For patrons interested in stories of personal growth and complex depictions of historical events. Illustrated in full color, this duology is likely to find a home with *Maus* and *Persepolis* on required reading lists. (print)

Conclusion: Trends in Graphic Novels

2014 was the year that marked the beginning of the We Need Diverse Books campaign, and graphic novels and manga are no exception to the rule. Some noise has recently been made about the rise in female readers, who now reportedly make up almost half of the total.[3] Ideally, documentation of this phenomenon will result in a corresponding rise in the number of graphic works featuring female characters, especially among mainstream publishers. There is a great need for diversity in other areas of comics, as well, and there will undoubtedly be movement in that direction with the proliferation of digital graphic and webcomics making small, independent artists' work more easily available to a large audience. Diverse titles can go out of print very quickly, so librarians should purchase as close to publication as possible to provide them to their patrons.

As with the traditional book format, graphic works are increasingly being published in unconventional ways: through online serials and subscriptions, financed by crowdsourced funding, and published independently in other ways. This is good for the diversity and robustness of the format, but not so useful for the librarian seeking to locate and add popular graphic works to the collection. The diversification of digital platforms available for readers of single issue and collected graphic works is an added complication. However, a librarian in this age is likely to have more demand for and choice of graphic items than budget to purchase everything desired. Librarians must continue to advocate for the role of comics, manga, and graphic novels—both in leisure enjoyment and in education—in order for the format to develop and thrive in the library setting.

Notes

1. *Critical Survey of Graphic Novels: History, Theme, Technique.*
2. http://newsok.com/ou-study-shows-graphic-novel-readers-retain-more -information-versus-traditional-textbook-users/article/3748784?custom _click=headlines_widget.
3. http://comicsbeat.com/market-research-says-46-female-comic-fans/.

References

Critical Survey of Graphic Novels: History, Theme, Technique. Eds. Bart Beaty and Stephen Weiner. Ipswich, MA: Salem Press, 2013.
Pawuk, Michael. *Graphic Novels: A Genre Guide to Comic Books, Manga, and More.* Westport, CT: Libraries Unlimited, 2007.
Price, Matthew. "OU Study Shows Graphic Novel Readers Retain More Information versus Traditional Textbook Users." *NewsOK.* January 25, 2013. http://newsok.com/ou-study-shows-graphic-novel-readers-retain -more-information-versus-traditional-textbook-users/article/3748784? custom_click=headlines_widget.
Schenker, Brett. "Market Research Says 46.67% of Comic Fans Are Female." *The Beat.* February 5, 2014. http://comicsbeat.com/market-research -says-46-female-comic-fans/.

About the Editor and Contributors

ALICIA AHLVERS currently works for the Henrico County Public Library as a Collection Development Selector specializing in Young Adult materials. She is active in the American Library Association and has served on numerous book award committees including the Notable Books Council Award and The Reading List Award.

ELIZABETH BURNS is a youth services librarian for a regional library of the National Library Service for the Blind and Physically Handicapped. On twitter, she is @LizB. She blogs at A Chair, A Fireplace, & A Tea Cozy at www.lizburns.org.

KRISTI CHADWICK is a consultant for the Massachusetts Library System, providing continuing education and advisory services for over 1,300 member libraries. She is the co-columnist for *Library Journal*'s Science Fiction/Fantasy column, and was named a 2014 *Library Journal* Mover & Shaker.

KELLY FANN is the executive director of the Hussey-Mayfield Memorial Public Library in Zionsville, Indiana. She holds master's degrees in library science from Emporia State University and public administration from the University of Kansas. Currently, Kelly reviews audiobooks and adult horror, science fiction, and fantasy for *Booklist* magazine and serves on *Booklist*'s advisory board. She presents regularly on readers' advisory practices, trends, and topics—her specialty being the horror genre, audiobooks, and incorporating digital mediums for enhancing and invigorating readers' advisory services. She serves annually as an Audies judge and has several book chapters and articles on audiobook and horror collections.

ERIN DOWNEY HOWERTON, MA, MSLIS is the children's manager at the Wichita Public Library, Kansas. Currently, she serves as the chair of the *Booklist* Editorial Advisory Board. She has worked with young people since 2000 in both library and school settings and has published various articles and book chapters about library collections, intellectual freedom, and technology topics concerning youth. Catch up with her online at hybridlib.net.

KELLY JENSEN is a former teen and adult librarian who currently works as a writer and editor for Book Riot (bookriot.com). She is the editor of the forthcoming collection *Here We Are: Feminism for the Real World*, a YA anthology about feminism, due out from *Algonquin Young Readers* in March 2017. Crossover reading is one of her areas of interest as both a librarian and a writer, and she has written and presented on the topic of "new adult" books since their emergence on the scene in 2011.

ILENE APPELBAUM LEFKOWITZ is the supervising librarian, Adult Services at the Denville Public Library, New Jersey. She has served as chairperson and vice chairperson of New Jersey Library Association's Readers' Advisory Roundtable. Along with C. L. Quillen, she is coauthor of *Read On ... Romance: Reading Lists for Every Taste* (Libraries Unlimited, 2014).

LUCY M. LOCKLEY is collection development manager for St. Charles City-County Library District, Missouri, and a strong proponent of readers' advisory, serving on RUSA's Listen List, Louis Shores Award, Zora Neal Hurston Award, Notable Books Council, and Reading List committees as well as the RUSA CODES Readers' Advisory Committee. Lucy contributes reviews to *Booklist* and has been a member of the Booklist Advisory Board. She is the author of "Keeping Up: Genre Studies as Continuing Education" a chapter in *The Readers' Advisory Handbook* (2010) and loves to discover new opportunities for promoting reading, listening, and viewing, both in person and through social media. Lucy is also addicted to audiobooks and a huge fan of trivia, animation, special effects, and action films.

ANNA GRACE MICKELSEN is a reference librarian at the Springfield (MA) City Library. She is an avid fan of science fiction, fantasy, romance, and graphic novels of all genres for both teens and adults. When she is not creating collection development spreadsheets or chasing her son, she shares her library experiences on Twitter (@helgagrace).

JESSICA E. MOYER is a visiting assistant professor and reference librarian at the Main Library of the University of Illinois at Urbana-Champaign, and is editor of *Integrated Advisory Service: Breaking through the Book Boundary to Better Serve Library Users* (Libraries Unlimited, 2010), as well as of *Research-Based Readers' Advisory* (2008); and is coeditor of *The Readers' Advisory Handbook* (2010). Previously Jessica was an assistant professor at the School of Information Studies at the University of Wisconsin-Milwaukee where she taught classes on reference and reader services. As a reviewer for *Booklist* and *Library Journal*, she has reviewed books, e-originals, and audiobooks, introducing "YA notes" to adult book reviews in several genres. In addition, Jessica has contributed her genre expertise and written chapters on adult science fiction and fantasy for collected volumes.

C. L. QUILLEN is the director of the Spotswood Public Library in New Jersey. She is a founding member of the New Jersey Library Association's Readers' Advisory Roundtable, where she has served as chair and vice chair. Quillen is the coauthor of *Read On ... Romance: Reading Lists for Every Taste* (Libraries Unlimited, 2014).

ANN CHAMBERS THEIS, collection management librarian, Henrico County Public Library. Active member of RUSA CODES, YALSA, VLA. Committee participation includes Reading List, Readers Advisory, Alex Awards, and Printz Award. Established Overbooked website in 1994, www.overbooked .com and www.overbooked.com/next-chapter.

JENNIFER HAAS THIELE is a library director for the Marinette County library system in Marinette, Wisconsin. Jennifer received an IMLS Laura Bush 21st Century Librarian Fellowship in 2011, and obtained her PhD in Information Studies from the University of Wisconsin, Milwaukee. Jennifer has published articles in *New Library World*, JASIST and Community and Junior College Libraries and has presented her research nationally and internationally.

MARY WEPKING is a former high school English teacher, and former academic and school librarian. Since 2007, she has been a lecturer and the school library coordinator at University of Wisconsin-Milwaukee in the School of Information Studies. Her areas of expertise as an instructor include collection management, young adult literature, and library services for children and teens in both school and public library settings.

Author/Title Index

Subject Index